Samuel A Bailey

Letters on the Philosophy of the Human Mind

Samuel A Bailey

Letters on the Philosophy of the Human Mind

ISBN/EAN: 9783742816504

Manufactured in Europe, USA, Canada, Australia, Japa

Cover: Foto ©Thomas Meinert / pixelio.de

Manufactured and distributed by brebook publishing software
(www.brebook.com)

Samuel A Bailey

Letters on the Philosophy of the Human Mind

LETTERS

ON THE

PHILOSOPHY OF THE HUMAN MIND.

BY SAMUEL BAILEY,

AUTHOR OF 'ESSAYS ON THE FORMATION AND PUBLICATION OF OPINIONS,' ETC.

THIRD SERIES.

LONDON:

LONGMAN, GREEN, LONGMAN, ROBERTS, & GREEN.

1863.

PREFACE.

It would be unreasonable to expect that the Third
Series of a work like the present, should attract
the attention of any but the possessors and the
readers of the two preceding volumes. To them
it may be of more or less interest to be informed,
that the Series now submitted to the Public, after
an interval of nearly five years, concludes the
Author's disquisitions on the Philosophy of the
Human Mind, at least under the present title.
He may repeat here what he said in his last
Preface, that the subjects treated in the following
Letters are not inferior in importance to their
predecessors; and he has certainly not bestowed
inferior care on the difficulties they present. In
the course of discussing them, he has had frequent
occasion, as a cursory inspection will discover, to
contest the opinions and to criticise the arguments
of several eminent living writers. If he has done

this with the freedom due to truth, he has not, he trusts, infringed that courtesy which men earnestly engaged in the cause of moral and intellectual advancement, have a right to expect from each other.

December 10, 1862.

CONTENTS.

LETTERS

ON THE

PHILOSOPHY OF THE HUMAN MIND.

LETTER I.

M. COMTE ON PSYCHOLOGY.

In the conclusion of my Second Series of Letters
on the Philosophy of the Human Mind, I held out
to you a promise, that if I should live to pub-
lish another series, I would examine Comte's doctrine that the direct contemplation of the mind by
itself is a pure illusion, and that hence there can
be no such science as the so-called Psychology.*
He goes on to tell us that the human mind can
observe directly all phenomena but its own proper
ones. For by what or by whom shall the observation be made? It is conceivable, with regard
to moral phenomena, that man can observe him
self as to the passions which animate him, for the

---

* Cours de Philosophie Positive, par M. Auguste Comte,
tome I. p. 35.

B

anatomical reason that the organs which are their
seat are distinct from those destined to the observing functions.

Such observations, however, cannot, he holds, be
of much scientific importance, and the best means
of knowing the passions will be to observe them
externally, for all marked state of passion is necessarily incompatible with the state of observation.

But as to observing in the same way the intellectual phenomena while they are passing, there is
in it a manifest impossibility. The thinking individual cannot divide himself into two, one of which
shall reason and the other look on. The observed
and observing organs being in this case identical,
how can the observation take place?

The passage in Comte's Positive Philosophy of
which the above is a faithful representation,* appears to me to abound in errors, and errors, too,
lying on the surface. I marvel that a man of his
powers could fall into such transparent fallacies.

These errors combined show an utter miscon-
ception of the way in which the knowledge of our
own minds arises, and prove, at the same time, the
danger of indiscriminately applying to purely
mental phenomena the language which originates
in our perception of what is external — an application which our author makes with unsuspecting
intrepidity. A great part of Comte's argument, it

* The original text is given in Note A at the end of the
present volume.

will doubtless have been remarked, turns on the word "observe."

If we borrow this term from the cognisance we take of external things, and apply it to that which we have of mental conditions, we must bear in mind that, like other language used to designate the incidents of thought and feeling, it is figurative; and we shall grievously err if, from the analogy implied in the term, we proceed as a matter of course to impose upon internal phenomena consequences which may be truly enough ascribed to those external events to which the term is literally applicable.

We "observe" external things, says M. Comte, through the eye, while we do not see the eye itself, nor the picture on the retina, or, to express the latter proposition in common but erroneous language, the eye does not "observe" itself. The fact, howsoever it may be described, is admitted.

It is admitted, too, that we may use the same term "observe" in speaking of mental phenomena: we may correctly enough say that we "observe" internal states and operations.

So far the expression can involve no mistake, but here the analogy between the cognisance of external and that of internal phenomena ceases.

There is nothing in the mind of which we can go on to say, as we say of the eye, that it cannot be seen by the observer in the act of observation; or in shorter phrase cannot observe itself.

The expression "we observe our internal states," simply means we are conscious of them, and the real amount of the assertion M. Comte makes is, that we, being the intelligent entities of whom states of consciousness are affections, cannot be conscious of them — that is, cannot be conscious of what we are conscious of. If we ascribe a more complex signification to the phrase " observing internal states," by including in it not only the consciousness of a direct mental act, but the subsequent recollection of it, or reflection upon it, the argument against M. Comte would be strengthened, were it for no other reason than this, that recollection and reflection are themselves modes of consciousness.

M. Comte, it is true, disguises this fallacy from himself by appealing to the phrenological organs, and in them finds an analogy with the eye. He has recourse to what he terms the anatomical reason, that as the eye cannot observe itself, so the organ of observation in the brain, although it may observe the organs of the passions, cannot observe itself.

This allegation, however, will not avail him, even if we admit the existence of phrenological organs. Organs of any kind, whether of the senses, or cranial, or cerebral, can neither observe nor feel. It is only figuratively that we talk of the eye seeing. It is not the eye that sees but the man through the instrumentality of the eye. So

with phrenological organs. If there is such an
organ as that of observation, it most undoubtedly
cannot observe itself or its own operations; and it
was quite needless for M. Comte to waste a word in
asserting the negative fact; but then it is equally
true that the organ in question cannot observe the
organs of the passions any more than itself, although
the author not only pronounces the process to be
conceivable, but speaks of it as actually occurring.
The observation of one organ by another of which
he talks so volubly, springing as it does out of a
'mere personification, is, in truth, as pure a fiction
as the volition ascribed by Kepler to the planets,
and has no foundation in nature. What then
becomes of M. Comte's argument, that we cannot
observe the intellectual operations within us because an organ cannot observe itself? The premises have vanished.

For the reasons here assigned, I conceive the
doctrine of M. Comte as to the impossibility of
observing our own states of consciousness, and
the consequent inanity of Psychology to be utterly
fallacious, to have no ground whatever to stand
upon; and it is really amazing or amusing, according as we may take it, that a positive philosopher
demanding realities at every step, should thus
have founded a theory on purely fictitious facts.

But the subject admits of farther elucidation.

The knowledge which a man has of any of his
own states of consciousness (except in the first

evanescent stage) implies two things: (1) having
been in that state; (2) recollecting it. The first step
in acquiring knowledge must be noticing, or discerning, or being conscious of something or other;
but as this is a fugitive event, permanent knowledge cannot be said to exist unless what was
noticed is remembered. Remembrance is essential
to it.

Now no one, not even M. Comte, would assert
that we are unable to recollect our states of
intellectual consciousness; that we have no remembrance of our reasonings, our imaginations,
our suppositions, our theories, our castles in the
air, as well as of our feelings and passions, our
being in love or being in a rage; and if we remember such states, we must have been in them,
and have been conscious at the time (if I may be
pardoned for uttering an identical proposition)
that we were in them. As we cannot recollect
what never took place, so we cannot recollect what
we never took cognisance of. Recollection presupposes both the actual occurrence and the mental
notice of what is recollected. If all this does not
imply internal observation, if it does not present
materials for discernment, comparison, classification, and inference, I know not what does; and
these are some of the processes which applied to
such materials constitute the Psychology which
our author condemns. If we can recollect mental
affections and operations, we can certainly discern

amongst them resemblances and differences, causes
and effects, co-existences and consecutions. What
is there to prevent us?

If we compare the materials and processes just
described with those of physical science, we shall
find the two although diverse in some things yet
parallel in the main, especially in reference to the
fugitiveness of the phenomena, and the great share
which recollection necessarily has in the act of
acquiring knowledge of all kinds.

Our knowledge of external things, in strict analogy with our knowledge of internal, implies, first,
observation of the phenomena, and secondly, as
equally indispensable, recollection of them. Whatever might be the acuteness and comprehensive-
ness of our observation outward, we should be just
as imbecile amongst external objects and events
without memory as we should be amongst those
which are internal. Recollection is alike indispensable for acquiring or using or constituting the
knowledge of either.

Nor (to make the parallel closer) are the phenomena of the external world, or at least a great
multitude of them that are subjected to scientific
observation, less fugitive than those of the mind;
but, as we all admit, the shifting or transitory
character of physical events does not preclude a
scientific acquaintance with them.

In making a chemical experiment, for example,
we see the phenomena pass before us with great

rapidity; the chemical union or the chemical separation of two substances is instantaneous; the
flash or the explosion is gone in a moment; they
are not events to be detained while we deliberately
watch them, and unless we could recollect what we
saw and heard, as we recollect the similarly transient events of consciousness, we could not possess
physical knowledge. Every step of the process,
so to speak, perishes in detail and becomes a remembered incident, taking its place in the connected sequence which appears in our mental
review.

An apposite illustration of the resemblance between mental and physical events in the circumstance here insisted upon, may be found in the
course of a ship at sea. She is constantly rolling
and pitching; frequently changing her direction;
going first on one tack and then on another;
having sails hoisted or lowered; reefs taken in or
let out; sometimes advancing rapidly, sometimes
floating like a log on the water; and we see her in
any one precise position only a single moment;
yet closely observing and noting and recollecting
every thing that passed, we can take a connected
retrospect and give a tolerably accurate account of
her proceedings.

So with the mind we are conscious of operations
and affections, mutable and fugitive as the motions
of a ship at sea; yet like those making an impression at the time, and subjects of distinct recol-

lection and reflection, comparison and classification afterwards.

There is another inadmissible remark in the passage cited from Comte, which may deserve a separate comment.

After allowing that a man may make internal observation of his own passions, since the organs of observation and of feeling are distinct, he goes on to say, " Such observations, however, cannot be of much scientific importance, and the best means of knowing the passions will be to observe them externally, for all marked state of passion is neces-, sarily incompatible with the state of observation."

On this I have first to remark that neither of the modes pointed out, neither external nor internal observation of the working of a passion, can be omitted in any full and accurate study of it. Both are requisite for complete knowledge.

If, however, a comparison, not needed, is to be instituted and any superiority be awarded to either over the other, it cannot with any shadow of reason be given to that to which M. Comte has assigned it.

While external observation is of undeniable importance, internal observation is absolutely indispensable. Unless a man had himself been the subject of any given passion, he would be utterly incapable of interpreting the actions of others to which it gives rise.

We can conceive a human being to be pretty

familiar with a passion he has often felt; with the circumstances by which it is aroused and directed, exasperated and mitigated; and with the conduct into which it leads him; although he has never had an opportunity of watching the effects of the passion on the behaviour of another. Self-study without extrinsic observation, might carry him a long way.

But, on the other hand, it would be plainly impossible for any one who had never experienced a passion himself to form a conception of the actuating motives of his neighbours while they were under its influence, and impossible to ascribe their actions to the right source. To him all would be inscrutable. They would be playing a game before his eyes of which he had never learned the moves, and which he would be wholly incapable of following.

There are obviously two different sets of circumstances to be learned in order to have the best possible knowledge of any given passion: (1) The course of the passion as we ourselves feel it in all its ebbs and flows, and their causes, together with the actions which it prompts us to do: (2) The actions which we observe it to prompt our neighbours to do, and which we attribute to the influence of the passion from extending to others the observations we have made on ourselves.

When any emotional law or mode of action is established by a concurrence of both kinds of

circumstances accurately noted, it has of course
better claims to be accepted than if it had been
founded on one, just as other laws derived from
full and accurate examination have a superiority
over such as are deduced from partial and incomplete evidence.*

The last part of the passage cited from Comte is
scarcely happier than the preceding. All marked
states of passion, he asserts, are incompatible with
the state of observation—a position vague enough,
but which means, I presume, or ought to mean to
be pertinent, that when a man is filled with intense
love or fear or joy or hope, he cannot observe the
course or procedure of the emotion by which he is
possessed. Why not? A man under the influence
of some strong passion has certainly vivid ideas as
well as vivid feeling, and what he so feels and
thinks and imagines, leaves a deep impression on
his memory. What is this but, as I have already
explained, internal observation? It would scarcely
have been more wide of the mark, had he said that
a philosopher enthusiastically devoted to some
physical science could not on account of his very

* The observations in the text may serve also as a reply to
part of Mr. Buckle's disparagement of Psychology in his " History of Civilisation in England," see vol. i. pp. 16 and 144.
With all his acknowledged ability and learning, he appears to
me, I confess, to give very loose and inexact representations
of metaphysical doctrines, and to be unacquainted with much
that has been done in mental philosophy. (This note was
written before his lamented death.)

enthusiastic devotion to it, observe the phenomena
which the science presented.   The author, I apprehend, was unwittingly thinking of a very different
position, which may be readily mistaken for the
one he has laid down, and which he seems accordingly to have confused with it — the position,
namely, that a mind possessed with a powerful
passion is often so engrossed with it and its acces-
sories as to overlook every thing else, the whole
attention, for the time, being absorbed by the pre-
dominant perturbation.   This, however, is a very
different thing from the mind not observing its
own state, or a man not observing his own mental
condition.

   Wherever there is strong passion, there must be
(for it is the same thing in different words) strong
impressions and consequent strong recollections and
reflections connected with it ; in a word, all that
constitutes vivid and active internal observation,
furnishing materials for thought and classification
and inference.   What is not compatible with such
a state of passion is the clear and full observation
at the same time of present objects and passing
events totally unconnected with it.

   It is a singular circumstance that Comte, who
was so hostile to those metaphysical entities which
he represents as having in the progress of mankind
long ruled the world, should not have discerned
that in his depreciation or rather attempted destruction of Psychology, he was proceeding on an

assumption of just the same kind of fictitious personifications. His faculties observing each other
are not a whit more real, have no more positive
existence, than the crowd of metaphysical principles
whose reign he traces or points to in the history of
the past.   .

And not only did he fall into this capital inconsistency, but he was at the same time overlooking
as subjects of systematic knowledge, the whole
world of the phenomena of pure consciousness, and
unphilosophically reducing or wishing to reduce
the science of man to little else than physical manifestations and external actions.

LETTER II.

IDENTITY.

An author who has written an able analysis of the
human mind, says that "identity is a case of belief;"
that when we affirm of an object to-day that it is
the same object we saw yesterday, we merely express our belief that it is a particular object.[*]

That we have the belief is certain, but surely
this is not all. Besides the belief there is the fact
which is the subject of belief. Belief may be correct or incorrect, but this does not affect the fact
which is what it is, however we may regard it.

Such an account of identity is evidently an imperfect one: it is a statement of what we do when
we affirm anything to be the same, not an explanation of what sameness consists in.

Let us try if something more precise and definite
cannot be wrought out. For this purpose it may
be requisite, perhaps, to hazard some trite propositions as stepping-stones to others not equally
evident.

1. Every particle in the universe is itself and

---

[*] Analysis of the Human Mind, by James Mill.

not some other particle:* it has an existence, an
individuality, distinct from that of every other
thing, and if we speak of it as existing at two
different points of time, we say it is the same particle at one time as it was at the other. Such
particles of matter we cannot know in their separate
or individual state. What we know are objects or
bodies formed of them, or congeries of such particles. So long as any body continues to be formed.
of precisely the individual particles of which it was
composed at any given time, and those particles
continue in the same relative position, it is precisely
the same body or object. This may be called Absolute Identity.

2. A body or congeries or object composed of a
certain number of particles may have those particles arranged in one order at one time, and in another order at another time, without any addition
or diminution. The same particles may be combined in a definite quantity of water or exist in the
state of a definite quantity of gas consisting of un-
combined oxygen and hydrogen. Here we have
absolute identity of substance but difference of
arrangement, and also a consequent difference of
relations to other substances. We may denominate

* In enunciating this platitude, I only follow Bishop Butler,
who knew how useful on occasion such identical propositions
are as aids to the attainment of something else. "Every thing
is," he says, "what it is, and not another thing."—*Preface to
Sermons preached at the Rolls' Chapel.*

it Substantial Identity, adding if we please, with Formal Difference.'

3. It is a common case that bodies or objects lose some of their particles while they retain the majority of them; or in other words they still continue to consist of the majority of their original particles. More accurately it may be said that the majority of original particles still remain con-.nected so as to form bodies or objects. In such cases we are wont to call the bodies the same, although more or less inaccurately. They are only partially the same. A counter case happens when the body retaining all its particles acquires others; and if these others bear a small proportion to the old ones, we still regard the object as the same.

A scythe may furnish an instance of both events: it loses something in the blade by use and often acquires additional particles by rust; or it may lose a portion or the whole of its handle which may be spliced or be replaced by a new one. In common parlance, nevertheless, it is still (however incorrectly) the same scythe. Here we have what may be appropriately termed, Partial Identity.

4. Organised systems whether animal or vegetable are continually receiving new matter and parting with old: yet every such system is regarded as the same organism so long as what may be called the circuit of organic action is kept up.

In this case the organised being may be said to preserve its Identity, but the Identity is obviously no more than partial: it is strictly neither absolute nor yet substantial identity. The important fact which may be expressed without reference to sameness of substance, is that organic action continues uninterrupted. We may call it Organic Identity.

5. So far I have been speaking of substances, but we apply the term identity to relations or relational facts. Two milestones, for example, are always at the same distance from each other. Two tables or two chairs or two peas (according to the common saying), may continue for a long period to bear the same resemblance to one another as they do now.

The two straight lines in the book before me forming a right angle always preserve to each other the same relative position.

This may be termed Relational Identity.

6. Although every particle has an existence of its own, an individuality, an identity, yet many particles or rather many of the congeries of particles which are all we can perceive, are so much alike, that it is impossible for us to distinguish one from the other : they are alike, that is to say, in knowable or perceptible properties. Hence two objects A and B, which are of course distinct entities, may be composed of equal numbers of particles possessing this exact resemblance and

c

arranged in precisely similar order; in which case
the objects themselves will not be distinguishable
by us.   Two portions of water for example from
the same spring, or two portions of wine from the
same bottle, may be so exactly alike that the
acutest eye and the nicest taste and even the finest
chemical analysis may not be able to discover any
difference between them or discriminate one from
the other.   This is plainly not Identity at all, but
Complete Similarity.   The same may be said in
regard to relations.

7. It is obvious also that as there is such a
thing as Partial Identity, so there is Incomplete or
Partial Similarity, as for example between two
portions of water or of wine differently coloured.

In instances of Complete Similarity and even of
high degrees of Partial Similarity we are constantly in the practice of calling the objects
between which the resemblance exists, the same.
For example, you do not hesitate to say that the
wine you are drinking to-day is the same that you
drank yesterday — which is convenient and allowable, but obviously not philosophically correct.

8. Under the head of Similarity must be placed
repeated acts of the same body.   There is, for
example, within view of the room in which I am
writing a tree waving in the wind.   As the wind
is steady every motion resembles its predecessor,
but we cannot say that it is the same motion.

In these cases of perfectly similar movements,

we do not say that the action or motion is the same, but that it is uniform, meaning that every individual movement is exactly similar to the rest.

Absolute Identity can be predicated only of substances and of certain fixed relations of substances. Every past motion of a particle has of course had an existence, has happened, but must, as an event, be different from any preceding or succeeding motion of the same particle: and so it must be with the motions of any congeries of such particles, or, in other words, with the motions of bodies.

Events may be completely similar one to the other, but no two events can in the nature of the case be the same, although the same agents may be engaged in both.

This proposition is important inasmuch as it applies to acts of consciousness as well as to physical incidents. Whether mental operations are considered to be the functions of physiological organs, or of a spiritual entity, they are things which pass or happen — events which in their very nature cannot last or recur, resembling in that respect all physical movements.

These views, abstract and metaphysically fine as they may appear, are yet capable of some useful applications.

In the first place I have to remark that the great principle of moral or probable or, as I prefer

calling it, contingent reasoning,* embraces not
only identity but similarity.

Not only do I reason that the identical substance or object in my hand, the plummet which I
am about to drop into the water, will sink, as I
have known it to do formerly; but, when the occasion arises, I infer that another and in fact every
plummet which I may chance to handle or to make
the subject of thought will do the like.   One inference is just as valid as the other.

Reasoning it is manifest would be extremely
limited and of comparatively little use, if it did
not comprehend cases of similarity as well as of
sameness; and accordingly it makes no appreciable
difference in the force of an argument whether it
is grounded upon complete or partial similarity on
the one hand, or upon complete or partial identity
on the other.

It is in truth instances of partial similarity
which form the great domain of probability, and
in proportion as the case *about* which we reason
approaches in resemblance the one *from* which we
reason, our conclusions are to be relied upon and
approximate to certainty.

Again : the exposition of the subject here given
may, as it appears to me, assist us to solve the
difficulties which have arisen regarding Personal

* For the considerations on which this preference is founded
I must take the liberty of referring to a former work, "The
Theory of Reasoning."

Identity, and which have exercised the sagacity of many distinguished philosophers.

The phrase Personal Identity seems applied by custom to human beings alone, and what it denotes is generally considered to be maintained in any man so long as the circuit of organic action is kept up. In simpler language, so long as he is living, he is considered without any other condition to be the same man, or the same person.

John Thompson in a trance during which all consciousness seemed to be suspended would still be considered as John Thompson — as personally the same being. Thomas Johnson lying in a state of complete insensibility from drowning would be regarded as Thomas Johnson just in the same way as he would be after he had been resuscitated.

In these cases we see that Personal Identity is considered to continue so long as Organic Identity continues, even when the organism is without consciousness.

John Thompson is the same person whether he is in a trance or stupor, or has all his faculties about him, because there is kept up in his body the same circuit of organic action — he lives.

This is I think a correct statement of the way in which the phrase is employed, or would be employed if uniform consistency of language were maintained.

It may still be possibly objected that consciousness

is essential to Personal Identity; that the latter cannot, indeed, be said to have place without Identity of Consciousness.

Nothing however can be clearer, as I have shown, than that Personal Identity remains, although Consciousness is absent. Such at all events is the way in which the phrase is generally applied: and if consciousness may be absent, identity of consciousness whatever is implied by it cannot be essential.

But, what is identity of consciousness? In what sense can consciousness be said to continue the same?

Surely nothing in the world is more variable. There cannot be a more diversified succession of events than the operations and feelings and affections that follow each other in human beings, and constitute what is meant by consciousness; or, to express it in other terms, constitute its phases. So far from any sameness existing, even in appearance, there is perpetual change.

In addition to these considerations, there is the conclusive one before explained, that every phenomenon of consciousness is an event, a function in fact of some substance corporeal or spiritual; and that events however alike they may be, are never the same; so that on this ground identity cannot be predicated of consciousness.

But then, it may be said, this view of the subject entirely overlooks the identity of the mind, or of the soul, which is surely an element in personal identity.

With regard to identity of mind, all that this term implies has just been discussed under the head of identity of consciousness, and I may pass on to the allegation of having omitted to consider the identity of the soul as included in personal identity.

I have most certainly omitted it, because it appears to me to be of some importance on any theory to discriminate and keep them separate, although the question is for the most part a question as to the application of words, the difference between the things themselves being acknowledged or admitted.

According to the general belief, that there is within the human organization a spiritual substance or entity distinct from it, spiritual identity must necessarily be different from organic identity, and must consist in that substance continuing the same whether in or out of the body—whether connected or disconnected with the organization. It is in fact a case of substantial identity.

The question then is, whether it would be more expedient to include this Spiritual Identity in the term Personal, which would make Personal Identity to consist in Organic Identity *plus* Spiritual Identity; or, whether it would be better to consider it as consisting in Organic Identity alone?

On both methods there would be no longer any thing after death to which the phrase could be applied. Organic Identity being terminated, the Personal Identity which it either constituted or helped to constitute, would also be at an end and only Spiritual Identity left.

It seems simpler then to let the latter have its own distinctive name throughout.

Besides, to the materialist who does not acknowledge a separate spiritual substance or entity, Personal Identity is a fact as clear as to the spiritualist, and this of itself is sufficient to show the inexpediency of mixing up Spiritual Identity with it under one name.

On this subject of personal identity much controversy seems to have arisen from a confusion of two distinct things—fact and knowledge.

The fact of personal identity is one thing: the kind and degree of knowledge we may, in any case, have of it is another.

What constitutes the identity of ourselves exactly corresponds with what constitutes the identity of other human beings; but the knowledge that we have of our own personal identity is evidently different in kind from the knowledge that we have of the personal identity of our neighbours.

We of necessity know our own existence as soon as we are conscious, and we know our own

personal identity as soon as we have experienced
two consecutive feelings, or two consecutive events
of consciousness, the first of which we recollect;
for as identity implies the existence of some individual entity not only at a certain time but
also at some other time, we cannot employ the term
in regard to either ourselves or others without
reference to at least two periods.

Hence recollection is essential to the knowledge of
our own personal identity. They manifestly imply
each other.   The recollection of an event implies,
of course, that the reminiscent knows himself to
be the same being as he was when the event
happened; and the knowledge of his own identity
implies the remembrance of a former occurrence.
Our knowledge of the personal identity of our
neighbour is evidently on a different footing.
It is simply perceiving him to be the same
organized being at one time as at another; or, in
different language, recollecting having perceived
him at a former period.   For as in the case of
self-knowledge, this also implies two periods and
presupposes recollection on our part.   We cannot in
any sense know him for the same person unless we
remember him.   It is requisite to remark, however,
that although recollection is essentially necessary
to the knowledge of identity in both cases, it is
not essential to the thing in either case.   My not
recollecting any one makes no difference in his

identity; and as to myself, were I no longer to
recollect a single past event, which I had taken
part in or witnessed, I should still continue to be
personally the same being.

Recollection implies or proves but does not
constitute personal identity. Our great country-
man Locke undoubtedly fell into the error
of making Personal Identity consist in recollection alone, and this arose fundamentally, I
think, from not allowing due weight to the
distinction, which I have here attempted to explain, between the thing and the knowledge of it;
and hence failing to discern or to keep in sight,
that while remembrance is necessary to the latter,
it has nothing to do with the former. Not seeing
this he launched into much verbal controversy.
Locke's disquisition on this subject, nevertheless,
is both acute and profound; and it has been well
observed by Dr. Thos. Brown, that his paradoxes
are most of them logical consequences of the
definition of " person " from which he sets out.
Grant him his own peculiar acceptation of the
term, and you must concur in nearly all the very
eccentric inferences which he seems almost to take
a pleasure, on account of their eccentricity, in
drawing from it. He was, indeed, half conscious
that he was mainly engaged on a question of
terminology.

But the errors of Locke on Personal Identity

have been so well elucidated by the Scottish
philosophers as to render any comments from me
superfluous.   M. Cousin following in their wake,
also brings some good objections against the
doctrine in question, but expressed loosely and
tinged, as his psychological disquisitions usually
are, with unsound philosophy.

LETTER III.

CAUSATION.

Of all the subjects which have perplexed human speculation few have proved more difficult to deal with than that of cause and effect.

Although it has been discussed by some of our acutest and profoundest philosophers, there is still an obscurity about it exceedingly annoying to the young inquirer.

In venturing on the attempt to clear away a portion of this obscurity, I am encouraged by the consideration that I may be able to bring to bear upon the subject some of the principles which I have already explained, so as to present it in a partially different aspect from that in which it has been generally regarded.

Putting aside language as far as practicable, let us think of some instances of connected events, the more familiar the better.

A lady touches a key of her piano, and draws forth the note c: a miller turns the stream upon his wheel and thereby sets it in motion: a boy drops a stone into the brook and it immediately forms concentric circles on the surface of the water: a secretary who has been writing despatches, presses a seal on some wax, and by so doing makes the figure engraved on the seal appear in relief on the outside of the letters.

Each of these cases presents us with a human act performed on a material substance; but it will equally serve the purpose if we take instances of mere physical action such as are expressed in the propositions the fire consumes the paper ; the stream turns the wheel of the mill; the carbonic acid in the well extinguishes the candle.

All these are events which are perceived through the organs of sense. No one doubts that he sees the fire consume the paper thrown into it, or that he sees the stream turn the wheel on which it impinges.

Having witnessed such incidents as these, I find that they afterwards recur to my mind; I think about them or recollect them : in other words I have ideas of them.

What I have perceived and recollect, I have or may have frequent occasion to describe; and for this purpose I employ names, some of which are proper and some are common. In describing the incidents above given as examples, I have used such names as are of the latter kind. Both the nouns and the verbs are common or general terms: but I might have substituted proper nouns in some of the sentences; instead of saying a boy drops a

stone into a brook, I might for instance have said
" Harry Smith drops the marble which his brother
gave him into the brook near my house:" where
the boy and the stone dropped and the stream into
which it fell are designated in language which by
its own quality or by particular combination becomes proper in contradistinction to common.

I might also have employed *more* general terms
to describe the events. I might have said the
stream causes the wheel to turn; the touch of the
lady's finger causes the key to sound the note c;
the flame causes the destruction of the paper; the
dropping of the stone into the brook causes concentric circles in the water.

Mark, however, that nothing is added in point
of fact and nothing more described or expressed
or indicated by the substitution of the more general for the less general term, except a resemblance
to a wider range of facts, while there is of course a
loss in particular significance.*

It is convenient to have a term which we can
use in respect of all the operations mentioned;
which can be applied to eliciting a note from the
piano, to making circles in the water, to consuming paper, and to extinguishing flame. In each of
these cases there is one thing giving rise to another,
there is a cause producing an effect, whether we

* In logical phrase the substituted term is greater in comprehension but less in extension than the one which it dis-
places.

describe the events which take place in terms less general or more general.

Here then we have before us, (1) Events perceived* to give rise to other events: (2) Ideas of those events: (3) Words of more or less generality to describe them.

What more do we want, and where is there any difficulty in the whole matter?

It may doubtless be said " So far all is well, but besides the three circumstances enumerated, the idea of causality or causation has sprung up in the mind and the great difficulty is to account for it or to show how we come by it."

This difficulty has I conceive been already met in a former letter, in which I showed that we have no idea of causation over and above the ideas of individual causes and effects: that these individual causes and effects are what we in the first place actually perceive when no " idea " is in question, and they are all we subsequently think of or can think of: or in other words all of which we can have ideas.

If any inquirer will only resort to his own consciousness instead of illuding himself by looking " through the spectacles of books," and ascertain what really passes in his mind when the word causation is used, or when he uses it himself, he

---

* The reader will please to bear in mind that I employ the word perceive to denote exclusively the act of discerning or observing through the organs of the senses.

will find that in his clearest mental state all that
he is conscious of, are representative conceptions
of individual objects or events in the act of producing others. Should he try to attach a precise
meaning to the word, he must think of particular
instances. If this statement is correct, we get
quit of all those perplexing questions as to the
idea of causation and its origin, which Hume with
all his acuteness and vigour proved himself im-
potent to solve.

We also get quit of the kindred inquiry " In
what does causation consist?" but only to find the
substance of it re-appear in a different form, namely,
what is the common circumstance, or attribute,
or quality, on account of which so many various
objects or events are designated by the term cause?
or to express it in other language, are classed under
that category?

You will probably be startled and will think me
dealing in paradoxes or in identical propositions,
when I say, in answer to this inquiry, that the
common circumstance cannot be better expressed
than by the term cause itself or its paronymes;
and that when we attempt to express it in any other
way we only vary our language and ring changes
on synonymous phrases.

The common circumstance in all causes is "causing." I may diversify the expression by saying
it is "producing an effect," or "effecting a change,"
or " operating upon an object," or " giving rise to

an event," or " modifying a substance:" but in all
this I am merely substituting equivalent expressions which themselves present the same difficulty,
if difficulty there really is, as the original phrase
which they replace.

If any one for example should make the inquiry
what is the common circumstance or attribute on
account of which one thing is said "to operate
upon another," I can resort only to the same mode
of reply.

I can as in the case of "causing" above elucidated, answer the inquiry only by equivalent
phrases. I may say that a thing operates upon
another when it produces a change in it, or alters
it, or effects a modification in it, but by employing such phrases I should in reality be no
nearer satisfying the question. It must be borne
in mind that the inquiry is something different
from asking the meaning of the expression.
Should the inquirer wish to know simply what
the phrase means, I should have no difficulty in re-
plying to him. I should not need to do more than
adduce particular incidents of the kind denoted by
the expression; I might point to the sun warming
the garden-wall, or the hot water in the tea-cup
melting the sugar, or the wind turning the vane
on the top of the house; which are all examples
of one body operating on another and would suffice
to convey my meaning.

So in the case of the kindred phrase " causing "

D

I cannot assign the common quality or property except by using equivalent expressions; but if you desire to know simply the meaning of the term, I can satisfy your inquiry by directing your attention to the flame of the taper liquefying the wax with which I am sealing a letter, or to the impression made by the seal on the melted substance, or a hundred other familiar instances of cause and effect which would at once put you in possession of the signification of the word.

And this is the furthest point that any one can reach; the utmost he can accomplish in the way of explanation. He may resort to equivalent phrases, or he may adduce individual examples. He can do no more.

This doctrine will I am aware be strenuously objected to at the first glance, not only by those who at once reject without examination everything not obviously consonant with their indurated prejudices, but even by those who may be disposed to bestow upon it due consideration. They may urge " we give a common name to two or more things because they resemble each other, and surely the circumstance or point in which they resemble each other may be assigned." Undoubtedly it may, but the question, according to what I have already said, is can it be assigned in any other way than by using the common name itself or an equivalent term?

In addition to the reply above given, — virtually

at least,—to this objection, let us test the soundness of it on the one hand and of the doctrine against which it is levelled on the other by taking some other simple instance of a common quality, and we cannot select a better one than a simple colour : let it be *red*.

We doubtless apply the common epithet *red* to the poppy and to the geranium because they resemble each other in a certain visible attribute or property.

But if you ask me to assign the particular property or circumstance or point or attribute in which they resemble each other I will not say they are alike in colour for that would be an evasion ; I can answer only that they are alike in being " red," in having a red colour. It is an ultimate fact that I perceive them to be similar in a certain visible respect which I designate by the epithet " red," and the inquiry is at an end.

Precisely in the same way I call the fire when scorching a piece of paper and the water when melting a lump of sugar or turning a wheel, by the common name cause, on account of their resembling each other in the circumstance of producing results. I call them causes for doing what I cannot better express than by the word causing.

Beyond this I am not able to go.

Each of these compared cases is an instance of calling a thing by a common name on account of a circumstance or property or attribute expressed by

the common name better, or at least not worse,
than by any other: and in each case the circumstance or attribute is a perceived object, and in
relation to thought or reasoning or speculation, it
is an ultimate fact. Objectors to this statement
would seem to require *two* names for the common
property, but even in the event of finding a second
one, they would be no nearer the end.

To show the truth of the doctrine in question
still more plainly let us take the very basis of all
classification and (inclusively) of all imposition of
general names, resemblance.

A portrait and the person whom it was painted
to represent are seen together and the spectator
discerns that the one has a peculiar relation to the
other: two mountains are perceived in the distance
both of which are peaked and blue: two pillars are
observed to support a building, both of the Corin-
thian order.

In each of these instances we discern two things
to resemble each other; and we further discern
that the pairs, as we may call them, do themselves
resemble one another in the fact that the two
individual members of each pair mutually resemble. A resembles B, C resembles D, E resembles F; and moreover the pairs AB, CD, and
EF are analogous to each other in being resembling
pairs.

Now to the objector who should want me to
point out the common circumstances on account

of which the name "cause" is given to the fire when scorching paper, and to the water when melting salt, I would say point out to me the common circumstance on account of which resemblance is said to exist in each pair of things in the above three cases, and also between the three pairs.

What is that which leads us to affirm in regard to the individual members of the pairs, and in regard to the pairs themselves, "these things resemble each other"?

What is the circumstance or respect or point or property which forms the ground of the assertion?

The only thing that leads us to say so, the only ground on which we make the assertion, is the resemblance itself. We *say* they are like because they *are* like. That phrase expresses precisely the whole fact.

We have reached the extreme length of our speculative and of our expositive tether.

We come in this case to one of those primary facts beyond which it is, in the nature of the case, impossible to go.

All that can be said is that we are so constituted as to perceive that things resemble one another.

So we perceive objects to be equal or near or opposite to each other, as well as a multitude of other relational facts — facts in which two objects at the least must bear a part, and which, if we wish to express in language, we must resort for that purpose to definite phrases not resolvable into others more significant.

It is just the same with "causing" as with "resembling": they are both general terms expressive of primary facts or circumstances of a relational character which we directly perceive.

Undoubtedly the generality of philosophers would explain or state the matter differently. They would bring in their general or abstract or simple ideas, to which I have already referred, and say that when we see a cause producing an effect, we not only see the sight but we have also the idea of causation or causality engendered in the mind. When they are asked, nevertheless, whether they ever have the idea of causation clearly distinct and separate from the perception or conception of some individual cause, they must be perplexed to return any but a negative answer, and a negative answer would be surrendering at discretion; it would at once admit the alleged idea of causation to be supererogatory or more correctly speaking to be a nullity.

For my own part, on scrutinizing my personal consciousness in every possible way, and especially the effects produced on it by general and abstract terms, I can find no such idea as causation; or, to speak with greater precision, I have not any idea in my mind corresponding to that abstract term, either when I am actually perceiving causes and effects or merely conceiving them; nor do I think of any thing when the words are used but individual events, specific instances of a cause producing an effect.

Besides, were this abstract idea of causation or causality upon which you insist to be admitted as an actual mental entity, I cannot see that it would carry us beyond the limit where I have shown that our knowledge and our speculations must stop. It would not advance the solution of the difficulty which presents itself to those inquirers who ask in what does causation consist.

It might still be demanded why is the idea of causation for which you contend raised up by, or attached to, or conferred upon, instances so widely at variance, in almost every respect, with each other as those which I have enumerated: and the answer must be, virtually if not formally, that which I have given.

There is still another consideration which is worth briefly adverting to.

If the perception of a cause producing an effect raises up as alleged the idea of causation or causingness *plus* the perception we have of cause and effect, an analogous phenomenon must be allowed to take place when we turn expressly to more particular cases (which are in truth all that are possible). The perception of fire burning wood must raise up the idea of burningness *plus* the sight of the fire consuming the wood. And so in every case: when water melts the sugar in your tea-cup,

or wets your coat, or quenches your thirst, you
must have the idea of meltingness, or wetting-
ness, or quenchingness, over and above the actual
perception of one or other of those several operations.

Indeed these more particular ideas, if such things
come into the mind at all, must precede the more
general idea of causation; for which in good sooth
it is not easy to find or fancy either a *hora natalis*
or a *nidus* to be born in.

We can witness the action of one particular
thing upon another but we cannot witness a cause
producing an effect generally or abstractedly.
There is no general or abstract entity called a
cause bringing about another general or abstract
entity called an effect; and if consequently the idea
of causation, as contended for, arise at all, it must
do so on some of the above described particular
occasions, along with the more limited idea appropriate to the case; and thus there would be both
a generic and a specific idea springing out of the
same causal event besides the representative idea
left in the mind by the event itself when it was
passed.

For example, in the case of a lighted taper
melting your sealing wax, there would on this
theory be the following ideas in your mind, besides
your perceiving through your sense of sight what
took place:

1. The simple or abstract idea of meltingness:

2. The simple or abstract idea of causingness:

3. The representative idea of the event after it had happened.

Those philosophers who maintain the doctrine of simple ideas merely (if any such there are) would be in a greater difficulty than those who maintain that of abstract ideas. On the former doctrine it is not easy to see how the ideas of meltingness and causingness could both be generated; but on the latter doctrine the idea of meltingness would be first abstracted from the concrete event, and then the idea of causingness would be abstracted from the idea of meltingness by a still higher process.

In such difficulties and incongruities are we landed by the doctrines of simple and abstract ideas in the matter of causation.

The plain and intelligible view which I have maintained extricates us from the embarrassment or rather prevents us from falling into it; namely, that in the case of a directly perceptible event, we perceive the cause producing the effect, and that the event so perceived bounds the consequent idea which represents it; or, in other words, the event is all that is or can be represented by the idea in its utmost possible completeness.

LETTER IV.

CAUSATION (*continued*).

IN the preceding letter I purposely confined my remarks to instances of causation which are directly perceived, which are the immediate subjects of observation through our organs of sense.

We see that the flame of the candle melts the sealing wax, and that the seal makes an impression on the melted substance; we see and hear that the touch of the lady's finger elicits the note from the piano; we feel that the sun gives warmth to the bodies exposed to his rays.

But besides the immense number of events constantly flowing from causes which we directly perceive in the very act of producing them, there are other events which we can only *infer* to be produced by certain causes; and there are causes which we can only infer to be productive of certain effects.

To take a familiar example, we do not perceive, we only infer that the moon causes the tides. We see the moon on the meridian, it is true, and we see the tide perhaps rising at the same time; but that one causes the other is a matter of inference requiring a great number of observations and many nice calculations to prove it.

Thus instances of causation naturally fall into two classes:

1. Instances of causation which we directly discern as such.

2. Instances of causation which we do not directly discern as such but which are the subjects of proof: in other words, events occurring in sequence or simultaneously which are determined by evidence to be causally connected: *i.e.* connected as those causes and effects are which we directly perceive. What we infer in this way can never go beyond the objects of direct perception.

Now one of the characteristics which we observe to belong to such instances of causation as we directly perceive, when we come to make them the subjects of comparison and reflection, is the invariableness of the operation. We observe when we compare numerous cases that a certain cause has always produced a certain effect.

It is obviously impossible for us to perceive this invariableness in a single instance, or in other words to perceive it from a cause once producing an effect; for the simple reason that it is a relation which can have place only amongst a number of instances. We may perceive a cause producing an effect without reference to any other similar event, but to perceive it *invariably* produce an effect, we must witness a number of similar events. Hence

although we expect similar results from similar
causes, it is only on comparison and reflection that
we come to consider invariable sequence or concomitance as a universal characteristic of the
causes and effects which are subject to our direct
perception; and it then becomes an important
criterion in the determination of the causal connexion of events in cases where that connexion is
not directly perceptible but is to be established by
proof.

When a cause produces an effect before our eyes,
no proof of the connexion between them is required
either from invariableness or from any thing else:
but when two successive or contemporaneous *
phenomena cannot be directly perceived to be
cause and effect, when, for example, they are separated by distance in space or in time, the invariableness of the sequence is indispensable, as
every one admits, to the proof of a causal connexion between them. If the tides did not invariably rise when the moon was in a certain relative position in regard to that part of the earth
where they once rose, they could not be concluded
to be the effect of that luminary.

But although invariableness of sequence or of

* I say contemporaneous to include causes which operate
continuously, so that the effects or some of them appear
simultaneous with the causes; but for the purpose in hand, it
is not needful to bring into view any but successive events,
and it simplifies the discussion to leave out the others which
may be assumed to be always tacitly included.

concomitance is indispensable to the proof of a causal connexion in such cases, it is not of itself sufficient to establish one, for the plain reason that it is an attribute of other sequences besides those of cause and effect. There are many phenomena taking place in succession with unbroken uniformity, without any causal dependence of the one on the other.

Amongst such may be mentioned joint effects of the same cause, or the same combination of causes, which are not always even simultaneous but precede and follow each other; as the flash and the report from a piece of artillery. The flash is the invariable antecedent but not the cause of the report. Other cases too abound of a different character.

In any given tune the notes follow each other in a succession which must be strictly observed, otherwise the tune is marred or rather prevented; but although to produce the tune they must follow each other in a certain order, or, if you prefer the phrase, in an invariable sequence, one note does not cause another; the first has nothing to do with producing its successor the second. Each note is proximately the effect of a definite number of vibrations in a string or other sonorous body, and not of the preceding note.

Hence invariableness of sequence, although it is indispensably requisite, cannot be held sufficient of itself to establish a causal connexion.

In the case of the moon and the tides, the now undisputed conclusion that one is the cause of the other, could not have been confidently drawn unless philosophers had been able, not only to show that the phenomena concerned take place invariably, but to account for them by the law of gravitation: *i.e.*, in truth, to show that the phenomena are analogous to instances of causation which we directly perceive. Otherwise the connexion between the moon and the tides would have been much in the same logical position as the uniformity of colour which led to the conclusion formerly prevailing that all swans were white.

Every case of *inferred* causal connexion must be analogous to cases which we *directly perceive*.

Thus there are two points to be noted in respect to invariableness of succession:

1. It is characteristic of other sequences beside those of cause and effect.

2. It is not included in the fact of a single cause producing an effect, nor of course in our perception of the fact.

Causation, therefore, is not the same thing as invariable succession.

Dr. Thos. Brown, who was a very able metaphysician, and in many respects an admirable writer, although too easily satisfied with his own speculations on points requiring protracted study and repeated examination, overlooked several of the considerations which I have presented to you in the preceding remarks.

In his celebrated " Inquiry into the Relation of Cause and Effect," the most elaborate and most carefully digested of his philosophical writings, he strenuously contends that causes are nothing but invariable antecedents, and that effects are nothing but invariable consequents. He says that to assert A to be the cause of B is the same thing as to assert A to be the invariable antecedent of B; and, conversely, to assert B to be the effect of A is the same thing as to assert B to be the invariable consequent of A. One proposition he contends affirms as much and no more than the other. To determine the truth of this doctrine let us look at a few obvious facts.

When it is affirmed that two propositions are identical or equivalent, the assertion is that the fact expressed in one is the same as the fact expressed in the other; that they are merely two modes of stating one fact.

Let us then take a single case of causation: I strike the table at which I am seated, and the stroke makes a sound.

According to my own view a cause here produces an effect, a stroke causes a sound, or to express it conversely, for the convenience of Dr. Brown's argument, a sound is the effect of a stroke; and I perceive it to be so. I perceive a

cause operate and an effect follow. According to
Dr. Brown this is precisely the same thing as the
sound *invariably* following the stroke. Nothing
more is contained in one description than in the
other.

Assuredly, however, the two propositions are
altogether different. One proposition asserts only
the happening of a pair of successive events without reference to any thing else : while the other
proposition asserts a relation between one pair of
successive events and other pairs of successive
events.

An instance of causation may take place and be
perceived as such unaccompanied by any connexion
with any other similar instance; it is complete in
itself; whereas by the very force of the terms, or
rather in the very nature of the case, more instances than one must occur to make it true that a
certain event is in those instances (not to speak of
all possible instances) uniformly followed by a certain other event. Applied to a single pair of
successive events, without reference to any others,
the designation "invariable sequence" has no
meaning, while to style one member of the pair
"the cause of the other" has a signification
obvious and complete in itself.

Perhaps this argument may be rendered clearer
by considering the several relations which may be
discriminated as concerned in the question.

The connexion of cause and effect is one rela-

tion: the succession of events is another relation:
and invariableness of succession is a third.

1. That one event is the cause of another is
clearly a relational fact which is complete in a
single instance, as I have shown, and is directly so
perceived. The whole case is, so to speak, in presence. The stroke falls on the table before our eyes
and we hear the sound occasioned by it. The causal
connexion is perfect in itself without reference to
any analogous events.

2. That one event follows another, is also a relational fact, which is complete in a single instance,
as well as perceived to be so, just as in the case of
causation.

3. That one event *invariably* follows another is
a third relational fact; but so far from the relation
of invariableness being one which can have place
in a single instance like the relations in the other
cases 1 and 2, it manifestly cannot subsist except
between several instances.

A stroke produces a sound in a single case as
completely as in a thousand cases, but it would be
absurd to speak of a sound *invariably* following
the stroke in a single case without reference to any
other. More instances than one being thus self-
evidently required for this relation of invariableness to subsist, a curious consequence results from
the doctrine under review. Since that doctrine
teaches invariable sequence to be the same thing
as causal connexion, it logically follows that a

E

single pair of successive events cannot by themselves be cause and effect: to become so they must
wait till other similar sequences have happened,
and then having emerged from their solitary state
they with the rest assume a causal connexion, not
in their own right but in virtue of the uniformity
of succession amongst the whole.

If Dr. Brown had simply maintained that causing and being caused are nothing more than preceding and following, and that the proposition " A
causes B " expresses no more than the proposition '
" A precedes B," he would not have exposed himself to the criticism just brought against his actual
doctrine.   It is a possible and on a first glance
even a plausible proposition that there is nothing
and that we can perceive nothing in a cause producing an effect but one event preceding another.
But he was too perspicacious not to see, that causation is only one kind of sequence, that numerous
other events which no one can mistake for causes
and effects also respectively precede and follow.
Discerning, then, that causes and effects are something besides mere sequences, he thought he had
found this something in invariableness of succession, not adverting to the obvious fact that this
circumstance can have place only when there are
more instances of sequence than one ; and therefore can have nothing to do with constituting the
causal character of the individual sequences amongst

which the relation of invariubleness comes to subsist.

I come back then to the doctrine already maintained that our perceiving a cause produce an effect, as for example, the flame of a taper melt sealing wax, is a primal fact which we cannot express more simply, just as our perceiving that one rose resembles another is a primal fact not to be more plainly or directly enunciated in language.

LETTER V.

EVIDENCE.

THERE is one important subject on which I hold some opinions difficult, I fear, to make as plain to you as they are to myself, but which you have frequently intimated you are anxious to learn — I mean the subject of evidence.

To clear the way, I must premise the obvious truth that there are two classes of facts more requisite than easy to distinguish, facts we know and facts we receive on evidence: in other words, facts discerned or felt, and facts inferred.

All that we can be strictly said to know are the mental affections of which we are conscious and the external objects which we personally perceive. Every thing else we learn from evidence and can learn by no other means.

Things thus known in the strictest sense of the expression, may be termed *primitive* facts; and *direct* evidence may be briefly defined as consisting in these primitive facts adduced to prove other facts.

Facts which have been themselves proved may be termed *derivative* or *secondary*, and when they in turn are made use of as proofs they constitute what may be denominated *indirect* evidence.

If we exclude from consideration mathematical and other demonstrative proofs which as being of a distinct character I purpose to omit in the following exposition, the definition of direct evidence may be stated thus: direct evidence consists in a fact or facts personally known to us employed to prove, or engaged in the function of proving, that some other fact not known, has taken place, is taking place, or will take place.

To some persons it may appear proper to limit the term evidence to the proofs of past events, but the inconvenience unavoidably arising from the repetition and prolixity consequent on such a restriction, would more than counterbalance the advantage gained by it. It would also be contrary to custom. For example, it is very common to speak of the evidence for a future state, or for the approaching appearance and probable track, in the heavens, of a comet.

When either primitive or derivative facts are brought to prove other facts, the operation may be styled either *discerning and adducing evidence** (in shorter phrase employing evidence), or *reasoning*.

* Discerning when we are engaged in silent thought, and both discerning and adducing when we are addressing ourselves to others.

It seems to be very commonly overlooked that these two processes are identical, or rather that the two phrases are different descriptions of the same process.

Facts adduced as evidence are the premises from which we draw a conclusion; and their being employed as evidence implies that they are adduced for the sake of establishing the conclusion.

The identity of these two processes needs to be pressed upon the attention, since it is altogether lost sight of by those writers who while they very properly and legitimately insist upon the evidences for the existence and attributes of a Deity and for the truth of revelation, are at the same time inconsistent enough to speak in the most disparaging and even contemptuous terms of " poor human reason." That miserable faculty being, however, a mere figure of speech, their contempt falls in reality on the very process of employing evidence in which they are so zealously engaged. They are decrying their own task. Nay more. They are with busy earnestness actually sawing off from the bole of the tree the identical branch on which they have seated themselves.

If, as their vituperation of weak human reason implies, we human beings are so constituted as to be incompetent, inefficient, and imbecile in dealing with evidence or drawing inferences from the facts presented to us, or rather if that process itself is fallacious and not to be trusted, why do these

writers who can pretend to no exemption from the
failings and feebleness of our common nature, pour
forth their confessedly wretched attempts at attaining truth by inference or deduction, into the
ears of those who partake of the same logical
incapacity ?

If they are to be taken at their word, they are
at the best engaged in nothing better than

> "—— the toil
> Of dropping buckets into empty wells,
> And growing old in drawing nothing up."

The course of the writers here alluded to, well
exemplifies the evils arising from the personification of mental operations. If reasoning had not
been spoken of as a faculty and if that faculty had
not subsequently been personified, or erected into
a separate entity, such futile invectives could not
have been put forth. No reasoner would have been
weak enough to directly disparage the process itself.

Further it is important to have a full and clear
apprehension, while considering the two classes of
facts above described, primitive facts and derivative facts, that the former do not admit of evidence
at all; they are not susceptible of proof ; or, in
other words, they are not the subjects of inference.
If direct evidence consists in known or primitive
facts adduced to prove facts not actually known,
the former class, it is plain, cannot themselves be
the subjects of evidence.

Thus all our own mental states and conditions,

operations and affections, our sensations, emotions, acts of perceiving, of reasoning, of recollecting, of willing, are things felt or done or experienced by us; they are facts known to us, primitive facts ; and they neither require nor admit of evidence or proof to us who experience them.

This truth holds good of, or more correctly speaking comprehends, our perceiving external objects. That I see the trees and the grass and the flowers in the landscape before me, is to me a primitive fact which is not susceptible of proof or evidence. I know it.

The employment of evidence has thus nothing to do with primitive facts; it is legitimately confined to showing either that some event has happened or is happening although unperceived by us, or that some event will happen, which therefore must be equally unperceived.

When any one attempts to prove the existence of objects actually present to our senses, or more precisely speaking perceived through the organs of sense, he falls (on the most favorable supposition) into the absurdity of adducing known facts to prove others equally known; and when he attempts on the other hand to prove the non-existence of such objects the self-contradiction, as I have shown elsewhere, if not equally manifest is not less real.*

* See Letters on the Philosophy of the Human Mind, First Series, p. 140, and Second Series, p. 132.

These conclusions seem almost too simple to require pointing out, yet they have been so utterly overlooked that philosophers in crowds have endeavoured to prove and others to disprove that we perceive external objects.

If they had duly reflected on the nature of evidence, they would have discerned the absolute futility of all such attempts.

Evidence having been thus shown to consist in known or already proved facts adduced to prove other facts, the next step is to consider in what property of the facts or the evidence the force of the proof lies; or, in different language, how some facts become or are fitted to become the proofs of other facts.

All facts it is plain cannot prove other facts indiscriminately. For one fact to have the capability of proving another there must be a connexion between the facts themselves or the classes of facts to which they belong.

This connexion is that of either causation or concomitance.

All facts adduced as evidence are and must be either causes or effects or concomitant circumstances.

When Robinson Crusoe (if I may resort to an example from fiction) was startled at seeing a foot-print on the sand in his solitary island, he instantly inferred that it had been made by a human being passing over the beach.

This was reasoning from the effect to the cause, or, to put the matter the other way, the print on the sand was evidence to him of the cause which had produced it — of the recent transit of a man.

On the other hand, should any one seeing a boat's crew about to land on the beach, predict from a previous knowledge of the consistence of the sand that they would leave their foot-prints upon it, he would reason from the cause to the effect, and the evidence to his mind would be facts before experienced of an analogous character.

In regard to the second kind of connexion, when concomitant facts like those here referred to are such as are always found together (for some facts are, I scarcely need to say, only casually conjoined) one is the evidence of the other just as in the case of causal succession, but to make them equal to the latter as proofs, they must be joint results of the same cause.   Thus the fall of the mercury in a thermometer to zero, or to a certain point above it, and the freezing of the neighbouring pond, are concomitant effects of a great abstraction of heat from the atmosphere; and on seeing the state of the thermometer we may infer the state of the pond without taking the trouble of going to look at it.   The state of the thermometer is not the cause of the state of the pond, nor, conversely, is the latter the cause of the former; they are con-comitant results of one cause and serve to prove each other.

These are doubtless trite and simple facts and explanations, but since they lie in the course of the argument, their triteness and simplicity do not diminish their importance.

Having thus shown the nature of the connexion between facts by which they become, or may become, evidence of each other, I will proceed to point out the limitations of this function.

At the first glance it is obvious that any given cause does not produce all sorts of effects but one precise effect, and from that particular cause, consequently, it is only that precise effect which can be inferred. The converse equally holds.

Thus we are limited in our inferences to similar cases of causation.

If we have seen A produce B at one time we can infer when we meet with it again, that it will again produce B: we cannot infer that it will produce C.

From no cause can we infer legitimately a future effect unless we have known directly or indirectly a similar cause produce a similar effect to that which we infer; and the same truth holds *mutatis mutandis* when from effects we infer past causes and past concomitant events the results of the same cause.

To put the matter the other way, we can have no evidence that an effect will happen from an assigned cause unless we have known similar effects to have happened from causes similar to

that assigned; or, more correctly speaking, an
assigned cause cannot be evidence to us of the
future event without the knowledge described.
When for example, a copper rod is fixed to a
church steeple to guard it from the stroke of the
lightning, there can be no ground for expecting
the rod to protect the building except the experience that the electric fluid in the atmosphere
has been conveyed harmless into the earth by
similar metallic conductors.

So with regard to the past: we can have no
evidence that an effect has been produced by an
assigned cause unless we have known similar
effects produced by similar causes; or again more
correctly, the effect cannot without that knowledge be to us evidence that the cause has been
in operation.

The shattered spire is proof to us that the
lightning has struck it, only because we have
witnessed or known or learned indirectly similar
instances of destruction from similar strokes of
the electric fluid.

The truth that we can infer none but events
similar to those which we already know, whether
the events inferred are causes, effects, or concomitant results, may be said in a certain sense to be
comprehended in another truth formerly insisted
upon, namely that we can conceive nothing or
think of nothing but such objects or events (how
differently soever arranged) as we have previously

perceived or been conscious of: but our inferences
are obviously much more limited than our conceptions; we must be able to conceive all that we
infer but we cannot infer all that we can conceive,
but only, as before said, such facts as are similar
to those which we have known to be connected by
causation or concomitance with the facts from
which we reason.

By separation and combination of known objects
and events, we may create in imagination scenes
and incidents more beautiful and interesting, vaster
and more sublime, of greater splendour and magni-
ficence, than any experienced realities; but for our
being able to infer that these will at some future
period take place, we must know that there are
causes at present in operation analogous to those
which have in past times produced similar scenes
and incidents.

Here doubtless an objection may naturally be
raised. It may be said by some of my readers,
"we may be told that events will take place at
some future period transcending our experience,
and surely we are right on sufficient authority in
looking forward to them, although bearing no resemblance to any thing in the past or the present."

Doubtless on sufficient authority you are; but
it is needful to bear in mind, (1) that you can
comprehend them only so far as you have known
like events, if not in their combination at least in
their elements. The tether that ties you here is

perfectly definite.   You must also bear in mind,
(2) that the evidence you have for such events is
the telling, *i.e.* the testimony or rather the predic-
tion of human beings; and the telling or the predic-
tion must be such in quality and circumstances as
you have always found to be trustworthy, always
found to announce no events but such as have
subsequently happened.   The same principles are
applicable *mutatis mutandis* to any narrative of
past events.   Thus testimony is brought within
the same principles as all other facts when they
become evidence.

This limitation of possible inferences to similar
cases may be applied to the doctrine, already
mentioned, of those metaphysicians who contend
that we *infer* the existence of an external world
from our own sensations which are caused by it;
and if I mistake not it will exhibit a striking phase
of that error.

If it is true, as I have shown, that in order to
be able to infer any facts of causation, we must
have known similar facts, *i.e.* both the causes and
the effects as connected, it follows that to be able
to infer the existence of the external world from
our own sensations we must have known a similar
world, and known it too as causing similar sensations : otherwise no inference is possible from one
to the other.

From this preposterous conclusion which strictly
follows from the premises we have no refuge but

in the truth or primal fact that we directly perceive the external world. It is impossible that we
can infer it. Its existence cannot be what is styled
in the loose language of some philosophers "a conclusion of the reason"; it is a fact which we know,
and which is consequently beyond the province of
reasoning.

It may appear that the limits here traced cir-
cumscribe too strictly the range of philosophical
speculation. The question, however, is not whether
the limits assigned are narrow, but whether they
are the true boundaries of legitimate inference.
Doubtless it is unpleasant to discover some of
our brilliant dreams to be mere dreams; to find
ourselves tied down to facts alike in our retrospec-
tive conclusions and in our anticipations of what
is to come; and to be fettered by restraints which
have been wisely submitted to by the greatest
thinkers.

I will not carry the subject farther in the present
Letter, but conclude by calling your attention to
the importance of the distinctions I have drawn.

It is of great consequence to have a clear apprehension of the difference between primal facts —
facts not within the province of proof—and facts
which rest on evidence: also to understand that
employing evidence, and the act of reasoning, are
one and the same process. We are also deeply
concerned in discerning how it is that one fact has
the power of proving another, or, in other words,

what are the characteristics of the facts which are capable of proving and susceptible of being proved.

It is likewise important to be aware that our inferences are unavoidably limited to causes, effects, and concomitant results, such or similar to such as we have already experienced.

Nor is it of inferior moment to be able to discriminate the facts we can legitimately infer, whether past, contemporal or future, from those creations of the imagination which, boundless as they may appear, are yet equally with our inferences strictly limited to the elements of knowledge supplied by the perception of external objects and by other forms of consciousness.

LETTER VI.

LAWS OF NATURE.

AFTER the complete exposure by Dugald Stewart of Montesquieu's confused employment of the term *law* at the commencement of his celebrated treatise "Esprit des Lois," it is surprising to find similar confusion frequently re-appearing in the present day.

Mr. Stewart's words are, "Even the great Montesquieu in the very first chapter of his principal work, has lost himself in a fruitless attempt to explain its meaning, when by a simple statement of the essential distinction between its literal and metaphorical acceptations, he might have at once cleared up the mystery. After telling us that 'laws in their most extensive signification are the necessary relations (*les rapports nécessaires*) which arise from the nature of things, and that in this sense, *all* beings have their laws;—that the Deity has *his* laws; the material world *its* laws; intelligences superior to man *their* laws; the brutes *their* laws; man *his* laws;' he proceeds to remark, 'That the moral world is far from being so well governed as the material; for the former, although it has *its*

F

laws which are invariable, does not observe these laws so constantly as the latter.' It is evident (proceeds Mr. Stewart) that this remark derives whatever plausibility it possesses from a play upon words; from confounding *moral* laws with *physical;* or in plainer terms, from confounding laws which are addressed by a legislator to intelligent beings, with those general conclusions concerning the established order of the universe to which, when legitimately inferred from an induction sufficiently extensive, philosophers have metaphorically applied the title of Laws of Nature." *

One of the particular evils which I am desirous of emphatically pointing out as resulting from the confusion of two meanings animadverted upon in the foregoing extract, is a very lax and inaccurate mode of speaking of the infraction or violation of the laws of nature.

It is plain enough that a law of morality may be violated, but it seems not to be generally understood that a law of nature is in a very different position; and accordingly the infraction of both is often indiscriminately spoken of, as if something took place with regard to material laws corresponding to a breach of moral laws.

Everybody understands what it is to violate a moral law. A thief breaks the law *thou shalt not steal.* He does steal. He does that which the law

* Elements of the Philosophy of the Human Mind, Vol. II. Chap. 2. Sect. 4.

forbids him to do. The deed is done although the law declares that it shall not be done.

But mark how different it is with a law of nature. It is a law of nature that the fumes of burning charcoal in a close room destroy life. A man inadvertently shuts himself up in a chamber without a vent and warmed by a pan of that substance in a state of ignition. He perishes. Here the writers I have in view would affirm that the man had violated a law of nature; but instead of a law of nature being violated, it was in truth completely carried out. Nature (if I may adopt the florid language common on such topics) proclaims her law that the fumes of charcoal destroy life, and she enforces it with unfaltering rigour.

What was violated on this occasion was clearly not any law of nature but a law of prudence or wisdom,—if we may dignify it by so high a name— that teaches us to avoid subjecting ourselves to the deadly action of the law which nature has clearly proclaimed and will unsparingly execute. In plain language the poor man in my hypothetical instance, was ignorant or heedless of the properties of the things he meddled with and suffered in consequence.

And so it is throughout. Prudential maxims may be set at nought or infringed, ethical rules may be broken, the enactments of the legislature may be violated, but the laws of nature cannot in any sense be correctly spoken of as the subjects of similar infraction.

It is obvious enough, however, that rules of conduct, maxims of prudence, and precepts of wisdom,
must, in order to be effectual for their purpose, be
founded on the laws of nature; or, in other words,
be conformable to the qualities of things. Wisdom
and prudence require for their perfection an accurate knowledge of the physical and mental agents
amongst which we are placed, so that wisdom may
select her instruments, and prudence be able to
point out what to avoid: but without the undeviating operation of these agents, or, in different language, the uniform connexion of causes and effects,
no rules of conduct could be formed and wisdom
and prudence would be vain.

There is one objection to the tenour of the preceding remarks which it may be worth while to
consider, especially as to do so will afford oppor-
tunities of further elucidating the distinctions here
drawn.

It may be said that the moral law *thou shalt not
steal* is just as unalterable as any physical law, so
that in this respect the two kinds of law are on an
equality, and one may be spoken of in the same
language as the other.

This brings us to a minuter examination of
what infringing, or breaking, or violating a law,
signifies.

When we say that a moral law is violated we
certainly do not mean that the law itself is altered.

The violation consists in some one acting contrary to it, while it still continues in force and unchanged. On one side is the unalterable precept; on the other the unconformable conduct. But the precept is as essential to the violation as the action which contravenes it; just as in the deviation of a right line A from parallelism with another right line B, the second line is as necessary to the deviation as the first.

In what is called a law of nature on the other hand the precept is wanting: there is no injunction and consequently it is impossible to act contrary to it. In truth the phrase *acting contrary to the law*, a phrase so clear and definite when applied to ethical precepts or legal enactments, has no real meaning when applied to the laws of nature. You cannot in any conceivable sense act contrary to them. Do what you will, you must submit to them as they are. Whether you stifle yourself with the fumes of charcoal in a chamber hermetically sealed, or preserve your life by providing a proper vent for the suffocating gas, the laws of nature are equally observed; a violation of such laws is equally impossible.

The laws of nature are in truth, as every philosopher knows and as Mr. Stewart clearly points out, nothing more than generalised facts, and it is only by a metaphor that the title in question is assigned to them. To deduce consequences from a literal interpretation of the figurative expression, is to plunge into error.

There is a further consideration which brings the present subject more especially under the Philosophy of the human mind, and may serve to vindicate, if that were necessary, the place assigned to it in these letters. Mental as well as material operations are concerned in the investigation.

Hitherto we have been engaged in contrasting laws of nature in the physical world with laws of conduct in the moral one. We must not suppose, however, that laws of nature and physical laws are co-extensive.

And this caution is the more requisite as it is much easier to confound a *mental* law of nature than a physical one with an ethical or civil law.

The distinction may be rendered more palpable by a brief explanation of the several kinds of laws relating to conduct.

(1) There are laws in the conduct of mankind which resemble physical laws in being *causal;* in other words uniform effects result from mental or moral causes as they do from physical causes: thus distrust is engendered by falsehood, and resentment is excited by injury.

(2) There are laws of wisdom or prudence, grounded on these causal laws, which we lay down for the government of our own conduct, or at least observe in practice from prudential considerations. Thus, as it is wise to avoid the fumes of charcoal, so it is wise to speak truth in our intercourse with our neighbours, and to refrain from inflicting in-

juries upon them, were it solely on account of the consequences predicated in the preceding causal laws, other motives apart.

(3) In addition to the preceding laws there are precepts given to us or enforced upon us by other persons, which are likely for the most part to agree with them. Thus we might receive from authority the precepts " thou shalt not lie to thy neighbours," "thou shalt not injure any one," as well as adopt maxims of conduct corresponding to them from enlightened views of our own nature and position as human beings.

In the first of these three cases, the laws resemble physical laws; they are what may be conveniently designated (as physical laws are) *natural* and cannot be, in any proper sense of the term, broken. Lying will engender distrust and injuries will provoke resentment.

If, neglecting these consequences, you utter falsehoods to your neighbour and injure his welfare, you do not break the natural laws, or in other words interrupt or alter the succession of causes and effects, but your conduct is an infraction of rule which comes within the second case: you violate the prudential maxims which prescribe that lying must be avoided if you desire the confidence of your fellow-men; and the infliction of injuries shunned if you seek not to provoke resentment and retaliation. Further, your false and injurious behaviour will be an infraction of rule also under the third case: you will contravene the precepts imposed by authority, and thus be additionally unwise by drawing on yourself the penalties of disobedience.

The inconsistency of speaking in the same breath of the uniform operation of the laws of nature and of the observance and infraction of such laws is exceedingly prevalent; and the impropriety of it is aggravated by the speaker's dilating also on the rewards and punishments respectively of such observance and such infraction.

One of the most striking instances of it is contained in the following passage from "Volney's Treatise on the Law of Nature," which, although the book may now be considered obsolete, faithfully represents what still continues to be uttered.

" It is a law of nature that water flows from an upper to a lower situation; that it seeks its level; that it is heavier than air; that all bodies tend towards the earth; that flame rises towards the sky; that it destroys the organisation of vegetables and animals; that air is essential to the life of certain animals; that, in certain cases, water suffocates and kills them; that certain juices of plants and certain minerals, attack their organs, and destroy their life; and the same of a variety of facts.

" Now since these facts, and many similar ones, are constant, regular, and immutable, they become so many *real commands, to which man is bound*

to conform under the express penalty of punishment
attached to their infraction, or well-being connected
with their observance. So that if a man were to pretend to see clearly in the dark, or is regardless of
the progress of the seasons, or the action of the elements; if he pretends to exist under water without
drowning, to handle fire without burning himself,
or deprive himself of air without suffocating, or
to drink poison without destroying himself; he
receives for each infraction of the law of nature,
a corporal punishment proportioned to his trans-
gression. If, on the contrary, he observes these
laws, and founds his practice on the precise and
regular relation which they bear to him, he pre-
serves his existence, and renders it as happy as it
is capable of being rendered."

Here the error of representing instances of the
natural connexion of causes and effects as things
enjoined, is conspicuously exhibited; for in order
to effect a parallel between violating precepts and
acting without prudent attention to the laws of
nature, the writer, bending before the inviolability
of natural successions, is obliged to resort to the
strange assertion that man sometimes *pretends* to
act contrary to those laws. But the whole passage
is fallacious and confused. No philosophical speculation should begin with a fiction, and it is
altogether a fiction to represent natural laws (*i. e.*
the qualities of objects around us) as commands.
No commands are issued and none should be

assumed. It is equally indulging in fiction to
speak of observing and transgressing the said laws;
of reaping the reward attendant on the first and
incurring the punishment appointed for the second.
The truth involved in this verbiage is nothing
more than that similar causes uniformly produce
similar effects; and that it is a knowledge of these
uniform successions which enables us to adjust
our conduct to them so as to avoid evil and to
secure good.

The same error runs through a work which
has obtained a large circulation, "The Constitution of Man considered in relation to External
Objects," by Mr. George Combe.

It is the production of an able, intelligent, and
to a certain extent clear-headed writer, who
grapples with a question manfully and seems to
have no aim but the discovery and inculcation
of truth. Taking for its basis the system originated by Dr. Gall, it is of course full of the language and of the errors of the phrenologists.
But although these deform and injure the work,
the substantial excellence of the matter is not
destroyed by them. The best parts of the author's
speculations might be expressed in common language exempt from all reference to phrenology,
not only without detriment but with great advantage to their perspicuity and force.

But besides phrenological verbiage, the great
and misleading error about the laws of nature

which I have above described, pervades the whole
book, and unavoidably detracts from the clearness
and philosophical precision of its statements and
reasonings.

This defect which consists, as we have seen, in
a confusion of certain things that ought to be kept
distinct and a consequent loose application of
language, leads Mr. Combe into a good many
trite truisms or nugatory propositions, the real
character of which would be at once disclosed
if they were expressed in common phraseology.

The substantial drift of his book is to trace and
exhibit the connexion of causes and effects in the
external world and in ourselves as far as they
concern human happiness — to awake attention to
the properties of mind and matter so far as they
produce pleasure and pain, good and evil: to
insist on the invariableness of these properties,
the undeviating uniformity with which causes
produce their effects: and to illustrate on the one
hand, the wisdom of regulating our conduct by
such facts, and on the other, the folly of expecting
any different results — the futility of anticipating
exemption from evil when we have taken the very
way to bring it upon our heads; or of looking for
a specific good depending on means which we have
not been at the trouble to employ.

All these truths, valuable as they are, may
nevertheless be explained and enforced without the
introduction of imaginary commands and the

fictitious infraction of them. There is not an instructive train of thought or a forcible representation of acts and consequences in the whole book, which would not be improved by being stripped of the phraseology of what may be called philosophical fiction.

Mr. Combe, however, from a deficiency in the power of precise thinking on the abstruser parts of philosophy, has fallen into the error of perpetually and systematically using such language. The two opposite courses of action which he has described, he designates respectively as observing and violating the laws of nature, not consistently seeing, what he sometimes positively and plainly enough asserts, that no violation is possible; that these expressions mean nothing more than prudently squaring our conduct to the properties of the existences around us on the one hand and neglecting to do it on the other. The whole discourse is an expansion of the common saying, " As you sow so shall you reap." He enforces what all know but are apt to forget, that as you will have to abide the consequences of your own acts you must take care what you are about. If you seek refuge under a tree in a thunder-storm, you will probably be struck dead; if you run into the fire you will certainly be burnt.

This is all. It is an excellent lesson to dilate upon; and he has illustrated it by striking examples of human conduct, and the happiness and

misery which may arise from that conduct being
well or ill directed by attention or inattention to
the laws of nature or the properties of surrounding objects; but there is no question at all of commands, of observance and infraction, of obedience
and disobedience, of rewards and punishments.
Such terms find their proper place in a different
connexion.   They relate to those precepts and
rules and maxims which grow up amongst mankind or are prescribed for the guidance of our
conduct, and which we may be properly said to
obey or to disobey, to observe or to infringe.

There is another incorrect view of the laws of
nature, or, more properly speaking perhaps, an
incorrect mode of using the phrase leading to
substantial incorrectness, which we occasionally
encounter in philosophical or historical speculations.   The fault in question consists in ranging
statistical results under that denomination, and
then attributing to them as laws, the power of
regulating if not of causing events.

Of this singular sort of attribution, the accomplished author of the "History of Civilization
in England," presents us with the most conspicuous
instances in his comprehensive speculations.   For
example, he cites the fact that in countries where
returns of the number of suicides in several consecutive years have been furnished, the annual
amount of those lamentable occurrences is nearly
the same.   He afterwards proceeds to say :

"These being the peculiarities of this singular crime, it is surely an astonishing fact, that all the evidence we possess respecting it points to one great conclusion, and can leave no doubt on our minds, that suicide is merely the product of the general condition of society, and that the individual felon only carries into effect what is a necessary consequence of preceding circumstances. In a given state of society, a certain number of persons must put an end to their own life. This is the general law; and the special question as to who shall commit the crime, depends of course upon special laws; which, however, in their total action, must obey the large social law to which they are all subordinate. And the power of the larger law is so irresistible, that neither the love of life nor the fear of another world can avail anything towards even checking its operation."[*]

In this passage he begins, you will observe, by ascribing suicide itself to the general condition of society which is a real if not a very definite cause; but when he proceeds to give us the law of the phenomenon, he states merely the uniformity of the effect; and in what follows he erects a simple statistical result into a powerful agent which nothing can withstand. Not only does he designate it as a large social law of irresistible force, but more strangely still, he speaks of certain

[*] History of Civilisation in England, by H. T. Buckle. Vol. I. p. 26.   1857.

special laws as obeying it (a novel feature in the
action of laws) and as, in their subordinate
capacity, determining who shall commit the crime.
This is perplexing enough; for the large social
law in question being, that in any given condition
of society a certain number of suicides necessarily
take place, which is a fact or result brought out
by a comparison of statistical returns, how can
this result, made up of the cases occurring, govern
the special laws by which the individual persons
concerned were determined to the fatal act ? How
can the numerical amount of the cases govern the
circumstances which produce them?

Instead of investing numerical results with the
attributes of power, Mr. Buckle would have done
more wisely if he had looked steadily at those real
causes on which he contents himself with casting
a momentary glance.

Why the number of suicides is in any given
year what it is, neither larger nor smaller, and
uniform with that in other years, must be dependent, it is plain, on some positive circumstances
or other: it is not a self-constituted fact.

The number is, in truth, determined by the
concurrence and conflict of various motives to
which not a few human beings are unhappily
subjected, impelling them to the rash act, or with-
holding them from it, the former motives being '
frequently suggested by external circumstances
obvious or assignable; the latter consisting for the

most part of that love of life and that fear of
another world, which Mr. Buckle describes as so
unavailing to check the numerical law, but which
are indisputably efficient causes and mainly instrumental in keeping down these melancholy
occurrences to their actual amount.

Should the motives which prompt to the act be
multiplied or strengthened, as, for example, by the
coming on of commercial distress, or by the increase of gambling or of drunkenness, there can
be no doubt that the love of life and the fear of
another world would oftener give way, and the
number of suicides would be raised. On the other
hand, should prosperity add a relish to life, and
judicious legislation withdraw the temptations of
the gaming-house and the gin-shop, the con-
servative motives would not only be fortified but
have fewer assaults to withstand, and a reduction
in the melancholy list would eventually follow.
If I am here stating trite and obvious truths, it is
because the character of the fallacies combated
naturally leads to them.

To show the nature of Mr. Buckle's doctrine in
a still clearer light, let us see how the position
assumed by him would do, if it were applied in
some analogous cases.

"Every year there is a certain number of panes
broken in hot-houses by hail-storms. Assume the
average proportion to be ten per cent. in the
whole country. What particular hot-houses will

be subject to this calamity will depend on special
laws which in their total action must obey the
large meteorological law, the power of which is so
irresistible that neither strength of glass nor any
skill on the part of the glazier, can even check it.
Ten per cent. of the panes must be broken."

This may appear absurd enough, but it is not, I
think, an unfair parallel with Mr. Buckle's representation on the subject of suicides.

A few pages subsequently, he furnishes another
instance of such laws (as he regards them) in relation to marriages, but it is really of a different
character, and it may be instructive to examine in
what the difference consists.

He tells us that " the number of marriages
annually contracted [in certain countries] is determined not by the temper and wishes of individuals
but by large general facts over which individuals
can exercise no authority." He then adds, "It is
now known that marriages bear a fixed and definite
relation to the price of corn, and in England the
experience of a century has proved that instead of
having any connexion with personal feelings, they
are simply regulated by the average earnings of
the great mass of the people: so that this immense
social and religious institution is not only swayed,
but is completely controlled, by the price of food
and by the rate of wages." *

* History of Civilisation in England, Vol. I. p. 30.

Here the large general facts, unlike those which
we have been considering, are actually *causes* that
affect the result, any marked prosperity among the
people increasing the marriages, and any marked
adversity reducing the number in a given time.

But instead of any hostility existing between
the action of these causes and the operation of
those personal feelings, which Mr. Buckle strips of
all influence, and places even in an antithetical
attitude, the great result necessarily depends on
both.   It may be true enough that the earnings of
the people and the price of corn control the number of marriages, and yet the temper and wishes
of individuals may none the less have a hand in
making that number what it is; for how do these
large causes operate? Not directly or immediately
as water quenches thirst or extinguishes fire; they
are not physical causes nor are they proximate to
the effects, but act through intermediate principles
or agencies, and chiefly through those personal
feelings, which Mr. Buckle discards as having
nothing to do with the result.   It is because work
is scarce or wages are diminished or food is dear,
that the young artizan hesitates to undertake the
charge of a family, and it is when these unfavour-
able conditions disappear and prosperity begins to
dawn upon him once more that he begins again to
entertain the design of marriage which he had before
found it prudent to lay aside.   The whole process
through which the price of food and the rate of

wages operate upon the number of marriages, is a
process of thought and feeling, of "temper and
wishes," nor can they operate in any other way or
through any other channel so as to affect the
result.

There is an additional fallacy implied, I think, in
some of Mr. Buckle's arguments, and not unfrequently to be met with in speculations on society
and social economy.

The facts with which the reasoning is concerned
are too often spoken of as if they were of a physical
or material nature, when they are in reality mental
phenomena, i.e. mental causes or effects.   Such
are the price of food, the rate of wages, and con-
tracts of marriage, which are all alike the results of
voluntary acts, and when any of these results are
affected by physical or political or social events, it
must be through the minds of human beings.   If
the error does not always take as broad a shape as
here described, it often happens that the mental
character of the incidents is manifestly either overlooked or not fully kept in view.

Nor does Mr. Buckle, as far as I can understand
him, see clearly into the subject of moral causation.
He appears to me not to discern the truth that
circumstances whether physical, social, or political,
may be so connected as causes in the chain of
events with human volitions and actions, that the
actions may be confidently predicted from the circumstances and yet be perfectly free.

Human life is, in truth, crowded with instances
of this description; and it may be laid down as a
general principle every day abundantly exemplified, that the freedom of human actions and the
power of predicting them are perfectly compatible.*

* See Letters XIV. and XV., Second Series, "On the
Causation of Voluntary Actions."

LETTER VII.

LANGUAGE.

I HAVE already had to consider several important points in the philosophy of language, but it is too intimately connected with mental operations to be passed over, in these letters, without express investigation of several questions involved in it.

One of these relates to the specific intellectual function of words considered singly; and another is, how words are affected when combined in sentences; neither of which has been so accurately and exhaustively treated as to preclude further discussion or elucidation.

When a word has indicated * or brought to mind the object or event for which it stands, it seems to me to have done all *intellectually* that it needs to do, or that it is desirable for it to do. It may cause an emotion of some kind as well as indicate an object or raise up a mental conception, and, by the thought or the feeling called up, may even awaken a multitude of associated thoughts

---

* I say *indicated*, to include cases in which the object designated by the word is actually present and consequently cannot be said to be brought to mind.

and feelings; but these are only incidental and variable effects; and irrespective of them, its direct intellectual function is perfectly accomplished when in certain cases it has indicated, and in others brought to mind, the object which it signifies.

The various ways in which words are connected with feelings constitute undoubtedly a subject of much interest and importance, and one also of much difficulty on account of the nicety required to distinguish the effects of the mere words from the effects of the ideas raised up by them.

A word while possessing the same intellectual significance in two successive ages, may cause a different emotion in each: and of two words in the same age meaning the same thing, one may excite pleasure, or shame, or loathing, and the other be heard with indifference. When, too, a word has raised up the precise idea of the object, that idea may suggest other ideas to an indefinite extent, but the latter, like the emotions just mentioned, do not enter into the meaning of the word. The influence of rhetoric, the beauties of poetry, the charm of personal conversation and epistolary intercourse, doubtless greatly depend not only on the precision with which words are used to raise up the ideas of the particular objects denoted by them, but on the tact (often instinctive) with which they are selected to awaken such emotions and associated ideas as will conduce to the purpose in view. Similar influences belong to the variable tones and inflections of the voice, but we do not on that account consider the signification of the individual words uttered to vary with them, although the total effect of what is said, will so vary.

At present I pass by these influences; I am concerned with language only as an instrument for recording and communicating knowledge and lending aid to reasoning — with its purely intellectual function

It may be objected indeed that if I admit a word to be capable of awakening other ideas than that of the object denoted by it, the intellectual function includes the rousing of associated thoughts; an objection, however, which is at once removed by a consideration of the circumstance that it is not the word which calls up the associated ideas, but it is the idea raised up or the emotion awakened by the word: and while the word ought to bring into the minds of all who use or hear it, one precise idea or one of a precise class of ideas, the associations with which that idea is connected may vary indefinitely in every individual without at all affecting the signification.

With regard to the intellectual power of words in certain cases, I have already shown that common names and abstract terms can do no more than bring before the mind particular objects or combinations just as proper names do.

Men know only individual things, although it may be in groups or sequences: there is in truth

nothing else for them to know; they can think
only of what they thus become acquainted with,
and it would be strange if words had the power of
enabling or compelling them to do otherwise — to
think of anything else.

It is no valid objection to this statement that we
think of many merely imaginary objects,

" Gorgons and hydras and chimeras dire,"

for a slight analysis suffices to show that every one
of these fabulous monsters, is made up of parts familiar to us through the organs of sense.   It cannot
indeed be otherwise.

In considering the efficiency of words, it is
important to bear in mind that a name, whether
articulated or written, is itself a real entity, a
sound or visible object, and it is probably owing
in part to this substantial existence that so many
fictitious entities are created by or rather out of
language.

The word itself being real, there is always something for the mind to dwell upon, so that even in
the use of an abstract term, which has no corresponding abstract idea (to speak for a moment of
a non-entity) but is suggestive only of shifting
objects each as individual as if it had been called
up by a proper name, the term presents itself to
us as a fixed independent thing audible or visible
or both.

Hence probably we are prone to conclude that

there is something equally distinct and independent in the consequent mental representation, to correspond with it.

For want of considering the precise intellectual office and power of words; that their special function is to bring before the mind objects and events already known (at least in their constituent parts) several singular doctrines have been maintained.

It is obvious that if the object named is brought before the mind clearly and fully by the name, it is of no importance in respect of the power of the word to perform its intellectual function, how it came to be associated with the object. Provided that the one directly suggests the other the utmost perfection of language, simply as an intellectual instrument, is attained. How extraordinary soever may have been the way in which the word came to be associated with the thing, that circumstance has not, nor can it beneficially have, any effect on the meaning when once the association has been perfectly established.

To trace the manner in which this took place is often interesting and instructive, and even amusing ; but when the name has become so familiar as directly to suggest the object, and the object directly suggests the name, the end of language as an instrument of reasoning and of communicating knowledge, is attained, nor can any etymological researches, whatever historical or philosophical interest they may possess, improve it. With

almost all people, this complete and direct connexion of name and object is established in the
case of external and familiar things.   The name,
in fact, comes to form an inseparable adjunct of
the thing designated by it, so that many of the
uneducated regard it as naturally belonging to the
object, just as much as the shape and the colour.

Hence their amazement when, on first going
into foreign countries, they hear children fluently
talking French or German.   They can understand
how a man or a woman may learn a foreign tongue,
as any one learns to play on the violin or the piano;
but that boys and girls who are only just able to
articulate, should speak one, seems to them perfectly unnatural.   I once overheard in Paris one
of those raw travellers from our country who are
often to be met with there — men scarcely sus-
pecting the existence of any language but their
own except as an accomplishment — say in an indignant tone to a garçon who addressed him in
French, " Why do'nt you speak English you
fool?" evidently thinking it to be very affected
and perverse in the lad to speak anything else.

So direct is this connexion and so little does the
derivation interfere with it, that even when a word
bears its etymological descent on its very face, as
in many compound phrases such as Christmas-box,
honey-suckle, snow-drop, butter-cup, candlestick,
it does not bring to mind the two things joined

together, but a single object, sometimes differing from both.

Amongst country people in the north, who in the fine days of summer are in the habit of spreading their clothes on the hedges to dry, it is very common to call the wooden frame or stand on which in bad weather they hang their linen within the house for the same purpose, " a winter-hedge "— in itself quite a poetical name but suggesting to the minds of those amongst whom it is used nothing but a convenient piece of furniture. No thought arises of the analogy between the wooden frame in the laundry in winter, and the hawthorn fence of summer: the latter indeed not being brought to mind, the analogy cannot occur.

I recollect passing some time in a family of both children and adults, who were in the constant use of the phrase "*ten-to-one,*" either as an adjective or as an adverb, to express probability. " It is ten to one," they would say, " that such a thing will take place," meaning it is highly probable; and this, without adverting in the faintest degree to the literal signification of the expression, to the relation between ten and one, or even to the numbers themselves; but actually considering the composite sound as one word.

I have said that the knowledge of the derivation of a word, when once we are acquainted with its precise signification, cannot improve the word as an intellectual instrument. I may even go

92   PHILOSOPHY OF THE HUMAN MIND.

farther and say that such etymological knowledge,
although it may sometimes help the learner to the
meaning of a word not understood, has a tendency
when much dwelt upon or habitually suggested to
pervert or render less definite our conception of
what the term denotes.

" It is in many cases," as Mr. Stewart well observes, " a fortunate circumstance, when the words
we employ have lost their pedigree; or (what
amounts nearly to the same thing) when it can be
traced by those alone who are skilled in ancient and
in foreign languages. Such words have in their
favour the sanction of immemorial use; and the
obscurity of their history prevents them from misleading the imagination, by recalling to it the sensible objects and phenomena to which they owed
their origin. The notions, accordingly, we annex
to them may be expected to be peculiarly precise
and definite, being entirely the result of those
habits of induction which I have shown to be so
essentially connected with the acquisition of language." *

In confirmation of this view, I may repeat an
observation which has been frequently made, that
the style of deeply learned men is apt to be
damaged by their knowledge of other languages
than their own, and of the derivation of the terms
they employ. Mr. Stewart gives a similar conclu-

* Philosophical Essays, 3rd Ed. p. 234.

sion as the result of his personal observation; " I
have hardly met," he says, " with an individual,
habitually addicted to them [etymological studies]
who wrote his own language with ease and ele-
gance," * and he quotes a valuable passage from a
French author to the same effect. " It is so seldom," says M. de Rivarol, "that the etymology of
a word coincides with its true acceptation, that we
cannot plead in favour of researches of this kind
that they serve to fix better the senses of words.
Those writers who are acquainted with the greatest ·
number of languages, are the persons who commit
the greatest number of improprieties.   Too much
engrossed with the ancient force of a term, they
forget its value in their own day, and neglect those
delicate shades of meaning which constitute the
grace and the power of composition." †
   The effect here described is frequently produced
even in those who are not professed etymologists
by the habit of composing in a foreign dialect
whether ancient or modern.   Such a habit almost
inevitably leads to the use of forms of speech not
consonant with the genius of the writer's native
language.   Idiomatic phrases intrinsically illogical
but sanctioned by long custom and therefore
not only justifiable but forcible in their original
place, are transplanted into a medium in which

* Philosophical Essays, p. 242.
† Ibid. p. 243. Mr. Stewart is not answerable for the
translation.

their logical deficiencies become glaring; while
concurrently the delicacies of indigenous phraseology are forgotten.   Any one who wishes to
acquire a pure English style should avoid habitual
composition in Latin or Greek, or indeed any
other tongue than his own, and should expressly
apply himself to the latter for the purpose of
acquiring a thorough knowledge of all its niceties,
an insight both into the structure of its sentences,
the allocation of its particles, epithets, and adverbs,
and the signification as well as the emotional
power of its words.   To pass through a mere
course of classical education is altogether insuffi-
cient in itself for attaining a mastery of his native
language.*

These remarks do not at all detract from the
value of etymology in its own sphere, but are
intended to show that its sphere is not to determine
from derivation the actual meaning of words, and
that to know the origin of the terms we employ
may rather hinder than aid their intellectual function.

What in truth, if we come to close analysis, is
the effect of etymological knowledge concerning the
origin and the changes in meaning of a perfectly

* See Note B. in the Appendix.   Since this letter was
written the study of the English language has been ably urged
by Mr. D'Orsey in a little volume, which will repay perusal,
entitled "The Study of the English Language an essential
Part of a University Course."

intelligible word, when such knowledge is awakened
in our minds at the sight or on the utterance of the
word? The effect is undoubtedly to divide the
attention between the present and the past significations, whence in the rapidity of discourse vacilla-
tion and confusion are naturally apt to arise.
Observe I am not doubting whether etymology
may assist us in the interpretation of a term which
we do not yet comprehend; but I am questioning
whether it is of any use, or rather whether it is
not positively detrimental, in the case of words
perfectly understood; or, to express the matter
differently, in the case of words that raise up immediately and clearly in ordinary minds the ideas
of the objects denoted by them.

Doubtless such knowledge on the part of individuals frequently helps them to recognize the
signification of technical terms in pursuits different
from their own; which is rather a personal and
accidental advantage arising from their particular
attainments than any thing else. A Greek scholar
ignorant of Geology, might know from the name
Icthyosaurus, should he happen to meet with it,
that by that uncouth designation some animal
must be indicated combining the forms of the fish
and the lizard; and so far his Greek would be
useful; but it could not give him any knowledge
of the thing worth speaking of. Contrast for a
moment his vague conception with that of an un-
learned man who had actually inspected the fossil

remains of the extinct species. Hugh Millar, who
had not classical learning enough to prevent him
from writing animalculæ for animalcula, had
doubtless as vivid and accurate an idea of that
monstrous Saurian, as if he had been fully charged
with Greek and perfectly acquainted with the derivation of its composite name. When the object
and the name are thus sensibly brought together
and directly connected with each other in the mind
of the observer, nothing else is required for constituting the word a perfect intellectual instrument.
To know that the name is derived from two Greek
words is simply to know that it is so derived — an
item of etymological learning, nothing more: it
does not in the slightest degree improve or increase
or make clearer our knowledge of its signification,
that is, of the object which it denotes, although it
may possibly help the memory to retain the
meaning of the term.

The considerations here adduced all confirm the
conclusions to which ·I before came, that the
present meaning of a word is a matter of fact not
gathered from its derivation but ascertained and
ascertainable solely from the actual usage of
writers and speakers current in our own age.

Etymology may show that the word ought not
to be applied in the sense in which it is used,
perhaps by uneducated or careless writers, and
may usefully restrain and retard or even wholly
prevent the perversion of it from its primitive

acceptation; but nevertheless if that perversion becomes general, even the learned and the fastidious must eventually submit to it.

Notwithstanding the unqualified condemnation passed by Horne Tooke upon the celebrated saying of Horace in his Art of Poetry; the poet, I venture to think, is both practically and philosophically right.

Mortalia facta peribunt:
Nedum sermonum stet honos, et gratia vivax.
Multa renascentur, quæ jam occidêre ; cadentque
Quæ nunc sunt in honore vocabula, *si volet usus,*
Quem penes arhitrium est et jus et norma loquendi.*

In a subsequent letter, I shall have occasion to examine some other advantages which have been attributed to the science of verbal derivation.

You may have remarked that in the preceding discussion I have treated words as immediately denoting things, without employing the customary designation "signs of ideas."

I have avoided the use of it because I do not see that it is needed, and especially because it has been employed in a way inconsistent with my view of the true intellectual function of words.

The practice of denominating words the signs of ideas, is certainly little short of universal in philosophical treatises of recent date.

But on my doctrine of ideas being all without exception representative conceptions, it follows

* De Arte Poetica, v. 68.

H

that words, if they can be called signs at all, are
primarily signs of things, and only in a secondary
manner the signs of the ideas of things. There
are not two names one for the thing and the other
for the idea of the thing, and consequently a sign
which indicates both, ought to be considered as
belonging to the former—to the substance rather
than to the shadow.

In my own opinion, however, the term sign is
not a happy designation for either.

Words are never called the signs of ideas except
in books of philosophy.

No one ever speaks of "John" as the sign of
the idea of a man, or of "apple" as the sign of the
idea of a fruit.

Nor is it according to usage to apply the term
even to objects themselves. We do not say that
"lily" is the sign of a flower, or that "lake" is
the sign of a sheet of water, but we say it is the
name.*

---

* In my objection to this phraseology, I find I have, in part
at least. the concurrence of Mr. Mill, with whom I am always
glad to be in accordance. He does not take exception at the
word sign as I have done, but he speaks of names as follows :
"Are names more properly said to be the names of things, or of
our ideas of things? The first is the expression in common
use; the last is that of some metaphysicians, who conceived
that in adopting it, they were introducing a highly important
distinction."—Logic, 5th Ed. Vol. I. p. 23. He subsequently
gives his reasons for adopting the common usage of speaking
of names as the names of things themselves and not merely
of our ideas of things.

We use, it is true, the expression that "lake"
signifies a sheet of water; but this is only one
amongst numerous instances of a great difference
in the application of paronymous words — a subject, by the way, of unappreciated interest and
importance.

If there are, as there possibly may be, cases in
which "sign" might be a more convenient phrase
than "name" I certainly am unable at the moment
to call any of them to mind.

LETTER VIII.

LANGUAGE (*in continuation*).

IN my last letter I was occupied in showing that
the perfection of a word as an intellectual instrument consists in its being so closely associated with
the thing denoted as to raise up the idea of it at
once; and that a knowledge of how the word and
the thing came to be thus connected, although interesting and in other respects valuable, is quite
needless for the perfection spoken of, and has
indeed rather a tendency to lessen it.

It is implied in this doctrine, or, perhaps more
correctly, it is the same doctrine varied in expression, that the intellectual effect produced by any
word, or in different language the object brought
to mind, or in still different language the idea
raised up, constitutes what is called the meaning
of a word.

The idea raised up by the word is not one thing
and the meaning another: they are one and the
same: the two phrases so employed are equivalent.

The importance of bearing this truth in mind
through all discussions of the subject is extreme.

It clears up not only the difficulties attending

the signification of general and abstract terms, but
also two other points on which there has been
much difference of opinion, namely, the alleged
intrinsic meaning of words, and how words are
affected in their signification when combined into
sentences. It is the first of these points which
I purpose to consider in the present letter.
Although it was virtually disposed of in my last,
it will not be useless to bestow on the doctrine, as
maintained by recent etymologists, a direct and
a fuller examination.

Horne Tooke manifestly proceeds on the assumption that words have an intrinsic meaning*
which they continuously preserve and which according to him is always distinguishable amidst
the various applications in which they may be
employed.

This able and ingenious etymologist but not
equally profound metaphysician, fell under the
criticism of a philosopher who saw with tolerable
clearness both the strength and the weakness of
the general speculations contained in "The Diversions of Purley," although he may have dwelt
more on the faults than on the merits of the work.
After quoting from it the celebrated passage about

* Mr. Tooke is often exceedingly shy of definite statement
and explanation where they are most wanted, and I cannot
find that he uses the phrase *intrinsic meaning*; but his ex-
positor, Dr. Richardson, employs it to show what the doctrine
of the Diversions of Purley is, as I shall shortly have to notice,
and employs it, I think, correctly for that purpose.

"right," Mr. Stewart, the critic to whom I allude,
proceeds as follows: " Through the whole of this
passage Mr. Tooke evidently assumes as a principle that in order to ascertain, with precision, the
philosophical import of any word, it is necessary
to trace its progress historically through all the
successive meanings which it has been employed
to convey from the moment it was first introduced
into our language; or, if the word be of foreign
growth, that we should prosecute the etymological
research, till we ascertain the literal and primitive
sense of the root from whence it sprung.   It is in
this literal and primitive sense alone, that according to him a philosopher is entitled to employ it,
even in the present advanced state of science; and
whenever he annexes to it a meaning at all different, he imposes equally on himself and on
others."*

After quoting this passage, one of the recent
expositors of the Diversions of Purley proceeds to
answer it as follows:

" To the Professor I reply, that Tooke's doctrine
is simply this: That from the etymology of the
word we† should fix the intrinsic meaning; that
that meaning should always furnish the cause of
the application, and that no application of any
word is justifiable for which that meaning will not
supply a reason; but that the usage of any appli-

cation so supported is not only allowable but indispensable." After adverting to a diversity of application and to changes effected by usage, he says: " The meaning, nevertheless, remains uniform, unvarying, and invariable; the application and subaudition as unlimited as the numberless necessities of speech."*

In commenting on these propositions the author of which I would treat with the respect due to him on account of his useful labours, and for which he is responsible only as having adopted the views of his predecessor and explained them in his own way, it is difficult to know how to begin from their being, as it appears to me, so completely wide of the truth.

It is obvious at the first glance that the writer uses the term "meaning" in a peculiar sense, as if it were a fixed steadfast something in a word which remained unalterable while the word could still be applied in various ways deviating more or less from it. Hence, according to him, the meaning and the application of a term are different.

The erroneousness of the doctrine will appear to any one who reflects that a word can have no meaning but in the mind of somebody, and that the meaning in every case can be no other than the intellectual effect produced, or, what is equivalent, the idea raised up by the word.

* On the Study of Language, by Chas. Richardson, LL.D., p. 190.

To assert therefore that a word always retains an intrinsic meaning is really to affirm that the ideas raised up by it in the minds of successive generations since the word was first uttered, have always been the same or similar.

Nor is it of any avail to allege that it is the application not the meaning of the word which varies. The distinction attempted to be drawn between the two is altogether untenable.

The application of a term can be nothing else than employing the term with a meaning, that is to say, for the purpose of raising up an idea of the thing denoted by it. To apply it in one way at one time and in another way at another time, is to employ it with two different meanings.[*]

That a word should have an intrinsic meaning besides its application by those who employ it, is simply impossible.

It may have one meaning to me and another to my neighbour, but this is not what is asserted: the theory maintains that besides the two meanings which we respectively have in our minds, there is another meaning of which neither of us may have the slightest knowledge, but which constantly

---

[*] I may support my views on this question, by the following extract from Mr. Garnett's Philological Essays, where, speaking of the verb-substantive, he says, "many of the extravagances promulgated on the subject have arisen from the utterly erroneous idea of an intrinsic meaning in words, constituting them the counterparts and equivalents of thought," p. 341.

resides in the word; it virtually affirms that in
addition to the idea produced in my mind and the
different idea raised up in the mind of my neighbour, there is a third idea perpetually raised up or
existing in the mind of nobody.

There cannot then be an intrinsic meaning, a
meaning over and above that which is contained
in the actual application of the word. In cases of
a change in signification, there may be the original
meaning manifested or recorded in ancient documents; but it is itself past and gone like any other
historical incident, and, like any other, may be
worth knowing for its influence on subsequent
events, especially for its influence on the present
signification of the term.

Every event or state of things which we witness
at present, is the result of a long train of circumstances without which it could not be what it is;
but our knowing its history cannot alter the fact
before us; and such is just the case with the present meaning of a word: we may sometimes trace
how the word came to mean what it does, but no
success in the search can alter the fact of the
actual acceptation in which it is now received, or
that in which it has been at any period heretofore
employed.

In fine, the present sense of a word which has
served various purposes in the lapse of ages, is the
result of the original signification subjected to the
modifying influence of various circumstances: but

this process and its consummation no more prove
an intrinsic meaning than the present existence of
a descendant of the Howards proves that, besides
the actual members of that family successively
appearing in the world and leaving it, there has
always been an intrinsic Howard.

These considerations will enable us to estimate
the value of the following passage.

After adverting to the instance of *sycophant* or
fig-shower the writer before us proceeds: " The
word *sycophant* still retains its meaning; *challenger,
informer, parasite, flatterer,* never enter into *it,*
never become whole or part of it : that word still
means, that is, means etymologically, and ever
must so mean, *a fig-shower,* and nothing else; but
in any *application* founded upon this meaning and
inferred from it, (as in the above explanation,
every application is inferred) the word may be
used to denote the meaning of the speaker, and is
so used with propriety."*

From the explanations I have already given it
is abundantly plain that instead of the word sycophant having retained the original meaning, it has
completely lost it, and never except by accident
raises up the idea of a fig-shower. The only
things in the case which remain unalterable, are
the historical facts that the word once signified
fig-shower, and has since undergone changes in
meaning. If, as here represented, it has been

* On the Study of Language, p. 193.

successively employed to designate a challenger, an informer, a parasite, and a flatterer, so often has its acceptation varied, and the enumeration of the variations can show nothing but the mutability of language in its specific function of raising up ideas, and the gradations by which it changes.

To say that the word still means and ever must mean *etymologically* a fig-shower, is nugatory or at the best only an incorrect mode of saying that the fact of its having originally meant so, cannot be undone — is irreversible — an attribute which it shares with all other facts.*

A good instance is adduced by Mr. Stewart to illustrate the way in which a word lapses from one signification into another until the original sense disappears.

" It has been remarked," he says, " by several writers, that the Latin word *intervallum* was evidently borrowed from the appropriate phraseology of a camp; *inter vallos spatium,*—the space between the stakes and palisades which strengthened the rampart. None of them, however, has taken any notice of the insensible *transitions* by which it came successively to be employed in a more enlarged sense; first to express a limited portion of longitudinal extension in general; and afterwards limited portions of time as well as of space. ' *Ut quoniam intervallo locorum et temporum disjuncti*

---

* " Factum est illud ; fieri infectum non potest."

sumus, per literas tecum quam sæpissime colloquar.'
The same word has passed into our language; and
it is not a little remarkable, that it is now so exclusively appropriated to *time*, that to speak of the
interval between two *places*, would be censured
as a mode of expression not agreeable to common
use." *

There is a case in our own tongue analogous
in the last mentioned circumstance to the preceding, which I have noticed in my Discourse
" On the Changes which have taken place in the
English Language." In reference to the word
punctual, I remark, " It was formerly applied to
space as well as time, but now seems to have
shrunk within the narrower limits of denoting
exactness in keeping engagements, or in attending
to appointed hours. In writers of no remote date,
we find such phrases as, " a punctual description,"
" a punctual relation," " a clear, full, and punctual
declaration," to express what we should probably
now denote by *particular* or *circumstantial*." †

In the two instances here cited there is severally
a complete change in signification. What greater
one could be imagined than that from denoting
the space between two stakes, to designating the
time between breakfast and dinner.?

It may possibly be alleged that still there is an
analogy in all these cases between the primitive

* Philosophical Essays, p. 267.
† Discourses on Various Subjects, p. 85.

and the present acceptation of the words; which
may be true enough; but an analogy between one
signification and another, although it shows a
relationship still preserved, does not constitute an
intrinsic meaning.

The question is, did the word raise up different
ideas in the mind severally at the two periods?
If it did then there has been a change in meaning,
whether the two things successively denoted by it
have a close or remote analogy to each other.

Such lingering analogies seem to be the natural
consequences of a fact which has frequently been
the subject of remark, namely, that the meanings
of words do not ordinarily change *per saltum;*
they deviate gradually (for a reason I shall immediately assign) and therefore it is no wonder
that what is ultimately denoted by a word after
many successive changes in signification, is often
found to possess something analogous to the original object. Where there has been a complete
estrangement as occasionally happens from the
primitive acceptation of a term, the steps (many of
them curious and interesting) by which it was
accomplished may be frequently although not invariably followed; and even in cases of a sudden
break, some slight trace of relationship or correspondence may still remain.

There are at present alterations in the meaning
of several words going on under our eyes, which,
should they be generally adopted, will afford so

many instances of a break in derivation, presenting
as marked a *fault* as is to be seen in any geological
stratum.

The term *defalcation*, which I many years ago
pointed out as employed by journalists in a sense
utterly at variance with etymology,[*] has now
become so current in that sense (although still
avoided by good writers) that it may be pronounced irreclaimable. It is used to designate the
act of a *defaulter.* I can account for this leap
only by supposing that writers and speakers of
little education, not finding ready to their hands
such a term as *defaultation* which, irregular and
barbarous as it is, would have expressed their precise meaning, were misled by the sound to seize
upon the existing but seldom used substantive
defalcation as the very thing they wanted; and
under this ridiculous misapprehension forced it
into their service:—a sort of press-gang violence
committed on that well-born noun, from a sheer
mistake of identity.

In this case we have the triumph of similarity
in sound over etymology; a change in signification
effected *per saltum;* a blundering change, undoubtedly, but likely enough to turn out a permanent perversion.

Even here, nevertheless, not only is there re-

[*] See Discourses on Various Subjects by the present author,
page 95, "On the Changes which have taken place in the
English Language."

semblance in the sound but analogy does not
altogether disappear in the sense.

No one would probably have thought of using
the word in the way pointed out, if he had not
attached to it some vague notion of its legitimate
meaning, so far as to understand that it implied
diminution or subtraction: it was therefore an
easy mistake to apply it under the influence of
similarity of sound to the act of a defaulter, of
which subtraction, although of a peculiar kind, is
an essential feature.

Both of the acts in question may in truth be
generalized under one name: they are both comprehensible under the same term: one is subtraction by lopping, the other subtraction by robbing.

Without this remote resemblance in the thing
thus miscalled, the similarity in sound would
scarcely have prevailed even with the dim or
illiterate understandings in which the perversion
originated. No one uses an old word in a new
sense without some reason, and this reason, except
possibly in rare cases, must be some kind of resemblance or analogy, however faint and whether
real or fancied, either in sense or in sound. This
seems essential even as the basis of such mistakes
as that which I have here pointed out, or, in
the phraseology of the day, even to make them
possible.

If similarity in sense cannot be pronounced
absolutely requisite in all such changes, yet, on

the other hand, it may be doubted whether similarity in sound could be effectual in any case if
between the things denoted there existed positive
contrariety.* We could hardly conceive, for instance, that the word defalcation could under any
circumstances come to be employed to signify an
increase, or addition, or excess.

Instances like the one just noticed present us
with changes of meaning in actual process. They
teach us that languages are not things which
transform themselves, although we are apt to speak
of them as doing so; and it is convenient enough,
from the succinctness of such expressions, to talk
of their growth, variations, corruption, decay and
so on.

All alterations however in the meaning of terms
are the work of human beings, and consequently
if we wish to ascertain the causes producing them
we must inquire into the circumstances which
have operated on the minds of speakers and writers
to determine them to employ words differently
from their predecessors. In the instance of *defalcation*, I have endeavoured to trace these operating circumstances, and surely to do this in all
cases, to discover the causes which have been at

* "This reflection of meaning from words of similar sound
but unconnected by their etymological origin, is necessarily
confined to words not repugnant to each other in signification,
but expressive of notions capable of coalescing." — *Discourses
on Various Subjects before cited*, page 102.

work in bringing about these changes and which are now acting on the understandings of ourselves and our contemporaries, is a part of the philosophy of language as interesting and important as chronicling the changes themselves when they have become accomplished facts.

The truth that not the slightest alteration in meaning takes place except as the mental act of human beings, enables the metaphysician to repel if not to retort one of the disparaging remarks thrown out by Horne Tooke against intellectual philosophy. Instead of the science of mind being as he represents it merely an affair of language, the single consideration just adduced shows that language itself with all its changes from first to last, is an affair of mind; and it is singular enough that any one should ever have regarded it in any other light.

From the first word uttered by human lips to the complicated dialect of our own day, we see the mind at work on its medium of articulate expression, adding, abbreviating, expanding, contracting, separating, conjoining; but in every mutation acting under the influence of circumstances or considerations which may, to some extent at least, be traced and classified.

Without a knowledge of the mental operations concerned it is impossible for the etymologist to have a full comprehension of the subject of his

I

own science, and in that knowledge the author of
the work before us was not an adept.

But I purpose in a subsequent letter, to examine
the heterodox notions of the Diversions of Purley
on the nature of Mental Philosophy.

LETTER IX.

LANGUAGE (*in continuation*).

ALTHOUGH I examined in my last letter one of the principal doctrines of Horne Tooke appertaining to mental philosophy, yet others remain which are more or less connected with the phenomena of consciousness, and which claim attention in discussing the subject of language.

Even the one already treated will be exhibited in a still clearer light by pointing out its place in the general range of his etymological speculations.

I purpose, therefore, in the present letter to show the philosophical bearings of what he has accomplished or aimed at, in this department of knowledge, and also the philosophical errors he has committed (from exclusiveness of view I am disposed to think), especially as to the nature of his own alleged discoveries and as to the conclusions deducible from them. My intention is not to enter except incidentally upon any purely philological questions, but to keep to such points as more immediately relate to the science which I am engaged in explaining.

Mr. Tooke has been generally considered (till

recently at least) by even learned men to have
established a theory, of which slight traces,
indeed, may be found in preceding writers, but
which, by the full development, the original
proofs, the copious illustrations of it contained in
his work, he may be said to have made his own;
the theory, namely, that in our own language, to
go no farther, not only grammatical terminations *
but all the subordinate parts of speech, the adjective, the pronoun, the adverb, the article, the
preposition and the conjunction, have alike been
derived from the noun or the verb: that they all
originally existed as independent words in the
shape of either the one or the other of those principal denominations; and that such of them as
are in our present language mere particles, apparently insignificant by themselves, then pos-

* Tooke has not devoted much space to the investigation of
such terminations, his principal labour having been bestowed
on the second part of the theory; but although what he has
said on grammatical inflexions is almost all comprised in a
single page, his merit in first showing their true character and
origin, is allowed even by those who call in question his theory
of the origin of particles. A recent writer who gives us the
results of the latest researches respecting language, and lays it
down as established that "what we now call terminations were
originally independent words," proceeds to say, "The true
nature of grammatical terminations was first pointed out by a
philosopher, who, however wild some of his speculations may
be, had certainly caught many a glimpse of the real life and
growth of language, I mean Horne Tooke."—*Lectures on the
Science of Language by Max Müller*, 3rd Ed. page 254.

sessed the full form and meaning which nouns and
verbs possess with us in the present day.

Their actual form of particles has arisen principally from the desire for despatch in communicating our thoughts; they are abbreviations, and
are not the signs of things but of other words;
of the words namely from which they have been
worn down to their present shape in the constant
attempts at prompt expression.*

* Amongst the most powerful objections which have been
brought against some of Tooke's views and especially his
theory of the origin of particles, are those of the late Mr.
Garnett, whose works have been pronounced by another
eminent writer in the same department, as "by far the best
works in comparative grammar and ethnology of the century."
(Dr. Latham.) After quoting Mr. Price's opinion that the
details in his [Tooke's] much-vaunted analysis of particles,
may be contested nearly as often as they are admitted, Mr.
Garnett proceeds, "We venture to go further, and to pronounce that it is, both in principle and execution, the most
erroneous and defective part of the system, and that it contains
very little indeed that can be safely relied upon.

"One copious source of error, affecting more or less every
branch of Tooke's system, is the assumption that Anglo-
Saxon and its sister dialects may be practically regarded as
original languages, and, consequently, that the bulk of the
abbreviated forms of speech, which we call particles, may be
traced to verbs or nouns, actually existing in one or more of
that tribe. All this is more easily asserted than proved: in
fact we have almost invincible evidence that the assumption is
a downright *petitio principii* and totally erroneous. Collateral
dialects, so closely related as those in question, as certainly
prove the existence of a parent language, as the co-existence
of brothers and sisters implies a father before them; and as
we have reason to suppose that Hecuba had a mother, though

In addition to his strenuous efforts to establish this view of the derivation of the inferior parts of speech, Mr. Tooke has with a confident hand traced a great number of our present words to a common origin, and shown that a multiplicity of terms which have at present no obvious connexion with each other, sprang from the same root.

This part of his work seems to have been undertaken chiefly with a view of showing that our abstract and general terms are descended from words signifying material objects or operations (in itself nothing new); and having successfully shown this in a great number of instances he thence concludes, with what validity I shall hereafter examine, that there is no such thing as the mental operation called Abstraction.

From the truths which, according to his own

we do not know who she was, it is at least possible, that this more ancient Teutonic, or whatever we choose to call it, might not itself be an original tongue, but a scion from a still older form of speech. If, therefore, Anglo-Saxon is a *mata naturum*, a language several descents removed from a primaeval one now lost, but in all likelihood closely related to Sanscrit, is it to be supposed that all its component elements are self-existent and self-derived?"— *The Philological Essays of the late Rev. Richd. Garnett*, page 20. The argument is pursued to a greater length and into some instructive details, and as far as I can see is irrefutable. The reader will probably be struck with what Mr. Garnett says about the little virtuous peace-making particle *it*, the very foundation of Tooke's theory of particles.

view, he has thus established, Mr. Tooke proceeds
to draw certain conclusions.

1. Inasmuch as the parts of speech recognized
in the present day were originally nouns and verbs,
he argues that they must be considered as still
retaining the same grammatical character, and
that our actual classification of them under eight
or nine different appellations is erroneous.

It is not difficult to see the fallacy of such
reasoning.

It might as well be argued that because the
chairs and tables in a room were made out of
trees, the unshaped trunks of which may have
formerly served the same purposes, they are still
to be regarded as trees.

To classify words which, although originally
used in one uniform way, have, in the progress of
language, been employed, under modified forms,
in different functions; and, further, to distinguish
them by names indicative of those several functions, are surely expedients of no little value, nor
would it be wise to confound things so essentially
distinct on the ground of a common origin.

Our rude ancestors (if you will permit me to
continue my parallel) might have used the trunk
of one tree for a seat and that of another for a
table, and perhaps interchangeably ; but their
successors after working up the trees into those
two distinct pieces of furniture, would habitually
regard each as adapted to its special purpose and

use it accordingly; nor would it be needful or
beneficial in using it to advert to its pristine shape.
The two diversely serviceable articles would stand
in their estimation and in their vocabulary as
widely different things notwithstanding their original existence in the same form.

So pronouns, prepositions, conjunctions, and the
rest, since they are respectively serviceable to us
in various ways and have their several grammatical relations with other parts of speech, are
very properly ranged under different heads,
although they may possibly all have been derived
from nouns and verbs.   Some one has styled them
"nouns and verbs in disguise;" but if this view
were correct and this phraseology received, it is
obvious that the propriety and utility of classifying
them by their distinguishing characteristics, i. e.
by their several kinds of disguises, would remain
unaffected.

Speech, according to Mr. Tooke's account of it,
was originally a disjointed series of unconnected
words, as insulated and as similar to each other in
function as the stepping-stones formerly used for
crossing rivers; but just as stones have been
shaped and compacted into continuous bridges
which save us from the jumping and jerking before
required, so words have been pared down and
connected together by abbreviation and modification into smooth and unbroken discourse.

It may be well to cite an instance of the way in

which this fallacy of the permanence of grammatical character is maintained in the Diversions of Purley.

The author enumerates the following words: —

Sheer, Sherd, Shred, Shore, Score, Short, Shorn, Shower, Share, Scar, Shard, Shire, Shirt, Skirt.

" All these," he says, " so variously written and pronounced; and now so differently and distinctly applied; are yet merely the past participle of Scipan, *to Shear*, to cut, to divide, to separate. And they were formerly used indifferently." *

Granting for argument's sake the etymology here to be quite correct, I beg you will observe the explicit assertion that all the words he enumerates *are* the past participle: he does not say merely that they are *derived* from it but that they are the participle itself.

Surely, however, the difference between the grammatical function of the noun " shore " and that of the participle " shorn " is as great as can well be conceived. The manner in which the two words are connected with other words in discourse, which constitutes their grammatical character, is wholly diverse.

Should any one doubt whether I have construed his doctrine correctly, and have not taken a casual expression for more than it was intended to assert, I will cite another passage. In reply to a critic

* Part 2, Chap. 4.

who maintains against him that Articles and
Pronouns are neither Nouns nor Verbs, he rejoins,
" I hope hereafter to satisfy the reader that they
are nothing else and *can be* nothing else." *

The author before us is remarkable for the care-
fulness with which he avoids throwing his doctrines
into general propositions, and the preference he
shows for adducing them as conclusions in particular cases, leaving his readers to make the general
inferences for themselves.   Although I am consequently unable to cite a passage containing an
equally comprehensive assertion with that in which
I have embodied his doctrine, I am fully justified
in it, I think, by the preceding quotations, and
accordingly the following may be regarded as an
accurate summary of what he teaches respecting
grammatical forms:—All the subordinate parts of
speech, as set forth in modern grammars, are
wrongly classed under the names of articles, pronouns, conjunctions, prepositions and the like;
they are all nouns or verbs and can be nothing
else, the proof that they *are* so being that they
originally *were* so.

2. But Mr. Tooke contends not only for permanence in the grammatical character of words,
but, as I have explained in a preceding letter, for
permanence in their meaning; two things which it

* Diversions of Purley, Vol. i. p. 221, Chap. 8.   The Italics
are Mr. Tooke's.

is not always easy to keep separate, and which he has accordingly sometimes mixed together.

Here again it is to be regretted that he leaves his general doctrine to be gathered from particular cases.

One of the most striking instances in which he maintains it is the word "right," which he traces to the Latin *regitum* or *rectum*, whence he maintains that the meaning of *right* is always "ordered;" a right action is an ordered action, a right line is an ordered line. *

Having already anticipated this instance in a former letter, I shall content myself with succinctly reminding you of the simple explanation and refutation of the fallacy which are afforded by considering what constitutes the signification of a word. Since the meaning is equivalent to the idea raised up in the mind by the word, and since it is quite obvious that when the expression "a right line" is used no one ever thinks of any order of which it has been the consequence; the epithet *right*, when applied to a line, cannot mean *ordered*, whatever may have been its origin.

The word Scipan, which has already come under review, may be taken as another instance. If, as Mr. Tooke says, all the fourteen words which he enumerates in connexion with that verb are only its past participle, it follows that they must all have one and the same meaning.

* Diversions of Purley, Part 2, Chapter 1.

He avoids the inference, it is true, not very consistently or logically, by stating that the fourteen words, although all of them are merely the same past participle, are now differently and distinctly *applied*—thus establishing or trying to establish the distinction of which I exposed the fallacy in my last letter, between the meaning and the application of the same term.

The distinction is still more explicitly laid down in the following passage:

"LID
LOT
DLOT
GLADE
CLOUD

These words, though seemingly of such different significations, have all but one meaning; viz. *Covered, Hidden.* And the only difference is in their modern distinct application or different subaudition."[*]

Which is really saying that although these five words have all of them but one meaning, they have, severally, different meanings.

Both the doctrines on which I have been animadverting, may be so clearly exhibited together in the case of the word *right* already brought under your notice, that you will pardon a little repetition.

In the first place *right*, according to our author, always retains its original grammatical character; it is always the past participle of the verb *regere*, and never can grammatically be any thing else. When by way of counsel you say to your friend "right yourself," although according to grammarians you clearly speak in the imperative mood,

* Diversions of Purley, Part 2, Chapter 4.

Tooke will have it that it is the past participle and nothing else, setting at defiance the consideration that the injunction respects an act yet to be performed.

In the second place, *right* always retains its original signification, always means *ordered* whether applied to an action, to an argument, to a line, to an angle, or to an arm; and it can never have any other signification.   Notwithstanding that your conduct may be right contrary [i. e. *directly contrary*] to what is ordered, it strictly follows from Tooke's premises that it is ordered to be contrary.

These two errors run through the whole of his speculations.   The permanence of grammatical character and the permanence of meaning in words are perpetually either expressed or implied.

But on these parts of the subject, after my exposition of the second of them in a preceding letter, I will no longer dwell; what I have said being sufficient to indicate their places in the general doctrine.

I will proceed at once to the author's view of the relation between Etymology and the Philosophy of the Human Mind, and his other extraordinary doctrines respecting mental phenomena.

He broadly asserts that the operations, or what are called the operations, of the mind, are merely the operations of language.

The passage in which this assertion appears, is one of the most confused and the least intelligible

to be found in the whole book; and as he does not
furnish the grounds on which he has come to so
extraordinary a conclusion, it is not worth while
attempting to discover and controvert them, or to
disentangle the confusion pervading the statement.*

It seems plain enough that the converse of Tooke's
position is true, viz. that the operations of language,
except in the purely physical incidents of speech,
are essentially operations of the mind.

Language is obviously not some entity or agent
distinct or independent of mental processes, but is
in every case the result of them. Speech would
be a series of unmeaning sounds unless certain
objects, ideas, and emotions, were connected with
it. Every word uttered presupposes at the least
an idea, a feeling and a volition, all of which are
states or operations of mind. Perceiving, remem-
bering, feeling, willing, are all causes of speaking;
and, at the same time, they are processes which are
so far from being operations of language, that we
are frequently conscious of them without reference
to words.

* "The business of the mind," he says, "as far as it concerns language, appears to me to be very simple. It extends
no farther than to receive impressions, that is to have Sensations or Feelings. What are called its operations are merely
the operations of Language. A consideration of Ideas or of
the Mind, or of Things (relative to the Parts of Speech) will
lead us no farther than to *Nouns:* i. e. the signs of those impressions, or names of Ideas."—*Diversions of Purley,* Vol. i.
p. 49, 8vo. ed.

On the other hand what operation of language (if such an expression has any meaning except when referring to physical processes) can be named which is not an operation of the mind upon language, or with, or through language? Language is not an independent entity to perform operations of itself.

Abbreviation, the incident connected with language on which Tooke so especially dwells, is the result of mental acts of several kinds; and the efforts to accomplish it could not have that permanent effect on any word which he ascribes to them, without repeated operations of the mind in a number of human beings.

It may be stated in truth to be one great deficiency in Tooke's work, consequent on his turning away from mental philosophy because he had really no vocation for it, that he seems to be unaware or perpetually loses sight of the fact, that every change in a language is brought about by the action of circumstances on the minds of those who speak it, i. e. it is the direct result of mental operations; and he accordingly makes no attempt, except assigning the desire for despatch as the cause of abbreviations, to account for the various forms which the same word assumes or gives birth to. For example, he tells us, as we have seen, that fourteen 'words enumerated by him are only the past participle Scɪpeð of the verb Scɪpan to shear, and that they were formerly used indifferently; but he says nothing of the circumstances which led our ancestors, in the application of this verb, to change the *e* into *a* when they named a *share*, into *i* when they spoke of a *shire*, and into *o* when they wished to indicate a *shore*: yet each of these modifications must have had its peculiar mental cause.

He registers the changes and shows, or aims to show, the origin of the words from the same root, and there he leaves us, without affording us a glimpse of the way in which the modifications were effected.

No doubt to trace the causes of such modifications to any great extent, is difficult, not to say impossible; but at all events, if any step could be taken in that direction, it must be by a careful study of the movements of the human mind when engaged in the process of utterance — a task scarcely hitherto attempted.

Amongst the operations of the mind, which Tooke denies or converts into mere operations of language, is, as I have already intimated, Abstraction. In his views on this subject, I partly agree with him, although on different grounds, as will appear in the sequel.

His mode of proving that Abstraction is not an operation of the mind is remarkable.

It consists in showing that certain general terms, such as Act, Fact, Debt, Right, have been derived from past participles; or in his own language that they "are all merely participles poetically embodied and substantiated by those who use them." *

After a great number of instances of the kind mentioned, H says to F, " You have now instances of my doctrine, in, I suppose, about a thousand words. Their number may be easily increased. But, I trust, these are sufficient to discard that imagined *operation of the mind* which has been termed *Abstraction:* and to prove, that what we call by that name is merely one of the contrivances of Language for the purpose of more speedy communication." †

Now mark the reasoning here; Act, Fact, Debt and a thousand other words, are all merely past participles in the form of substantives; therefore there is no such operation of the mind as that which is termed Abstraction.

It is plain enough that here we have a complete *non sequitur.* Anyone may admit the derivations, and still hold that there is a process rightly called Abstraction.

If Tooke, instead of limiting his view to words, had ascended to the causes of all words, namely, our states of consciousness, his wider survey would have comprehended the truth.

The term Abstraction has been employed by philosophers (without always being aware of it) in two different ways; first, to denote the alleged

* Diversions of Purley, Vol. ii. Chap. 2.
† Ibid. Vol. ii. p. 394.

formation of abstract ideas from the concrete;
and, secondly, to designate the exclusive attention
bestowed by the mind on some object or circumstance to the neglect of everything else.

Taking the first sense of the term, I quite concur in Tooke's doctrine, that no such abstraction
takes place, and that we have no abstract ideas;
but not for the reason he assigns. I concur in it
because, on examining what passes in my own
mind, I am conscious that when abstract terms
are used, just the same kind of ideas come into
my mind as when proper names are used; the only
difference being one of limitation: that, in brief,
all ideas being representative of objects or things,
internal or external, and there being no abstract
objects or things, ideas must be particular or
concrete like their archetypes.

Tooke mistakes the kind of proof required to
show that we do not and cannot form abstract
ideas.* Such proof must consist in an accurate

* In a very defective and inaccurate account of the doctrines
of Horne Tooke, put forth by Lord Brougham, the former is with
singular infelicity represented as holding the existence of
general and abstract ideas, the following being part of the account : "As for other ideas of a general or abstract nature, they
are still later of being distinctly formed."—*Historical Sketches of
Statesmen in the Time of Geo. III.* What says Tooke himself?
Nothing surely can be more explicit: "They are not ideas but
mere'y *terms,* which are *general* and *abstract.*"—*Diversions,*
Pt. 1, Chap. 2. He repeats this over and over again : in truth,
a great part of his work is devoted to showing it by examples.

appreciation of what passes in our consciousness, not in any verbal derivations. It is altogether a mental investigation.

With regard to the second application of the term Abstraction (to which Tooke, if he recognizes it at all, does not distinctly advert), in the sense, namely, of partial attention, no one assuredly who looks into his own mind, or at the conduct of others, can entertain a doubt that there is such an operation; but, as I have already treated this part of the human constitution in its proper place, an exposition of the subject here would be redundant.

Another great error into which our author falls in regard to mental phenomena is his doctrine on the composition of terms.

Speaking of Locke he says, " the supposition [of a composition of ideas] is unnecessary. Every purpose for which the composition of ideas was imagined, being more easily and naturally answered by the *composition of Terms.*"

What, nevertheless, does the latter phrase signify? On revolving the question in my own mind, I can find only three cases which can with the least propriety be so designated. (1) There is putting together the letters of which a term is formed, as making the word *sun* out of the letters *s, u, n.* (2) There is putting together two or more separate words so as to form one compound word, as *sun-flower*, a case which includes words formed by

prefixes and suffixes as *preposition*.   (3) There is
putting together words, so as to form sentences,
as, *the sun-flower is full-blown.*

Having these meanings before us, let us examine
Tooke's recommendation that in reading Locke we
should substitute *composition of terms*, wherever
the author has supposed a composition of ideas.
Well, Locke tells us that the composition of ideas
may be seen in the meaning of such words as
beauty, man, army, which, according to him, denote
complex ideas made up of simple ideas.

Let us then make the substitution recommended
by Tooke in the case of the last-mentioned term,
" *army:* "

How can *army* be said to be a composition of
terms?   In which of the senses already explained?

The word denotes a multitudinous thing, an
assemblage of soldiers: all the putting together in
the matter is the putting together of men.   The
composition of terms is here out of place; utterly
inapplicable.

Although Locke's doctrine on the subject of
general and abstract ideas is fundamentally such
as I dissent from, yet he has here a manifest
advantage over his critic.   When the word army
is used, what takes place is, that the image or
idea of a number of congregated soldiers is raised
up in the mind; and since soldiers actually so congregated form a composite body, the idea of that
body may be said to be composite too.

But as to the mere word itself, there is no composition that can possibly be in question, and with regard to the application of a term to a compound object (if that were Tooke's meaning) it can, in no sense, be called a composition of the term.

The tendency in the author of " The Diversions " to reduce everything mental to an operation of language, is so strong, that he considers Locke's Essay — the whole of it — " as a philosophical account of the first sort of abbreviations in language," namely, abbreviations in terms; * while in another place he describes the whole business of the Essay to be the consideration of the force of terms; † and, again, he gives it as his " opinion, that Mr. Locke in his Essay never did advance one step beyond the origin of Ideas and the composition of Terms." ‡ Further, " it is merely a Grammatical Essay, or a Treatise on Words, or on Language." § These seem to be, on the face of them, incongruous descriptions of the immortal work which they are intended to characterise; but it is not worth while attempting to reconcile them.

" Abbreviation in terms," whatever may have been intended by it, can legitimately mean nothing but shortening words; which is no more the object of consideration with Locke than the composition of terms which has just had our attention. In

* Diversions of Purley, Vol. i. p. 29. † Ibid. p. 51.
‡ Ibid. p. 31. § Ibid. p. 30.

regard to "the force of terms," the phrase is
equivalent to "the meaning of terms," or to some
quality of the meaning, and of course the consideration of it can scarcely fail to be mingled with that
of mental processes : but to represent the consideration of that one quality as the whole business
of a work which takes into view a large number of
the most important questions of intellectual philosophy, shows an incapacity in the author of the
representation to comprehend what the Essay on
Human Understanding has effected.   Valuable as
its third Book is that great work is assuredly
something more than a mere Treatise on Words.

I will extend this notice of Tooke's psychological
errors by citing one more instance of his tendency
to reduce mental processes to what he calls operations of language.   He will not allow that affirming and denying are anything else than verbal.

Doubtless, language is usually employed to make
known that we do affirm or deny; and so far,
affirmation and denial are in a verbal form: but
words could not be put together in these modes
without previous mental acts which they are
employed to indicate.

We discern that a thing has a property or that
it has not; and this discernment, positive or negative, is expressed in a proposition, whence the
proposition is said to affirm or deny; but if there
were no mental act or state prior to the utterance
of the words and represented by them, they would

be unmeaning sounds; or, to speak more correctly, were there no act of discernment, then no proposition affirming or denying could be uttered. For these reasons mental affirmation and denial (whatever objection may lie against the mere phraseology) are real facts equally with verbal affirmation and denial, and are perfectly distinct from them. It seems to be the fate of Tooke, as soon as he touches on the Mind, to plunge into error.

LETTER X.

LANGUAGE (*in continuation*).

It is a logical consequence of my doctrine regarding the specific function of words in intellectual operations, and what constitutes the perfection of language as an intellectual instrument, that I should dissent from the extravagant powers and qualities which have been ascribed to words in their individual capacity and in virtue of their etymological origin.

Perhaps I cannot better show the extreme, as I think it, to which this lavish attribution has been carried, than by citing passages from a recent work of considerable merit and popularity.

" There are few," says the author, " who would not readily acknowledge that in worthy books is laid up and hoarded the greater part of the treasures of wisdom and knowledge which the world has accumulated; and that chiefly by aid of these they are handed down from one generation to another. My purpose in the present and some succeeding lectures, which by the kindness of your Principal, I shall have the opportunity of addressing to you here, is to press on you something

different from this; namely, that not in books
only, which all acknowledge, nor yet in connected
oral discourse, but often also in words contemplated each one apart from others, and by itself,
there are boundless stores of moral and historic
truth, and no less of passion and imagination, laid
up, — lessons of infinite worth which we may
derive from them, if only our attention is awakened
to their existence." — *On the Study of Words, by
R. C. Trench,* page 1.

Another writer of reputation speaks in the same
strain :

" A language," he says, " will often be wiser,
not merely than the vulgar, but even than the
wisest of those who speak it. Being like amber in
its efficacy to circulate the electric spirit of truth,*
it is also like amber in embalming and preserving

* Unfortunately for this similitude amber, although an
electric, is a non-conductor of electricity : it stops the circulation of the electric fluid. But the whole comparison is very
confused and imperfectly brought out. Amber is represented
as circulating not electricity (which was the obvious design)
but the spirit of truth, and as preserving and embalming not
material objects but the relics of wisdom. Even if we rectify
the comparison, the first material fact will still remain incorrect; and, as to the second, since amber, according to common description, is found to enclose nothing better than leaves
and insects, we obtain but a sorry counterpart to the relics of
the wisdom of our ancestors. The whole passage is an apt
illustration of what I shall hereafter insist upon at greater
length — the peril of pushing such analogies beyond a single
point, in the vain endeavour to make them elucidate truths on
which they are incapable of throwing light.

the relics of ancient wisdom, although one is not seldom puzzled to decipher its contents. . Sometimes it locks up truths which were once well known, but which in the course of ages have passed out of sight and been forgotten. In other cases it holds the germs of truth, of which, though they were never plainly discerned, the genius of its framers caught a glimpse in a happy moment of divination. A meditative man cannot refrain from wonder, when he digs down to the deep thought lying at the root of many a metaphorical term employed for the designation of spiritual things, even of those with regard to which professing philosophers have blundered grossly; and often it would seem as though rays of truths, which were still below the intellectual horizon, had dawned on the imagination as it was looking up to heaven." — *Guesses at Truth*, 1st Series, p. 333, 4th ed.

These passages appear to me to contain a most singular misrepresentation of an interesting subject, and if they are not diametrically opposed to the sober truth, they greatly exaggerate the little foundation which there is for them. They also appear to mix up the case of metaphorical symbolization with that of etymological significance.

A word by itself, contemplated apart from other words, cannot surely be said with correctness (except in certain particular cases which will be hereafter expressly noticed) to give us any information, yield us any truth whatever beyond its ordinary meaning, much less to impart any profound wisdom or contain lessons of infinite worth. All other knowledge we may happen to possess or can obtain about it, is historical knowledge which has been or must be collected from "books or connected discourse," whether oral or written.

Thus the origin of the word and the various meanings which it may have borne at various times, are directly or indirectly matters of history, circumstances obviously not to be gathered from contemplating the word alone and apart, but to be learned from extant records, and, in every case, by means of that combination of words with words in propositions, which, strangely enough, in one of the quotations before us is expressly excluded. The particulars in question cannot with any verisimilitude be described as laid up in the word; they are simply incidents connected with it, and to be collected like other past incidents from suitable evidence.

The author of the Lectures proceeds, in the same style of exaggeration, to say, "Many a single word is itself a concentrated poem, having stores of poetical thought and imagery laid up in it. Examine it, and it will be found to rest on some deep analogy of things natural and things spiritual, bringing those to illustrate and to give an abiding form and body to these."

He illustrates his position by the word "tribu-

lation," which, he says, is derived from the Latin
" tribulum," " the threshing instrument, or roller,
by which the Romans separated the corn from
the husks; and 'tribulatio' in its primary significance was the act of this separation. But
some Latin writer of the Christian Church appropriated the word and image for the setting forth
of a higher truth; and sorrow and distress and
adversity being the appointed means for the
separating in men of their chaff from their wheat,
of whatever in them was light and trivial and
poor, from the solid and the true, therefore he
called these sorrows and griefs 'tribulations,'
'threshings,' that is, of the inner spiritual man,
without which there could be no fitting him for
the heavenly garner."

Here, according to my views, we have a good
instance of what a word singly and apart cannot
do. We can learn nothing from the term *tribulation* considered by itself, apart from external evidence; or, in different language, it can suggest
nothing to us, except accidentally, beyond that
mental condition which it simply denotes.

As we are of course supposed to understand
ordinary language, we know what the word means
when we happen to meet with it; that is to say, it
raises up in our minds the idea of a peculiar
kind of distress. If we proceed to discover that
the term is derived from the name of a Roman
agricultural implement, we must gain the informa-

tion from external sources: if we further learn
that it was analogically appropriated by a Christian
writer and that "this deeper religious use of the
word tribulation was unknown to classical, that is
to heathen antiquity, and belongs exclusively to
Christian writers," all this, supposing we admit it
to be unquestionably true, is likewise information
drawn from the records of the past *about* the
word: it is not truth laid up *in* the word and
extracted from it by contemplating it by itself and
apart.

The author appears to me to blend two very different things, to mistake the knowledge which is to
be learned from various sources respecting a word
and its acceptations, or respecting the objects denoted by it, in different ages, for something which
is intrinsic and laid up in the bare term itself.
Such knowledge may be properly described as being
accumulated about the word not contained in it
nor drawn from it.

Investigating the history of a word, i. e. of the
modes in which it has been employed, may lead
us to acquire a good deal of knowledge connected
with the term, but in no other way than investigating the history of an article of dress, a social
custom, or a useful implement, may lead us to
gather much information connected with the object
of our inquiry.

We have elaborate historical accounts, for example, of the various machinery formerly resorted

to in grinding corn down to the latest inventions,
interspersed with episodes on the particular kinds
of food of different nations and on the commerce
in grain.   Hence if the historian of these inventions were disposed, as most historians are, to extol
the subject of his researches, he might say that
boundless stores of historic truth are laid up in
a mill-stone; and the assertion would be quite as
appropriate and correct as the doctrine that they
are laid up in a word : but this, I apprehend, would
scarcely be accepted as solving the ancient problem
of seeing into that visually impenetrable body.

Nevertheless it seems to me, with great respect
for the authors of the theory, that looking into
a word for past wisdom is much like looking into
a mill-stone for the history of grinding.

There are cases, nevertheless, in which, as I
have already admitted, words may be said with
more correctness to contain knowledge when considered singly as words in their literal meaning;
cases where the very presence of certain terms in
the vocabulary of a people, may indicate modes
of thinking, feeling, and acting, for which we have
no other evidence, or which lie beyond the evidence
we possess.

But even here disconnected words are only on a
level with other insulated relics of antiquity, implements and arms and sculptures, which have
been dug up from buried ruins or handed down

to us by accident, and which serve to give us a
few glimpses into the story of past times.

The most striking instances of this kind of
lingual evidence are when we have no information
regarding a nation or tribe, but some relics of its
vocabulary, and when from the terms contained
in that wreck of a vocabulary, or from the absence
even of certain classes of terms, we are able to
infer that the people were agricultural or nomadic,
or warlike or peaceful. And even with regard to
nations of whom we have historical records, a word
may indicate some feature in their social condition
or manners or customs or fortunes, of which their
written annals furnish no explicit account.

All these circumstances in the past state of a
people, are evidently inferred from the mere
existence of the words in the vocabulary which
has come down to us ; and we may speak of them
with sufficient accuracy as information furnished
by the words considered singly and apart; but at
the same time we must admit that the information
so gathered is in the very nature of the case
exceedingly meagre at the best; so meagre, indeed,
though valuable in its place, that we cannot for a
moment suppose it to be all that was in the view
of those writers who have so highly extolled the
deep wisdom and concentrated poetry laid up in
solitary terms; who have eulogized words contemplated "apart from others and by themselves,"

as boundless stores of moral and historic truth
and pregnant with lessons of infinite worth.*

* The lecturer quotes Niebuhr to show the knowledge which
words can furnish, and particularly the circumstance that while
Latin and Greek correspond closely in their agricultural terms,
they differ altogether in those denoting the operations and incidents of war ; and hence the inference is drawn (how I do
not exactly discern) that the Italians once stood in a similar
relation to the Greeks as the Normans to the Saxons in
England. More recent comparative philologists than Niebuhr
maintain, on the other hand, that the Roman language is as
perfectly original as the Greek and the Sanscrit, and hence the
assertion that the Roman people were a mixed nation " is de-
prived of its linguistic support." " Even Niebuhr's ingenious
hypothesis—one which O. Müller has adopted—that the
names of the objects of peace belong to the Greek and those of
a warlike character to the Italian portion of Latin, does not
hold good after comparative researches. The inhabitants of
Italy share the names of the peaceful household, not only with
the Greeks, but with almost all the nations of the common
stock. There is, therefore, nothing especially Greek in them.
Words for the business of war and warlike implements are also
hardly to be found in the cognate languages : and every
nation forms them in part herself. We may, therefore, say
that these words of the Latin language are not German, not
Slavonic, with just as much right as when we maintain that
they are not Greek. Much of this points to the fact, that the
cognate nations were, during the period of their living
together, more addicted to peaceful occupations than to warlike
pursuits, and that they marked each of the weapons which at
the time of their separation they used against each other with
a particular name."—*The Results of Comparative Philology, by
Dr. G. Curtius, Eng. Trans,* p. 12. *Non nostrum tantas com-
ponere lites.* I have introduced this extract for the purpose of
showing, not only the uncertainty which may belong to the
grounds afforded to us by philology, but also the vague and
scanty inferences which we are able to draw from them.

Taken as a whole the study of the Origin and Progress of

Although single words, considered apart in their
literal signification, may thus constitute grounds
for inferring certain features in the condition of
those nations to whose vocabulary they belong,
yet inasmuch as they cannot in any proper sense
be said to present us with either deep wisdom or
condensed poetry, we must seek further for these
treasures, if they exist at all, in the figurative character of the words; to which, indeed, we are expressly referred for them by the authors before us.
Let us therefore inquire whether they can be found
in the metaphors sometimes contained in such
single words so considered apart; and this involves
the general question of the value of analogical
applications of terms designating material operations and events, to such as are mental.

As the point is one respecting which precise
thinking is exceedingly desirable, I purpose to
take some pains to exhibit it in what appears to
me the proper light. In the first place, it may be

Languages is doubtless a noble and an interesting pursuit, and
may throw light on the unity and separation and migration of
the former inhabitants of the earth, as well as on the mental
processes concerned in the evolution and vicissitudes of human
speech. It may also present us with detached intimations of
manners, customs, and modes of thinking; but I have yet to
learn that it can supply, or even do much to illustrate, trains
of national events when historical documents fail; or furnish
us with instructive information of the conduct, condition, and
career of nations, which to be instructive in any high degree
must be definite and connected. I can nowhere find the alleged
" vast harvests of historic lore garnered often in single words."

L

remarked, that we human beings are under the absolute necessity of applying terms borrowed from
outward objects to designate our mental operations
and affections: we have no other possible resource
when we wish to speak of them to others; and
there is in human nature a general power of discerning and relishing analogies of all kinds—analogies between the phenomena of the outward and
those of the inward world, as well as between the
phenomena belonging respectively to each.

The employment of terms denoting external
objects to designate figuratively the phenomena of
consciousness being thus unavoidable in the ordinary intercourse of life, and being consonant with
our natural propensities and endowments, any new
application of a word in this way cannot be truly
regarded as, in general, indicating any deep wisdom
or any great stretch of poetical imagination.

Nor can it be so regarded in the particular case
of past times, even the most remote, when there
was doubtless a greater call for the transference
of terms from material to mental phenomena.

The farther we push our investigations into our
own language (which I instance in order to limit
the discussion), the clearer will be the truth that it
originated in the scanty vocabulary of a rude tribe;
scanty, because the knowledge to be uttered was in
the same condition. It was the very meagreness
of their language that, as their knowledge widened,
seems to have forced the barbarous speakers into

those metaphors which are now ascribed to profound thought or strong imagination; but which
resulted, for the most part, from the urgent desire
for utterance, in the dearth of literal phraseology,
seizing hold from sheer necessity of obvious analogies to accomplish its purpose.*

In other cases, although comparatively few, such
metaphors have doubtless originated in mere fond-
ness for figurative expression, or in the glow of
passion, or in the leisurely play of fancy delighting
in its own creations.

In the second place, necessary as the transfer of
terms from matter to mind is, and pleasing as in
every stage of civilization such metaphors when
newly and happily applied may be, they do not
and cannot convey any knowledge of the mental
states which they are employed to indicate or designate, beyond, in each case, raising up in the
mind of the hearer a conception of the precise
mental state intended by the speaker.

It may be laid down as a law in the science of
mind (and a most important law it is), that no
analogy between mental phenomena and material
phenomena can make us better acquainted with

* It has been shown by recent philologists that some nations
whom we regard as uncivilised have a great many synonyms,
many words for the same object or event; but this is no real
store of language from which names for new objects may be
taken without effort, and does not militate against the position
in the text. On the accession of fresh knowledge, such a
nation would still have suitable terms to seek.

either. Such analogies can only help us to each
other's meaning, or fix it more deeply in the
memory, or excite us to think on the separate
characteristics of the two things brought into
comparison.

This may be a startling, but it is a true and by
no means a novel doctrine. It may be found in
Descartes, as was long ago pointed out by Mr.
Stewart, who, while giving an account of that
philosopher's opinions, has expressed his own view
of the subject with clearness and precision in the
following words: —

"He [Descartes] was led to perceive with the
evidence of consciousness, that the attributes of
Mind were still more clearly and distinctly knowable than those of Matter; and that in studying
the former, so far from attempting to explain them
by analogies borrowed from the latter, our chief
aim ought to be, to banish as much as possible
from the fancy every analogy, and even every analogical expression, which, by inviting the attention
abroad, might divert it from its proper business at
home."* In a subsequent page Mr. Stewart proceeds to add, "Descartes laid down as a first principle that *nothing comprehensible by the imagination
can be at all subservient to the knowledge of Mind;*
and that the sensible images involved in all our
common forms of speaking concerning its opera-

* Dissertation on the Progress of Metaphysical Philosophy,
p. 60.

tions, are to be guarded against with the most anxious care, as leading to confound, in our apprehensions, two classes of phenomena, which it is of the last importance to distinguish accurately from each other."*

In the next place it may be remarked that if such metaphors could convey any knowledge of the nature or laws of mental phenomena, or assist us in any way to comprehend those phenomena better, there is another feature belonging to them which would inevitably render their assistance of little worth: it is, that the analogy seldom extends beyond a single point, or is at all events exceedingly vague and imperfect when carried farther; and if we attempt it we are in danger of losing ourselves in inconsistency or confusion. Metaphors are dangerous tools to handle, if handled long.

* Dissertation, page 61.

On carefully reading over the Second Meditation of Descartes, I do not find the doctrine to be so fully and so explicitly enunciated by him as it appears in the language of Mr. Stewart, but it is there in substance. The passages on which the latter philosopher grounded his representation are the following:—

"Itaque cognosco, nihil eorum quæ possum *Imaginatione* comprehendere, ad hanc quam de me habeo notitiam pertinere, mentemque ab illis diligentissime esse avocandum, ut suam ipsa naturam quam distinctissime percipiat." Descartes had already explained in what sense he used the term Imagination: "Nihil est *imaginari* quam rei corporeæ figuram seu imaginem contemplari." This limited meaning of Imagination must be borne in mind, otherwise the doctrine may be misconstrued.

In order to illustrate both this and the preceding remark, I will take the analogy which is dwelt upon at so much length and with so much fervour by the intelligent lecturer whom I have before quoted, and which is contained in the word "tribulation." As I have so recently extracted the passage referred to, I will beg you to turn to it that you may fully enter into the following comments.

The vagueness and imperfection of the analogy will be seen from a brief analysis.

1. In the case of wheat previously to its being threshed, there are obviously three things adhering together, the straw, the grain, and the chaff.

In the human counterpart there are, according to the representation, the spiritual man, his solid qualities, and his light qualities. In this comparison there is certainly to be discovered a rude but only a rude kind of resemblance between the objects compared.

2. Let us proceed next to consider the material operation. The threshing of wheat consists in loosening from each other all the coadherent parts, leaving the grain and chaff mixed together it may be, but disunited, and the straw separated from both, with the exception of the unremovable husks.

In the mental process there is nothing corresponding to this: the salutary effect of adversity, as intended to be shown by the metaphor, ought to consist in loosening the spiritual man not from *all* his qualities light and solid (which would indeed reduce him to a mere man of straw), but only from his light and trivial qualities. The ex-trusion of both kinds out of him, which would be needful to complete the analogy with the process undergone by the wheat, would be not a moral purgation but a spiritual extinction.

To add to the discrepancy and confusion which almost always attend pushing a resemblance too far, the spiritual man, in the final sentence of the quotation, is suddenly transformed from being the straw — the holder of the metaphorical grain — into the very wheat itself: he is spoken of at least as being *fitted for the garner*, and you are compelled, in consonance with that description, to consider him, for the time being, as the grain, unless, to escape from the inconsistency, you seek refuge in the sack in which the wheat may (conveniently for the metaphor's sake) be presumed to be depo-sited, and which, in this rhetorical strait, may be taken to shadow forth the human being. But, alas! even here, as the sack itself has not been threshed, a rock lies in our course, and the meta-phor is still fated to be wrecked. *Incidit in Scyl-lam qui vult vitare Charybdim.*

So difficult is it to manage these analogies at all, if we push them beyond a single point of re-semblance, (in itself perhaps somewhat indefinite), or aspire to make them subservient to the expo-sition of mental phenomena. The attempt to

extract knowledge or wisdom from such a source
must inevitably fail.   How can there be deep
wisdom (other considerations apart) in an analogy
which breaks down?   Were it possible (which I
venture to think it is not) that such a treasure
could lurk in the figure, it could be only in virtue
of the apt tallying of the subjects compared, the
close correspondence of the several physical circumstances adduced for the purpose of illustration,
with the several mental circumstances to be illustrated.

In ordinary cases all this criticism of a metaphorical passage which could be disposed of in half
a sentence, might appear to be only "breaking a
butterfly upon a wheel;" but it is not (you will
observe) merely the correctness of the figures that
is here in question, but also the justness of extol-
ling them in the large, lofty, and extravagant terms
employed.   It is a question of philosophical truth
even more than of purity of taste.

Pray do not mistake the position I have taken
up.   I by no means intend to deny that great
depth of thought and richness of imagery may be
connected with the word "tribulation" or any similar term, or with the analogy presented by its etymological origin.   These however, according to my
view, are adventitious or rather adscititious, supplied or gathered together by the meditator himself; and so far from being extracted out of the
word, they are and must be brought to the naked

term and thrown around it by his learning and
imagination.*

Nor will I deny that analogies of this kind, particularly when they are vague or remote, may be
readily associated with profound emotions; re-
membering the observation of Coleridge, "that
deep feeling has a tendency to combine with
obscure ideas, in preference to clear and distinct
notions."†

As a conclusion to the subject, I must solicit
your attention for a moment to a judicious recommendation made by Descartes and confirmed by
Stewart, which you may possibly have overlooked;
and I do so for the purpose of contrasting it with
the doctrine on which I have been commenting.

The recommendation referred to is contained in
a passage already cited, and is to the effect that,
in treating of the mind, we should banish as far as
practicable analogies and analogical expressions.
The wisdom of this, against which the first impulse of many may be to rebel, will be more
clearly seen the more it is reflected upon.   I

* The passages on which I am commenting seem to be
little more than a reproduction, as a grave philosophical speculation in reference to words, of what appears in Shakespeare as
a play of fancy in reference to natural objects.

"And this our life, exempt from public haunt,
Finds tongues in trees, books in the running brooks,
Sermons in stones, and good in every thing."
                    As you like it, Act II. Scene 1.

† The Friend, Vol. I. p. 177.

would follow it up by observing, that when the
transfer of a term from material to mental phenomena has been once effectually accomplished and
generally adopted, the sooner the analogy drops
out of the mind and leaves the expression a literal
one, the better for precise thinking and accurate
investigation.   The more completely, for example,
we forget the pedigree of the word "tribulation,"
when we make use of the term, and the more exclusively we think of the mental state itself and its
immediate accompaniments, the more clearly (as I
conceive, in direct contrariety to the lecturer) shall
we discern its nature, its causes, its effects — in
brief, understand all about it.   The imperfect
analogy of the threshing implement can tend only,
as it appears to me and as I have endeavoured to
point out, to confuse the mind with incongruous or
ill-assorted images, "similes unlike" and " passages
that lead to nothing."   A great part of the loose
thinking (if thinking it may be called*) which so
generally prevails in regard to the phenomena of
consciousness, is made up of vague tropes, in which
the mind seems to repose, without going or seeking
to go farther.

Figurative language in description, in rhetoric,
in sentiment, in the expression of feeling, in rousing to action, is, when it chances to be happy,
prolific of delight, and powerful in the impressions

* "How many never think who think they do!"—*Jane
Taylor.*

which it leaves; but in the communication of knowledge, the finest and best fitting metaphor, pleasing as it may be to the imagination, can do nothing better than convey to the hearer and vividly imprint on his mind, the precise idea which it was intended to indicate, while it is perpetually liable to become the substitute of the reality which it shadows forth.

There is another passage, in an earlier work of Mr. Stewart's, which so happily corroborates the views maintained in the preceding discussion, that I cannot forbear to present it to you here. It will form an appropriate close to the present letter.

After quoting as examples of metaphorical language the expressions "*the morning of our days; the chequered condition of human life; the lights of science; the rise and the fall of empires;*" he proceeds, " In all these instances, the metaphors are happy and impressive; but whatever advantage the poet or the orator may derive from them, the most accurate analysis of the different subjects thus brought into contact will never enable the philosopher to form one new conclusion concerning the nature either of the one or of the other. I mention this particularly, because it has been too little attended to by those who have speculated concerning the powers of the Mind. The words which denote these powers are all borrowed (as I have already observed repeatedly) from material objects, or from physical operations, and it seems to have been very generally supposed, that this implied something common in the nature or attributes of Mind and of Matter. Hence the real origin of those analogical theories concerning the former, which, instead of advancing our knowledge with respect to it, have operated more powerfully than any other circumstances whatever to retard the progress of that branch of science." *

* Philosophical Essays by Dugald Stewart, p. 270, 3rd ed.

LETTER XI.

LANGUAGE (*in continuation*).

I HAVE been hitherto occupied, chiefly at least, with words regarded singly or apart from their connexion with other words.

I have next to consider the second question before proposed, namely, how words are affected in their signification when they are combined in sentences.

In a former letter (First Series) I endeavoured to show, that common names and abstract terms differ from proper names, not in the character of the representations or ideas suggested, but in the more limited range of suggestion appertaining to the latter.

Precisely the same difference may be remarked between a word when standing alone and when united with other words to form a sentence, or in composition. In the latter case, the range of the ideas raised up by the word is much narrower than in the former.

This may be exemplified . by a very simple

instance.   If some one standing at the window of
the room where I am sitting utters the sentence,
" I see a man walking through a field," a picture
immediately presents itself to my mind representing
a man in the act of walking and a field in which
he walks.   The man must be conceived or mentally
depicted as engaged in that particular act in that
particular sort of ground.

But if the supposed spectator standing at the
window, uses the shorter phrase, " I see a man,"
I am by no means under the same restrictions.
I may then think of any man in any position or
attitude or act; either sitting or standing or
running, either in the field or in the lane or in the
garden, in short as doing anything anywhere .
within view of the window.

It is to be remarked, too, that if any of these
my conceptions should be expressed in words,
they would necessarily take the form of a sentence
or proposition not less complete than the one
which I first supposed to be uttered, and having
a meaning equally definite.

On this account if it were advisable to confound
under one name things essentially distinct, and
most usefully discriminated, it would be nearer
the truth to say that every word is a sentence,
than, as an able and ingenious writer contends, *
that every sentence is a word.   Even a proper

* Mr. B. H. Smart in his Sematology and other Works.

name brings to mind very variable things, none of which could be described except by a proposition.

For instance, the name of Sir James Mackintosh, whose memoirs I have just been reading, when I dwell upon it, brings that distinguished man to my mind as sitting in a particular room where I once met with him when he was making a temporary sojourn in Yorkshire; or as I saw him and listened to his eloquence at a meeting in London on behalf of the Greeks; or as I heard him speaking in the House of Commons: and in the same way, every name that denotes an individual person or thing brings to your recollection, if you pause upon it, that person or thing in some particular attitude or employment or condition, or with some particular accompaniments, which could be told only in one or more sentences.

That when a speaker utters a sentence instead of a word, or, more correctly, when after uttering a word as "man" he proceeds to use it in a sentence by describing a man walking in a field, he thereby limits the variety of conceptions raised up by the word in the hearer, is a truth which deserves to be further elucidated. Nor is it less worthy of attention that the restrictive action is the same as ensues when a common term is replaced by a proper name. The two cases, indeed, may be presented in combination.

Had the speaker in the preceding hypothetical instance, after telling me there was a man, and

that the man was walking in a field, proceeded to
say that it was a cornfield, and that the man who
was walking there was my servant John Jones,
my conception would have been still more nar-
rowed by the description of the field and by the
proper name, than it had been by the previous
particulars; and yet, after all these limitations, it
is to be remarked, that I should be at liberty to
conceive the object with considerable variations of
appearance.   I might conceive John walking
rapidly or walking slowly, in a cap or a hat or
bareheaded, with a coat or without one, singing or
silent, smiling or serious.

Thus the real effect produced on the representations raised up by a word, when other words
are added to it so as to form a sentence, is a
limitation of possible conceptions, but not an ex-
clusion of variety, corresponding in this respect to
the effect of replacing a common term by a proper
name.

This explanation of the matter will perhaps serve
to show the real value of a passage in Dugald
Stewart's Philosophical Essays of a somewhat questionable character.   In his " Essay on the Tendency
of some late Philological Speculations," he asserts
" that our words when examined separately are
often as completely insignificant as the letters of
which they are composed; deriving their meaning
solely from the connexion or relation in which they
stand to others.   Of this a very obvious example

occurs in the case of terms which have a variety of
acceptations, and of which the import, in every
particular application, must be collected from the
whole sentence of which they form a part."

If we suppose that in this passage Mr. Stewart
intended to assert that all the words in a sentence
are individually insignificant, a curious result will
ensue. It will follow that words, every one of
which is without meaning when standing alone,
must give and take meaning reciprocally when
they are combined in a sentence: each must give
what it has not got. Surely a term completely
insignificant can stand in no relation of meaning
to other terms equally insignificant, and can derive
no meaning from them. We must suppose, then,
that Mr. Stewart intended to say that some of the
words in a sentence are or may be insignificant
when considered by themselves, and are made
significant by other words which are already so :
and to exemplify this he cites the case of words
having *various* significations, his reasoning on this
supposition being, as far as I can discern, that
because the meaning of some words which have a
variety of significations is determined by the con-
text, therefore the meaning of those which are
non-significant is determined in the same way.

He has, I think, mixed up two cases and not
accurately stated either of them. The first case,
as given, is wrong in point of fact. Words taken
separately, so far from being insignificant, raise up,

M

or may raise up, as I have just explained, a wider
range of conceptions than when they are combined;
and the precise effect of one word being joined to
others is not that meaning is imparted to what
was before destitute of it, but that the word is
thereby limited in its latitude of suggestion.

But the case of a word with two or more
meanings is a different and more complicated one.
When a term has two distinct acceptations, the
meanings of the other words associated with it
undoubtedly determine in which of the two senses
— both being present to the mind — it is to be
taken; or they cause one of the senses, perhaps, to
be suggested alone; and they at the same time
limit the latitude of suggestion which the word
possesses in the sense so determined.

In no case, however, can words be insignificant
except from the ignorance of the hearer or reader
— which is not here in question.

Tooke puts the matter in very positive terms:
" There is not," he says, " nor is it possible there
should be, a word in any language, which has not
a complete meaning and signification even when
taken by itself."*

This kind of determination of the import of a
word employed in several distinct acceptations, or
(as the fact is more properly described when certain cases are spoken of) in several distinct modes,

* Letter to Dunning.

is a pervading feature in language, far beyond
what is generally understood and far beyond what
Mr. Stewart seems to have apprehended.

Language would be overburthened with words
if there did not prevail a sort of economy by using
the same term for various purposes; not any intentional economy, but an economy arising from
several causes, and principally from speakers laying
hold instinctively of the first known term which
presents itself, to serve their purpose of conveying
to others, although it may be irregularly and
figuratively and elliptically, what they wish to
express.

The circumstance here described forms, in truth,
one of the most important points to be attended
to in the use of words in combination; and is
especially important in all philosophical speculations. This will appear manifest on taking a cursory
glance at some examples of the fact that the same
word is made to do different duties in different
positions, or under different circumstances, and frequently without any recognised or even suspected
change of meaning.

In a preceding letter (Second Series) when
treating of what are styled necessary truths, I
pointed out one mode in which we are accustomed
to do this, unconsciously making the same epithet
serve different purposes, by placing it in situations
where it cannot directly qualify the noun to which
it is joined, and can be regarded only as an elliptical

indication of what is meant : and by way of illustration I showed how in thus economising language, we apply the term *criminal* both to the act of a culprit and to the court in which he is tried.

This is a common, and probably an unavoidable, expedient, without which our vocabularies might become cumbrous and unwieldy; but it is nevertheless a defect in language as an intellectual instrument, and great care is required, I scarcely need to say, in guarding against the natural consequences of it in our reasonings. We must sedulously and rigorously avoid drawing inferences which would be quite correct were the epithet intended, as in ordinary cases, to qualify the noun associated with it, but which would be utterly erroneous because it was intended for an entirely different office.

Such inferences, I have shown, have been made from the term "necessary" when translocated from its proper position and elliptically applied. The ignorance or the oversight of this kind of translocation and elliptical usage on the part of Leibnitz, Kant and other philosophers, has resulted in their bewildering themselves with difficulties about necessary truths and *à priori* principles, which admit of the simplest solution when this expedient of language is once thoroughly understood and appreciated.*

* See the Second Series of these Letters, p. 110.

As what I have ventured to name the translocation of terms, has not, I think, received that share of attention, since I first pointed it out to the notice of thinkers, which its importance deserves; and as its bearings on philosophical speculation seem to have been little understood, I will take occasion to repeat briefly here how it affects the question of what have been called *necessary truths*.

The phrase *necessary truth* or proposition is, in regard to the inappropriate allocation of the epithet, precisely on a level with the phrase *criminal court*.

By the latter expression we do not intend to charge a court of law with crime, but we intend to convey to the hearer that it is a court in which crimes, or culprits accused of crimes, are tried. Thus the epithet criminal is not appropriately placed, but is transferred for the sake of brevity from its proper position before acts or agents, and prefixed to the noun *court* to which it is really inapplicable.

What is here so clearly seen and acknowledged has place equally in the phrase " necessary truth." A truth is simply a true proposition, or the knowledge which a true proposition expresses ; and when it is styled a necessary truth, the meaning is that the proposition expresses a necessary fact. It is the *fact* which is necessary not the knowledge of the fact, nor yet the proposition embodying the knowledge; just as it is the culprit that is criminal not the court which tries him nor the hall

in which he is arraigned: and the reason (it may
be added) why the fact is styled *necessary* is, that
it includes conditions which are essential to each
other's existence; or it exists only as inseparably
connected, both in reality and in conception, with
some other fact.

In this view there is no longer any question
about such things as the necessary cognitions of
the German philosophers. Certain facts are discerned by us to be necessary, as certain lines are
discerned to be straight or curved, and certain
angles to be acute or obtuse, simply because they
are so: and, setting custom aside, it would be as
philosophically correct to designate a proposition
about lines a straight or curved proposition, and
a proposition about angles an acute or obtuse proposition, as a proposition about necessary facts a
necessary proposition or a necessary truth.

The word *fact* itself, of which I have here made
so free a use, will exemplify another shape which
this sort of verbal economy assumes; the shape, in
truth, of a solecism, in which a noun is made a
party to the contradiction of its own meaning by
the epithets annexed to it. The old logicians called
it "*oppositum in apposito*," and "*contradictio in
adjecto.*"* No one hesitates to speak of pretended

* "Siquando non explicitè ponitur hujusmodi negatio sed in
verborum saltem significata implicite lateat; dicitur *implicari
contradictio*, ut si dicatur *Homo irrationalis*, quod sensu im-
plicat *Hominem et non hominem*. Atque hæc dici solet *contradictio in adjecto;* item *oppositum in apposito*."—Institutio
Logicæ per J. Wallis, Lib. I. Cap. 16.

or fictitious or false facts. Thus it was the saying of a well-known physician, that there are
more false facts current in the world than false
theories.

Now facts are obviously realities which exist or
have existed, and a contradiction is involved in
styling them otherwise; but to be debarred from
coupling the word with the epithets cited or other
similar adjuncts would occasion great prolixity.
Although it is manifestly not false facts but false
assertions regarding facts, which the physician
affirmed to be more current in the world than
false theories, yet to be obliged to express all this
in full would render the communication of thought
exceedingly operose.

Another economising expedient in language
occurs when two things being of necessity combined in one phrase, we use the phrase sometimes
for one, sometimes for the other. In the 12th
Letter of the First Series I pointed out this du-
plexity in meaning in the case of the word *perception*, which sometimes designates the act of perceiving, and at other times the object perceived.
The word cannot be used without really implying
both act and object, as the former cannot exist
without the latter; but it may be so employed for
only one as to lead to false conclusions; a liability
which I have explained in the letter referred to.

The word *cognition* may be adduced as an
example under this head. It implies both the act

of cognising and the fact cognised. When writers
speak of a dormant cognition or an innate cognition of which there is no consciousness, they
appear to drop the mental act and consider alone
the substance (so to speak) of what is cognised.
But cognition being the conscious act of an intelligent being, it cannot be dormant, or laid up in
a repository. The fact itself may exist dormant
enough, that is, unknown or unperceived, but for
the existence of a *cognised* fact—a fact in the condition of being known — a knower is requisite;
nor can we consistently speak of a cognition apart
from him. It undoubtedly saves trouble to use
the word first for one purpose and then for the
other, but it is, as modern speculation shows, a
perilous expedient.

The great lesson to be learned from such instances is to be continually on our guard in reasoning, so as not to draw any inferences from elliptical
expressions or translocated epithets, or a one-sided
use of two-sided designations, which could not be
legitimately drawn if all the ellipses were supplied,
the translocations readjusted, and both sides of
ambiguous phrases brought into view.

Such economical expedients in language as I
have here described unavoidably occasion a good
deal of trouble and perplexity to lexicographers in
their definitions and explanations. But inasmuch
as the business of a lexicographer is to explain
all the modes in which a word is used by good

writers, they are difficulties not to be avoided
without depreciating the value of his work. Throwing together a word and its paronymes, tracing its
derivation, assigning its radical import, and then
subjoining passages from various authors in which
the terms are variously applied; and doing all this
without any attempt to point out their different
shades of signification, the elliptical modes in
which they are employed, and the deviation in
meaning of the paronymes from the principal form
and from each other, may be, to a certain extent,
useful, not only etymologically but by the mere
accumulation of materials, as we see in the case of
Dr. Richardson's English Dictionary: but it is
really shirking the principal intellectual difficulty
of a lexicographer's task, and omitting what constitutes the principal utility of a lexicon to nine
hundred and ninety-nine out of a thousand of
those who have occasion to consult it ; leaving
them, in truth, to do for themselves what it was
the author's business to do for them; to pick up,
as they best may, what the lexicographer should
have presented ready to their hands.

In manfully encountering this labour and per-
forming it with a success marvellous in a single
individual, Dr. Johnson stands pre-eminent, as far
as our own language is concerned; and it will not
be by discarding this feature of his great work
that a better English Dictionary will ever be produced.

LETTER XII

LANGUAGE (*in continuation*).

In writing the preceding Letters on Language, several years ago, I was of course assuming it to be one of the legitimate subjects of Mental Philosophy. Such it has been regarded, as far as I know, by the most eminent philosophers.

I was, therefore, not a little surprised to find the investigation or methodical treatment of it ranked amongst the Physical Sciences, in a work of merit which has recently excited a good deal of attention.*

I had always been accustomed to consider the most general division of the Sciences, founded on the subject-matter, to be into two great classes, the Physical and the Mental.

When the subject investigated is matter and its properties, the science is regarded by most people as a physical science; when the subject is the mind and its operations, as a mental science. In the latter case the majority of philosophers would perhaps designate it a moral one.

It is obvious that the character of the subject

---

* Lectures on the Science of Language by Max Müller.

must determine to which of these classes any science
can be properly referred.

A few considerations may suffice to show that
on this principle the methodical treatment of Language can be no other than a branch of Mental
Philosophy, or, if the expression is preferred,
Mental Science.

The investigation of the sounds issuing from the
organs of speech, and of the structure and the sono-
riferous functions of those organs, doubtless belongs
to acoustics and physiology, and so comes under
the denomination of physical; but the indication
of our thoughts and feelings by such articulate
expression is in every case a mental act, which,
although it causes a series of physical motions in
the body and the atmosphere, does not on that
account lose its psychical character. Both the
original cause of this mixed train of events and the
ultimate effect on the hearer, are affections of the
mind ; and the material nature of the intermediate
movements can be no ground, and has never probably been alleged as a ground, for treating the
whole process as belonging to the domain of physical
science. The origin and the result are alike of a
mental character, and clearly determine the place
of language as a subject of methodical investigation.

It will be at once seen by all who enter into the
preceding argument, that the propriety of the
classification therein maintained does not depend

in the least on the answer to the inquiry how language first arose, or how it attained to its present
exuberance; its origin and its growth are in this
question alike immaterial considerations. If we
suppose it to have been originally given by inspi-
ration or supernatural instruction, that circumstance could not, any more than the nature of its
subsequent changes, enter at all into the determination of its character now. It is what it is; and
we have to gather from its actual efficiency the
functions it performs and thence to refer it to the
class of subjects to which it belongs.

Now if you will just cast a backward glance on
the five preceding letters and on some other discussions, in the two former Series of these Letters,
relating to words, you will observe that they are
occupied with such questions as these: whether
we can think or reason without language? what
passes in the mind on the use of proper and
common names and abstract terms? what is the
specific intellectual function of words taken singly?
how far it is connected with the emotions? and
what modification takes place in the mental effects
of words when they are combined in sentences?
what is the true definition of meaning itself? and
as that word denotes an intellectual affection,
whether there can be such a thing as an intrinsic
meaning? how is it that certain terms produce
different mental effects by their position? and
other analogous inquiries.

Surely if there is a science of language, all such

questions not only belong to it but form a main part of it, and are quite sufficient to rescue it from being classed with the physical sciences, or rather are utterly inconsistent with such a classification.

The considerations here brought into view do not appear to have duly engaged the attention of Mr. Müller, who, although expressly adverting to some of them,[*] decides the question on other grounds, and in so doing narrows the range of the science which he had half acknowledged to extend over the field I have assigned to it.

His lectures are in the main a dissertation on only one part of the subject, namely the formation and genealogy of language and languages; and it is on this limited view that he determines the place of the entire department of knowledge among the sciences. Whilst I, with most others (I imagine) maintain that the classification should be decided by the nature of the functions which language performs, he contends that it is to be decided by its birth or origin, and by its growth or development. Language, he asserts, is a subject of physical science (1) because it is originally the work of God or nature, and (2) because its subsequent growth and changes are governed by laws which mankind obey without being conscious of

* "Many of these problems," he says in one place, "which have agitated the world from the earliest to our own times, belong properly to the science of language;" and he afterwards mentions as an example of them the controversy about Nominalism and Realism.—*Lectures,* pp. 11, 12.

them, and without intending the general results
produced.

In order to make the point at issue clear to
those who have not heretofore attended to the
subject, it may be needful to state that the researches of philologists have led them generally
to the conclusion that what are called the Indo-
European or Aryan languages "together point to
an earlier period of language when the first ancestors of the Indians, the Persians, the Greeks, the
Slaves, the Celts and the Germans were living together within the same inclosures."* The language
they primitively spoke was monosyllabic, consisting
of roots about five hundred in number.   Up to this
point the philologists advance by resolving words
made up of more than one syllable or composite
terms into their elementary parts, and by com-
paring various languages as to both verbal and
grammatical forms.   The species of evidence on
which they proceed being thus essentially the
decomposition of compound words and the comparison of varying forms, necessarily vanishes
when nothing remains but primitive roots.   So
far their conclusions may be accepted; or, at
all events, they cannot be effectively called in
question, except by a critic possessing equal erudi-
tion to that of the eminent philologists with whom
they have originated, or by whom they have been
supported.

* Lectures, p. 213.

Here, however, etymological evidence ends. It lands us in a primitive language of five hundred roots and there it leaves us: it cannot take us a step farther. This is its utmost achievement.

Mr. Müller, nevertheless, is not content to stop here. He attempts to account for the origin of the roots themselves. He concurs with several preceding philologists of eminence in ascribing their production to a creative faculty which man possessed at that period, but which was speedily lost.* This creative faculty "gave to each conception, as it thrilled for the first time through the brain, a phonetic expression," and "became extinct when its object was fulfilled."†

Never surely was a philosophical hypothesis propounded by an accomplished scholar so completely destitute of evidence to support it. The whole is a series of gratuitous assertions: the creative faculty is purely conjectural; a conception thrilling through the brain is not only merely hypothetical, but, in any case, must be incognoscible or beyond knowledge; and, lastly, the creative faculty giving phonetic expression to the conceptions is the assumed action of an imaginary power.

Admitting that philologists have traced the

---

* The same hypothesis, or a similar one, is to be met with in the speculations of F. Schlegel, Wm. Von Humboldt, Dr. Prichard, and other philologists.

† Lectures, by Max Müller, p. 392.

Aryan languages to a monosyllabic state * and to
a few roots, it seems to me obvious, for the reasons
already assigned, that when they attempt to
account for the origin of these roots, they are
proceeding without the least shadow of evidence,
trying to wing their way in a vacuum.

.But that which directly concerns my subject is
the consideration, that supposing the hypothesis to
be well-founded, it could afford no ground for
designating the science of language a physical
science; the creative faculty postulated by it would
belong, while it lasted, to the mind of man; the
conceptions would of course be mental, and the results effected or contemplated would be intellectual
or emotional or both.   What would there be in all
this to constitute language a physical phenomenon
or an appropriate subject of physical science?   Or
how could it, even in its bare radical stage, be
called the production of nature more than anything else proceeding from the human mind?
Doubtless, the assumed faculty described as so
efficient and so fleeting, would itself be the work
of nature; but this would be of little avail to the
doctrine: for, first, the circumstance of its being
a temporary and transient endowment would not
make it more the work of nature than the per-

* Dr. Latham remarks, in his Elements of Comparative
Philology, that the doctrine which affirms all roots to have
been originally monosyllabic can scarcely be taken absolutely.
See page 699.

manent parts of the human constitution: and,
secondly, although the human faculties may be
characterised as the work of nature, yet what
proceeds from them cannot; otherwise Art itself
would come under the same denomination.* With
no propriety can the smith who makes the sickle
for the labourer of the field, be called the reaper
of the harvest.   It is precisely because an effect is
accomplished through the mind of man that it is
not attributed to nature.†

Let us next examine whether the growth and
changes of language, or their causes, can be con-
.sidered as taking it into the domain of physical
science on the ground that in effecting them man
obeys laws of which he is unconscious, and pro-
motes, without intending it, the results which
ensue. Such, I apprehend, is the drift of the
following passages:

"Let us consider first," he says, "that although
there is a continual change in language, it is not in
the power of man either to produce or to prevent
it. We might think as well of changing the laws

* Vide Note C.
† This truth is well insisted upon by St. Gregory in a passage
quoted by the Lecturer himself: "Though God has given to
human nature its faculties, it does not follow that therefore He
produces all the actions which we perform. He has given us
the faculty of building a house and doing any other work, but
we surely are the builders and not He. In the same manner
our faculty of speaking is the work of Him who has so framed
our nature, but the invention of words for the naming of each
object is the work of the mind."—*Lectures*, p. 30.

N

which control the circulation of our blood, or of
adding an inch to our height, as of altering the
laws of speech, or inventing new words according
to our own pleasure."[*]

Again, speaking of the individual: " He can do
nothing by himself, and the first impulse to a new
formation in language, though given by an individual, is mostly, if not always, given without
premeditation, nay, unconsciously.   The individual
as such is powerless, and the results apparently
produced by him depend on laws beyond his
control, and on the cooperation of all those who
form together with him one class, one body, or.
one organic whole."[†]

Further on in reference to the laws of what he
styles phonetic decay, he says, "these laws were
not made by man: on the contrary, man had to
obey them without knowing of their existence."[‡]

Hence the author infers, if I understand him
aright, that language belongs to the domain of
physical science.   It does not belong to the other
great department of science (which for the present I
will designate the non-physical) because it is not the
product of individuals consciously and intentionally
engaged in forming or altering it, but of a number
of men constituting one body or one organic whole.
The argument seems to me to comprise implicitly
two separate allegations which are not perhaps

* Lectures, p. 37.   † Ibid. p. 40.   ‡ Ibid. p. 64.

kept sufficiently distinct and which are both erroneous: (1) that when we are unconscious of the
principles which guide our acts, those acts are not
mental but physical; (2) that when the concurrent
acts of individuals resulting in some general effect,
are not purposely done with a view to that effect,
not only the individual so acting has no share in
producing it, and is to be regarded as powerless,
but the act is to be ranked amongst physical
events.

I. The first of these positions is confuted by
a great number of mental phenomena: it will be
sufficient to name the association of ideas,* and the

* "Courteous readers" will excuse the introduction of a
passage in relation to this point taken from a work by the
present author which from the small number of copies printed,
they are not likely to have seen: "Our thoughts are suggested,
combined, associated, and uttered, without any advertence to,
nay without any knowledge of, the principles on which these
incidents depend, unless we purposely make them objects of
attention. A hypothetical example will elucidate this. Our
convenient friend A (by supposition) meets with a certain
person in the street; that person, by having on some peculiar
article of dress, brings to his mind a scene in Wales, where he
first saw it worn; hence follows the recollection of the Welsh
mountains; thereupon certain geological phenomena are immediately suggested; these take him to pre-historic periods —
to the igneous rocks, to the earliest traces of vegetable and
animal life; to the first appearance of mankind on the mutable
crust of our diversified sphere; and so his ideas run on till he
is landed, perhaps, in the 'Vestiges of Creation,' or in Mr.
Darwin's 'Origin of Species.' Through this long train of
conceptions, you may trace that some were suggested by proxi-
mity, some by resemblance, some by causation: but whatever

process of reasoning. To take the latter: Every
man reasons as every man talks; he does it inces-
santly; he cannot avoid it; but he is not conscious
of the principles on which he proceeds, nor even,
for the most part, of the nature of the process in
which he is engaged. We do not, however, say on
this account that particular acts of reasoning are
not his own and are not mental events; and in
like manner we cannot say that the changes in
language are not to be attributed to man as the
work of his own mind, on the ground that he is not
distinctly conscious of the principles of his nature
which influence him to make them.

2. The second position is equally groundless.
A hundred instances might be adduced in which
individuals without intending it, concur in producing a joint result of which their volitional
agency is alone the proximate cause. A farmer,
for example, for some purpose of his own brings
his stock of wheat to market; a thousand other
farmers in various parts of the country happen to

---

were the relations that brought them into his mind, our friend
A was (a thousand to one) utterly unconscious that any such
governed his thoughts, or were circumstances on which the intellectual procession depended."—*On the. Received Text of
Shakespeare's Dramatic Writings and its Improvement*, p. 234
(1862). As the author is now addressing those who are interested in philosophy, he may venture to add that the work
just cited is, to some extent, an application of psychological
principles to the emendation of corrupt passages in those immortal dramas.

do the same about the same time; and the result
of so many contemporaneous sales is a fall in the
price: but not one of these farmers has probably
the slightest intention of producing such a decline.
His aim must be on the contrary to sell his produce at the highest price he can get.   Of course if
he were foolish enough to entertain the design of
depressing the general market by his individual
act, he could not succeed; which is only affirming
the truism that an individual cannot himself effect
what in the nature of the case must be the result
of the joint acts of many: but without any design
on his part, what he does is, nevertheless, efficient
towards the issue, and consequently he cannot be
considered as not concerned in producing it by
volition although not by intention.   The whole of
the individuals produce the whole of the effect
through their voluntary acts.   So in language, a
change cannot establish itself except by the concurrent volitions of a number of unconnected
persons acting for the most part without a view to
the general result; but still it is properly regarded
as the work of the human mind: there is no other
agent to do it, and above all it must ever stand
apart from physical phenomena.

From the considerations here adduced the general
conclusion may be briefly stated to be, that although
the changes in language may take place according to
laws in the human constitution of which the men
who make the changes are not cognisant, and may

be effected by the concurrent acts of numerous
individuals, without any view on their part to the
general result, they are still accomplished through
the human mind, and the investigation of them
belongs to mental science.

The preceding observations notice the substance
of the principal arguments and allegations of the
Lecturer intended to show the science of language
to be one of the physical sciences: and if my refutation of his doctrine is valid, it is scarcely requisite (except for the sake of obviating objections
founded on the omission of what some may consider
to be important) to advert to the singular positions
on the subjects of history and growth which he has
laid down in support of it.

On these subjects, notwithstanding his general
perspicuity and mastery of the English tongue,
he appears to me to have fallen into such indefi-
niteness and confusion as can scarcely fail to
perplex any students who wish to thoroughly comprehend his treatise.   His aim, as far as it is to
be gathered from an exposition marked by such
qualities, seems to be to show that *history* and
growth are to be contra-distinguished and are in
some way incompatible, and that as language *grows*
and consequently has no history, it comes within
the domain of the physical sciences.   Now, that
history and growth are different every one must
admit; they are so different, indeed, as to be what
is logically termed disparate; and hence although

they may be distinguished, they cannot with propriety or for any useful purpose, be *contra*-distinguished or drawn into comparison or contrast.

To elucidate this, let us take the title of his second Lecture, which runs: " The growth of language in contra-distinction to the history of language."

Here two things are placed in opposition which are really not opposed to each other.

By *history* we mean a narrative of successive events; by *growth* the increase of some body, or substance, or appearance, or other entity; and as the latter consists or may consist of successive increments, those increments may be observed and recorded, and thus growth may become the subject of history. Hence to contra-distinguish these two things is to make an unmeaning or a false antithesis.

In another passage the Lecturer not only makes the same false antithesis between history and growth, but he combines a second with it: he contrasts certain departments of knowledge not with another department, but with *the subject* of another department. "Art, Science, Philosophy and Religion," he says, " all have a history; language or any other production of nature, admits only of growth." ·

Here Science, and of course any science,— the science of the stars for example, — is brought into comparison not with the *science* of language but with the *subject-matter* of that science, with

language itself, and hence it is no wonder that the
proposition turns out to be nugatory.

If this defect were remedied by saying, "the
stars have a history, language has only growth;"
or, "the science of the stars has a history, the
science of language has only growth;" in either
case a proposition would be obtained not certainly
destitute of a precise signification but clearly
untenable, for, contrary to what the first asserts,
language has a history; and, contrary to what the
second asserts, the science of language has a history.

As the passage stands in the Lectures, it not
only embodies both the defects pointed out, but
presents us with a proposition altogether purpose-
less. It is impossible to draw from it any conclusion ; and if impossibility admitted of degrees,
it would be especially impossible to draw from
it the conclusion deduced by the Lecturer, that
language belongs to the domain of physical not
of historical science.

The inference itself, however obtained, does not
call for discussion here, since I have already shown
that the nature of those changes in language which
he sums up in the term growth, constitutes no
ground for classing the investigation of that interesting train of human events with the physical
sciences.

With regard to the term historical, nevertheless,
as here and elsewhere applied to the whole class of
the sciences which are not physical, it may be

necessary to say something in addition. The epithet so applied is objectionable in itself, and inconsistent not only with the acceptation required in other parts of the Lectures, but with the necessities of English speech. It seems needless to use it at all in the designation or classification of the sciences, but if it be admitted it should be employed in consonance with its customary applications.

Properly speaking, an historical science is one that investigates the principles on which a series of connected or kindred events, whether physical or moral, have taken place, and would again take place, were the same circumstances to be repeated.

Such a series of events may either have been expressly recorded, in which case they would clearly belong to history; or have left their traces behind them without any human testimony to vouch for what had occurred, and in this case their scientific position might be questioned, and the application of the term not so clear. But if from such traces we could deduce a connected succession of occurrences, they would properly come, it seems to me, within the same province.

On this ground Geology might be appropriately denominated historical, although there is no direct testimony to the great bulk of the events with which it deals, and which are, indeed, usually styled in the narrow sense of the word pre-historic. They must have happened at any rate in regular sequence and through successive periods, and are thus essentially historical in character. They belong to what Dr. Latham, in the treatise cited below, terms Pre-historic History.

For similar reasons, comparative philology (or whatever else we may term this department of knowledge) might be designated as historical.

It is almost altogether occupied in tracing the connexion of successive events, namely, the changes in language; which are to be gathered, indeed, from human writings, but not for the most part from direct and positive testimony. They have perhaps in one point a better claim to the title in question than geological mutations, inasmuch as they are to a far less extent pre-historic in the sense before cited.*

But geology may not only be regarded in a certain sense as historical in character but be correctly styled a science, since it investigates the causes of the phenomena which it describes, as well as traces the succession or order, or contemporaneousness of their occurrence.

Comparative philology, on the other hand, although in the same sense historical in its cha-

---

* I should have liked to cite here Dr. Latham's opinions on some of these points in his recent work on Comparative Philology, but that it would not be easy to give them in other words than his own, and to quote the passages I allude to *verbatim* would occupy too much space. I must therefore refer the reader to the book itself. See p. 747 et seq.

racter, is scarcely in its present state to be called scientific, because while it traces the order and the manner in which the changes in language happen, it bestows little attention on the causes producing them.

These causes can be nothing proximately but states or movements of the human mind. They are occasionally adverted to in the work before me, but I seem to myself to miss in these Lectures, as well as in the writings of other philologists, a systematic explanation of them.

There are great learning and ingenuity displayed by the authors in tracing the ancestry of a word, and even its country cousins as well as its remoter relatives and foreign kindred; and in showing how words have been gradually modified into more or less resembling and even occasion. ally very dissimilar vocables; how likewise certain stages in language have succeeded each other, and the particular stages in which the languages of the world now severally are.

But we are not told, except occasionally and incidentally, on what principles or from what causes these changes took place, or, in more explicit terms, we are not told what motives or views or purposes influenced men to make them.

No doubt to assign these causes would be a work of great labour, thought, and difficulty, and frequently not to be accomplished even by the most strenuous efforts: but until some systematic attempt to do it has been made, comparative philology may be very valuable and very admirable in its way, but can scarcely be regarded as scientific. If it is to be distinguished by the appellation of a science at all, it can be termed only a phenomenal science. In its actual condition it appears to me to be something like a branch of natural history disconnected from physiology; or like Geology, were that science a mere account of the changes successively produced on the crust of the globe and of the order of their occurrence, without any reference to their causes; or, in other words, without recourse to Natural Philosophy, Botany, Zoology, Chemistry and the rest, to explain them.

I may perhaps make my views on this subject more readily and fully understood if I cite some instances in which what I here suggest (for it is nothing new) has been done.

The first writer I will quote in exemplification is Horne Tooke, who, although like most of his fellow-labourers in philology, exceedingly sparing of observations on this point, yet almost at the outset of his book insists on one great mental principle operating to produce changes in language, namely, the desire for despatch. " The first aim of language," he says, "was to communicate our thoughts; the second, to do it with despatch."* The latter purpose, he affirms, " has had a much

* Diversions of Purley, Vol. I. p 27.

greater share in accounting for the different sorts
of words than the former." He afterwards recognizes that alterations and additions may have
been made "for the sake of beauty, ornament,
ease, gracefulness or pleasure" — points nevertheless which he does not undertake to discuss.[1]

Mr. Müller scarcely bestows more attention on
this aspect of the matter than Tooke. He only occasionally assigns the principles on which changes
are effected: once at least he does it explicitly,
and several times, implicitly. For example, he
permits us to catch sight of such a principle,
when he tells us that the sense of grammatical
justice, the generous feeling of what ought to be,
has eliminated many so called irregular forms.[*]
And in the same page, he traces the change from
the Latin *illius* to *de illo*, to the *inconvenience*
people felt.

More frequently, however, while doubtless aware
of the real facts implied, he personifies language
(as we are all apt to do), speaks of it as an agent
or power, and attributes the changes which it
undergoes to itself. Thus he says: "We may
well understand that a root having the general
meaning of mingling or being together, should
be employed to express both the friendly joining
of hands and the engaging in hostile combat; but
we may equally understand that language in *its*

[*] Lectures, p. 66.

progress to clearness and definiteness, should have desired a distinction between these two meanings, and should gladly have availed *herself* [sic] of the two derivatives, *yuj* and *yudh*, to mark this distinction." *

This can be interpreted to mean only that the men who spoke the language entertained the desire and gladly marked the distinction, † so that we have here the implicit recognition of another mental principle effecting verbal changes, the desire to mark differences of meaning couched under one word by some modification of that word — the desire, in fact, for definite and distinct expression.

These passages and a few others of similar tendency are slight indications, at the best, of the principles at work in the human mind when directed upon language, but they point to an important path of inquiry.

I will add that Mr. Garnett, in his able Essays, also gives a few similar indications.

He remarks that " in the Indian languages

---

* Lectures, p. 269.

† Mr. Müller excellently observes in an early lecture, " To speak of language as a thing by itself, as living a life of its own, as growing to maturity, producing offspring and dying away, is sheer mythology : and though we cannot help using metaphorical expressions, we should always be on our guard, when engaged in inquiries like the present, against being carried away by the very words which we are using."—Ibid. p. 41.

(American) there is an evident *anxiety* to leave nothing implied that can be expressed "—almost the opposite to the desire for brevity and despatch insisted upon by Horne Tooke.

Another principle to which Mr. Garnett attributes great effects is the taste or craving for agreeable sounds. " In some of the leading tongues, more particularly in Sanskrit and Greek, a vast number of articulations have been sacrificed to considerations of euphony." * In a former Essay he had mentioned that " in Sanskrit, *finals* are changed exclusively for the sake of euphony " † —in itself a notable fact for my present purpose.

Collecting into one view these scattered and incidental notices, we obtain a small body of mental principles, to each of which, casually introduced as they are, important effects on language are ascribed, not, let it be observed, by myself, but by the writers who furnish them.

Thus a *preponderant share* in originating the different sorts of words, is attributed to the desire for dispatch; the sense of grammatical justice has (it is affirmed) eliminated *many* irregular forms; certain changes which from their nature must be numerous, are referred to a desire for definite and distinct expression; in a large family of languages there is manifested, we are told, a desire to express *everything* with fullness; in Greek and Sanskrit a

* Philological Essays, p. 325.　　　† Ibid. p. 81.

vast number of articulations, it is stated, have been sacrificed to a taste for euphony; and in the latter language, finals are said to be changed *exclusively* from the same principle.

These specimens, while they proclaim the importance, and the extensiveness of the field open to inquiry, are enough to indicate what might be accomplished by a systematic attention to a part or aspect of the subject, which seems hitherto to have attracted only casual notice.

LETTER XIII.

MORAL SENTIMENTS.

It has been one part of my plan in the foregoing
discussions, to take hackneyed and yet unsettled
questions, as far as possible, out of the language
in which they have been unsuccessfully mooted,
and put them into other and simpler forms. Thus,
instead of concerning myself with human powers
and faculties, which are fictitious entities or mere
personifications that have too often engrossed and
misled philosophers, I have treated directly of
mental operations and affections, which are real
events not to be questioned by any one without
transparent inconsistency.

In pursuing the investigation of moral science,
I purpose to adopt the same method by avoiding
those venerated personifications "the moral sense,"
" the conscience," and " the heart;" all very convenient and unexceptionable phrases in ordinary
speech or rhetorical discourse, and dear to the
lovers of vague and indefinite speculation, but not
easily reconcilable with close and consecutive
thinking; and which I shall attempt to show,
before I conclude, are superfluous and even
detrimental forms of expression in philosophical

o

inquiries.   Instead of such fictitious entities, I
shall speak of the feelings, thoughts, and actions
of mankind which we all recognize as real things.

The field of morality is human conduct, and our
moral sentiments being the feelings with which
that conduct inspires us, my present purpose is to
trace their rudiments, follow their development,
and ascertain their nature.

The facts in the human constitution in which
moral phenomena originate, or on which they
depend, mainly at least, are the following :

1. Man is susceptible of pleasure and pain of
   various kinds and of various degrees.
2. He likes and dislikes respectively the causes
   of them.
3. He resents (in the widest sense of the term)
   or desires to reciprocate the pleasure and
   the pain received, when they are intentionally given by other sentient beings.
4. He expects them to be reciprocated when he
   has himself given them to his fellow-men ;
   coveting the reciprocation in the one case
   and shunning it in the other.
5. He not only is susceptible of pleasure and
   pain given directly to himself, but he feels
   under certain circumstances more or less
   sympathy with the pleasures and pains
   given to others, accompanied by a propor-
   tionate desire that those affections should
   be reciprocated to the givers.

It would be mere supererogation to attempt to prove a statement of this kind, since every man can readily verify the facts for himself from consciousness and personal experience amongst his fellows.

Concurrently with the feelings here described, there are certain intellectual operations going on within him, which although they may be intimately blended or take place simultaneously with the emotions, it is yet useful to discriminate. When he experiences pleasure or pain, he frequently perceives the agent in the act of producing it; which is intellectual discernment: and he likewise infers that it has been given intentionally; which is reasoning. When, in consequence, he likes or dislikes the agent, the pleasure or the pain is connected with the latter in his thoughts; which is memory and what is usually called association of ideas.

When, moreover, he looks forward to a reciprocation of the pleasure and the pain which he has himself caused to his fellow-beings, he both recollects and reasons as well as hopes and fears. In fact it is impossible, as a moment's reflection will show, for moral sentiments to exist without the accompaniment of intellectual conditions and processes.

These rudimentary affections, states, and operations of consciousness, are found more or less developed or manifested in all, or nearly all, the

o 2

human race; and from them may be traced the
rise and formation of moral sentiment in all its
various phases.

It may appear a superfluous limitation to say
"nearly all the human race," but tribes have been
found with some of these mental principles so
obscurely, or rather so dubiously and uncertainly
manifested, as to make it questionable whether we
can be said to have sufficient evidence that they
possess even the rudiments of such principles.
Amongst the feelings of which sometimes no
certain indication can be discovered, may be
particularized the desire to reciprocate kindness
or benefits, and also the emotion of sympathy or
fellow-feeling with the enjoyments and sufferings
of others.

In the natives of the Andaman Islands,* and in
certain tribes inhabiting the Philippine Islands,
according to accounts recently brought before the
public, the indications of several of these rudiments
are non-apparent. In reference to some of the
Indians of the latter region, one of the friars once
resident there said, " Did all mankind hang on a
single peg and that peg were wanted by an Indian
for his hat, he would sacrifice all mankind:" †
a statement which if it could be taken as un-

* An account of these people was given by Professor Owen
to the British Association at Manchester, Sept. 1861.

† 'A Visit to the Philippine Islands,' by Sir J. Bowring,
p. 138.

exaggerated would strip the subjects of it of all
pretension to fellow-feeling.

Another statement has the same tendency:

"I had once occasion," says the author from
whose book I have taken the above, "to examine
in the prison of Kandy (Ceylon) one of the real
'wild men of the woods,' of that island, who had
been convicted of murder; the moral sense was so
unawakened, that it was obvious no idea of wrong
was associated with the act, and the judge most
properly did not consider him a responsible being
on whom he could inflict the penalties of the
law."* This, as I understand it, is intended as
a representation not merely of an individual but
of the race.

Such cases of moral deficiency in tribes and
nations, however, even if unquestionably established, may for my present purpose be left out of
consideration, and cannot disturb the course of
my argument. My disquisition may without
detriment and without any impeachment of its
general applicability, be regarded as not embracing
them if they exist, and may accordingly be
designated as an endeavour to trace the nature
and development of moral sentiment in those
human beings who possess the rudimentary powers
and susceptibilities described.

In attempting to do this it will be necessary for

* 'A Visit to the Philippine Islands,' by Sir J. Bowring,
p. 167.

me to draw some distinctions not always sufficiently
adverted to, premising that although the objects
by which the susceptibilities are affected can be
no other than human beings acting in particular
ways, yet it will be convenient, for the sake of
brevity, as is usually done, to speak of the actions
themselves in the character of the objects, instead
of the human beings acting.   Adopting this convenient and even unavoidable mode of speech (not
however without occasional recourse to the fuller
expression and a constant tacit reference to the
whole meaning implied) I shall proceed, in the
next letter, to point out the distinctions to which
I have referred.

LETTER XIV.

HAVING laid down the principles of our nature which I conceive to form the basis of all moral sentiment, I purpose in the present letter to examine and describe more particularly how these rudimentary affections unfold themselves.

Actions giving pleasure or pain and intentionally done with a view to produce those effects, may be conveniently ranked for the purposes of investigation and exposition under the following predicaments:

1. Actions done to ourselves by others.
2. Actions done to others by others.
3. Actions done to others by ourselves.

In each of these cases our feelings are so unavoidably modified in regard to the same or similar actions, that it will be needful to examine them separately. If an action is done to ourselves, we feel in one way; if it is done not to us but within our cognizance by A to B, we feel in another way, or in the same way but in a different degree; if we ourselves do it to another person, we feel in a still different way or in a still different degree.

To make these distinctions, which I shall hereafter more fully enter into, perfectly clear at the
outset, let us suppose a man half starved and
voraciously hungry to have at length obtained a
supply of food, which he is just on the point of
devouring when another man, for the gratification
of his own appetite, snatches it from him and
carries it off; and let us further suppose that we,
without being able to prevent it, are spectators of
the iniquitous spoliation.

The man who is robbed of what he prizes at
the moment beyond all things, will be seized with
violent indignation and deadly desire of vengeance:
the robber, as soon as the engrossment of his whole
being in the satisfaction of his appetite has subsided,
will feel more or less uneasiness and dread of the
vengeance he has provoked; while we the spectators
shall sympathise with the injured starveling and
be filled with indignant reprobation of the wrong
committed:—a reprobation, nevertheless, tame in
comparison with the passionate exasperation of him
who has suffered the injury.

This hypothetical instance will be sufficient to
show the necessity of considering our different feelings with regard to actions generically the same,
when such actions come under the several predicaments already enumerated: in other words, the
different sentiments occasioned in us by similar
actions, according as we are the subjects, the
spectators, or the doers of them.

1. We will first inquire, then, into the nature of
our feelings in regard to actions done to ourselves
by others.

It is these feelings which lie at the foundation
of the rest, and they are therefore to be carefully
examined and discriminated.

When we are placed amongst our fellow-creatures
in almost any situation, they intentionally contribute, or may contribute, in many ways to our
pleasure. One offers us shelter or refreshment;
another brings us an agreeable object to look at;
a third guides us on our way; a fourth relieves us
from some annoyance. In these simple cases we
feel pleasure at the thing done; we feel a liking for
the person intentionally conferring the pleasure,
i.e. we feel his presence or even the thought of him
to be agreeable; and we feel an inclination to give
pleasure in return. These two last feelings—liking
the cause and inclination to reciprocate the pleasure,
constitute what we mean by moral approbation, or,
I may say, constitute the simplest form of that state
of mind which is termed moral approbation. Even
if no other considerations occurred to us we should
have the feelings described.

The contrary case it is scarcely necessary to do
more than indicate. Our fellow-creatures are able
not only to confer pleasure upon us but to inflict
pain. One deprives us of property, another fetters
our movements, another wounds us in some part
of the body. Here we not only suffer the pain,

but feel dislike of the individuals who intentionally
inflict it, and a desire to make them proportionately
suffer in return.

These feelings of dislike and resentment constitute the simplest form of moral disapprobation.

In order to have the sentiments here described,
it is not essentially necessary that we should in
every case directly know that the action was done
by the person to whom we attribute it, and that it
was beneficial or injurious to us: it is sufficient if
we conceive or infer these several particulars.
Even an unaccountable caprice of fancy or a misapprehension of what is seen, may excite our liking
or aversion towards an action with the consequent
desire to reciprocate the pleasure or displeasure
received, when there is no actual foundation for
either the one cast of sentiment or the other. Mis-
conception is sometimes as strong a ground of
approbation or disapprobation as fact itself.

For the purpose of exhibiting the feelings or
sentiments of approbation and disapprobation in
their pristine or rudimentary form, it will be well
to put an imaginary case. If all the actions of
those of our fellow-creatures with whom we lived,
were of a kind that affected only ourselves and did
not affect any body else; if the acts of A affected
us but did not affect B, and the acts of B affected
us but did not affect A, we should manifestly still
feel approbation and disapprobation of them according to their quality. Or to state the illustration

differently, if we lived with only one fellow-creature A, and had no intercourse of any kind with other human beings, we should still feel the sentiments in question; they would not fail to be excited by the conduct of even one individual towards us; so that they would be direct effects of actions done to ourselves. They would be moral sentiments in what may be called their purely selfish form.

If we advert for a moment to the feelings engendered in our minds by material objects, it may throw light on the subject before us, and especially enable us to distinguish mere liking and disliking from the combination of those feelings with the desire to reciprocate good and evil which constitutes moral sentiment. Certain inanimate objects give pleasure through our organs of sense; others give pain. The rose pleases us by its colour and its fragrance, and we not only see it with gratification, but when we merely think of it, we have a similar although fainter emotion: we like it. The nettle, on the contrary, stings and is avoided. It becomes a disagreeable object to handle either actually or in imagination.

If we attend to our feelings on such occasions, we shall find, (1) An organic pleasure or pain; (2) A liking or disliking of the object when it is presented to us either actually or merely in idea.

The same feelings are engendered in our minds by the lower animals with whom we come in contact. They exhibit in their actions certain qualities

which please us, and other qualities which displease
us, and we may trace in ourselves, (1) The primary
pleasure or pain; (2) The consequent liking or disliking, just as in the case of objects without life.

But, in addition to these, we feel also an instinctive desire to reciprocate the pleasure or the
pain arising from such qualities, similar to that
which we experience towards human beings, and
which is not (except perhaps by children or savages,
or for a bare moment) usually felt towards inanimate objects.

In the latter case kindness or resentment is
instantly checked if not prevented, by its manifest
inutility and inappropriateness—by its being obviously misplaced—while in the case of animated
beings, there is no such perception of inutility or
misapplication, but on the contrary, an instinctive
or quickly following apprehension that to manifest
those sentiments by some outward act, will tend to
encourage or deter.

Thus if a human being were solitary in the world,
destitute of the society of any of his fellow-creatures, a Robinson Crusoe from his very infancy, he
would still have a system of feelings engendered or
rather developed in his mind, of what even then
might be called a moral character.   He would like
and dislike material objects; he would more strongly
like and dislike the inferior animals, and towards
the latter he would feel a disposition to reciprocate

pleasure and pain, which is the peculiar distinction
of moral sentiment.

We thus clearly see that sensibility to pleasure
and pain, the consequent liking and disliking felt
towards the agent concerned in giving them, and
the desire of reciprocation when they are intentionally given to ourselves, are respectively essential
to moral approbation and disapprobation in their
simplest forms.

There are two objections which may possibly be
taken to styling these sentiments when directed
upon actions done to ourselves, moral approbation
and disapprobation: first, it may be alleged that
the affections in question are frequently too violent
to be characterised by so temperate a designation;
and secondly, it may be contended that as they
originate in purely personal feeling and are (by
supposition) destitute of sympathy, the epithet
moral is scarcely appropriate to them.

Undoubtedly when, as the first objection supposes, they become intense, when they rise into
passions, we usually call them gratitude and resentment, or eagerness to return benefits and desire
of revenge, reserving the former denominations, if
we employ them at all in the case, for the cooler
feelings which in point of warmth do not exceed
such as we generally have when we are spectators
and actors, not immediate subjects or sufferers.
Unquestionably too there is some foundation (chiefly

from the ambiguity of terms) for the second objection.

(1) As to the first exception here taken, it must be considered that the sentiments we experience in respect to any given action, whether we suffer it, witness it, or do it ourselves, are all liable, although not equally so, to be intensified, while they are in certain respects so similar, so allied in origin and effects and become so blended and mutually influenced, that it is exceedingly convenient if not unavoidable to speak of them under one general designation, notwithstanding that they may occasionally be carried to such extremes as demand peculiar appellations.

Such peculiar appellations may be very properly employed to designate the higher and more marked degrees of the affections in question, but if you attempt to draw a strict line of application between them and the lower degrees, you find as you descend in the scale that it is impossible to do it.

(2) In answer to the second objection, it is sufficient to allege that the term *moral* carries with it an ambiguity seldom avoided by even our most precise writers, and exemplified by the objection under notice. It is, in general, used more or less designedly in antithesis to *immoral*, and hence is eulogistic; but in philosophy strictly it is neutral, and means relating to conduct whatever that conduct may be; whence we speak of moral offences and moral depravity as well as (in the same neutral)

sense) of moral speculations and moral excellence.
Hence selfish approbation and disapprobation may,
equally with disinterested or sympathetic, be correctly spoken of as moral sentiments.

It is in savage and uncultivated life that the
violent desire for reciprocation is seen in its extreme
degree; but the violence usually takes place only
when the desire is for the reciprocation of evil.

Amongst barbarians gratitude is commonly weak,
while the craving for revenge absorbs the whole
nature, and is sometimes perpetuated to the third
and fourth generation.

We are told by a recent traveller that an African
race, the Namaquas, are unable to appreciate kindness, and seem to have no word in their language
expressive of gratitude.*

With regard to the other passion, another traveller states that in Australia " the holiest duty a
native is called on to perform, is that of avenging
the death of his nearest relation."†

Both passions, however, are sometimes exhibited
with extraordinary intensity in the same race.
Speaking of the American tribes about Lake
Superior, Kohl tells us that the blood of even
the youngest Indian children appears to be im-
pregnated with revenge. If, nevertheless, you
have once done a service to one of these savages,

---

* Lake Ngami, by C. J. Anderson, 2nd Ed. p. 28.
† Journals in Australia, by George Grey, Vol. II. p. 240.

he will bountifully repay you whenever he has it in his power.*

2. Having taken a brief survey of actions done to ourselves, and our consequent feelings, let us next consider our sentiments towards actions under the second predicament (namely, actions done to others by others) when such actions are within our cognizance: a class necessarily more comprehensive than either the preceding or the subsequent one. Actions under this predicament, however, would obviously have no meaning to us (for the most part at least) unless we had had some experience of actions more or less analogous done to ourselves.

When we witness them, we are affected with certain feelings allied to those already described, although not generally speaking in the same degree of intensity as when actions are directed to us personally.

It will assist us to trace the course of these feelings, if we take into view one or two further distinctions in a very complicated set of phenomena where it is impossible to consider all. Actions done to others by others may be,

1. Actions done to those whom we love;
2. Actions done to those who are indifferent to us;
3. Actions done to those whom we hate.

* Kitchi-gami, or Wanderings round Lake Superior, by J. G. Kohl, pp. 272—77.

And a similar discrimination may be made as to actions done *by* these several parties, but it will suffice for the purpose of exposition to consider the former, viz. actions done *to* the parties standing to us in the respective relations given.

When we witness an action done to one we love, which we should approve if done to ourselves, we naturally regard it with similar complacency; and we feel an analogous desire to make a return of pleasure to the agent. To love a person is to extend our own sensibility to the pains and pleasures of the beloved object. I need not do more than allude to a mother's affection for her child.

The contrary case is equally true. We naturally feel displeased to witness an injury done to any one we like; and we feel resentment against the perpetrator, much in the same way and often in the same degree as when an injury is done to ourselves.

In fine, our sympathy with the pleasures and pains of a beloved object is generally strong, and is sometimes carried to an intensity which transcends that of our own personal enjoyment and suffering. In such cases our gratitude and resentment are of course proportionately excited towards the actor.

Proceeding to the next division of actions done to others by others, we find the result somewhat modified.

When we witness an action done by one man to another, where neither party is particularly inter-

esting to us, where, for example, they are both
entire strangers, there is not the same excitation
of feeling as in the last case.

But mankind naturally sympathise with each
other's pleasures and pains, except (and it is a very
large exception) when some cause is at work to
counteract or supersede the sympathy; and
apart from this, we naturally, by the law of association, feel some degree of pleasure at witnessing
an action which would have pleased us if done to
ourselves or to those we love; and some degree of
pain at an action of the contrary tendency. The
bare imagination of anything which has caused us
pain is disagreeable, although no one really suffers,
as in a tale of fiction; and when we see the pain
actually inflicted on a human being, however indifferent to us he may be, we must, in the absence
of counteracting causes, be similarly affected.

In a word, as we dislike evil actions done to ourselves, and dislike even to think upon them, we
cannot fail (sympathy apart) to dislike them when
obtruded on our thoughts by being done to others,
nothing (it is assumed) intervening to countervail
or subvert the influence of the association: and as
sympathy is usually called into play as well as
association, the resulting emotion may be and often
is strong and lively.

The pleasure and the displeasure we feel on the
occasions here described, are also attended by a
desire, sometimes faint, sometimes strong, that the

agent shall experience pleasure or pain in return for the good or evil which he may have caused. When we ourselves are personally concerned we have, as already explained, this desire habitually as well as instinctively, and if it did not instinctively spring up in our minds, as it really does, in these other cases, it would cling to us by the force of association.

Nevertheless the sympathy which human beings have with other human beings not personally or specially connected with them, is not found to exist in a high degree except under peculiar circumstances, and frequently disappears altogether. A certain measure of civilisation, or of intellectual culture, or some other special cause, seems required to bring it out. Amongst the rude and uncultivated it is extremely weak, perpetually liable to numerous counteractions, and easily extinguished. We are too apt to ascribe to men universally what belongs only to instructed men, and to them not by any means with the uniformity of a law.

If we look into the accounts we possess of savage or semi-barbarous people, we shall find the utmost indifference to the sufferings of each other where there are no family ties or special connexions to rouse a fellow feeling in the spectator, and not unfrequently even then.

A recent traveller presents us with a remarkable but easily paralleled instance of this utter want of sympathy.

"A large number of artisans (Burmese) were employed in gilding the lofty spire of the pagoda, for the accomplishment of which object they were mounted on a high bamboo ladder, about thirty feet broad, and some hundred and fifty in height, very loosely constructed and not fixed as a scaffolding, the top merely resting on the spire, and the feet on the ground at the base of the building. I should think there were at least a hundred workmen on this ladder at the time, busily engaged in their occupation, apparently confident in the safety of the bamboo upon which they had trusted their persons. It had however been raining a little while previously, and the ground beneath them had become slippery from the wet. Suddenly the feet of the treacherous ladder were seen to recede from their original position, and the destruction of the workmen above appeared imminent. Slowly slided the frail support, and the poor wretches upon it must certainly have felt that they were moving towards their doom. The world was literally slipping from beneath their feet. There were hundreds of their fellow-countrymen below, gazing upon the gradually descending concourse, and awaiting the apparently inevitable result, not in breathless and fearful apprehension, but with every demonstration of intense delight. They laughed, actually laughed uproariously, as the bottom of the ladder neared a declivity still more greasy than the level ground around the pagoda; and not one stirred to arrest

its downward progress, although but a little effort
would have prevented what seemed an impending
frightful sacrifice of life.   Had it not been for a
party of artillerymen, who had observed the affair
from a distance, and who had providentially arrived
at the spot in time to render assistance, every one
of those unhappy men upon the ladder must have
perished, with their countrymen around them
laughing at the fun."*

Where there is such indifference as this amongst
men to the sufferings of each other, even of those
amongst whom they live, moral approbation and
disapprobation can scarcely exist except in their
selfish or self-interested forms.   These people who
could laugh at the frightful catastrophe to which
their neighbours were hurrying, would probably
have resented any inhumanity shown to their own
sufferings or any injury inflicted on themselves,
or even on the objects of their love; although even
this degree of sensibility is in some cases more
than can be perceived.   "It is said that many a
time an Indian has allowed his wife and children
to perish in the flames when his house has taken
fire, but never was known to fail in securing his
favourite *gallo* [game-cock] from danger."†

The third division of actions under the second

* Four Years in Burmah, by W. H. Marshall, quoted in the
Athenæum.

† A Visit to the Philippine Islands, by Sir J. Bowring,
p. 8.

predicament, namely actions done to others by others, comprises such as are done by others to persons whom we dislike.

As we already feel a degree of resentment against persons we hate, we naturally feel displeasure when this resentment is contravened by the circumstance of the objects of it being made to rejoice instead of being made to suffer; when, in other words, they receive the benefits of the good actions of their neighbours.

This displeasure, however, is liable to be modified and even overcome by the habitual associations established in our minds with actions of that character.

In the opposite case, when an evil action is done to our enemy, we naturally rejoice, but the joy again is modified by the disagreeable emotions which are associated in our minds with an evil action. We already dislike and condemn it, and although we dislike the sufferer we may dislike the action still more. In savages and uncultivated people this dislike of the mere action is weak or wanting, and their joy at seeing an enemy suffer the acutest torments, justly or unjustly, is intense, and often unqualified. The same casting away of humanity occurs amongst nations who have reached the highest point of civilisation yet attained, when they are at war with each other. Then deceit, lying, robbing, murdering, are all not only com-mitted without compunction but witnessed without

condemnation, nay even with universal applause.
It is needless to discuss the real height reached by
that civilisation with which such things are compatible.

3. Having considered in the first place actions
done by others to ourselves, and secondly actions
done by others to others, I now come to those
which fall under the third predicament, namely,
actions done by ourselves to others.

An important observation presents itself at the
outset. Whatever feelings we have in regard to
actions under the two first predicaments, will be
naturally awakened by analogous actions which
come under the last. When we intentionally do
an act to another person which gives him pleasure,
we enjoy in some degree the gratification naturally
attached to an act of beneficence in the other two
cases. We have commonly a lively impression of
its effect on him from recollecting the emotion produced by similar acts done to ourselves, and also
done to others by others.

But while we are thus naturally affected, more
or less, by the sentiment with which actions of
that kind come to be generally associated, there is
a new feature in the case not appertaining to the
other cases. Instead of the desire of reciprocating
good, which here of course can have no place, we
have now the expectation of receiving a return of
it from our neighbours. Without that expectation
having at all entered into the motives of the action,

we feel when it has been done that the natural
tendency of the benefit is to excite in the breast of
the receiver, as well as in that of the spectator, a
disposition to reciprocate the kindness. We look
upon ourselves as the proper object of grateful
thoughts, good wishes and courteous behaviour, not
only on his part but generally.   In a word, we are
affected at once, although it may be transiently
and faintly, with the gratification of a benevolent
desire, with self-complacency, and with undefined
hopes.

The contrary case is perhaps more remarkable.
When we inflict pain or injury upon another, we
contravene our own benevolent instincts, and we
have generally a more or less lively sense of what
he suffers — an idea which is in itself disagreeable
to us. But here, as in the opposite case of doing
good, there is a new feature. Instead of a desire
for retaliation, which is of course out of the question, we now feel an apprehension of resentment
on his part and on that of the community. We
are aware of his strong wish to avenge himself,
and we dread its consequences: we are sensible,
too, of the public opprobrium ready to overwhelm
us, and we cannot avoid associating with our own
act (veiled as it is in the haze of self-illusion)
somewhat of the same bitterness of condemnation
which we should have experienced, had we ourselves been the sufferers.

The combination of these feelings, which are at

times exceedingly strong, usually takes the name
of remorse, and it is often greatly aggravated by a
vivid sense of having offended a higher Power.

The sentiments here described, I must again
remark, are such as can scarcely take place with
any regularity except in minds of some cultivation
or under special circumstances; and they are constantly liable to be prevented or counteracted by
civilised ignorance, bad habits, and strong passions,
as well as by barbarism. Little remorse is felt by
the savage when his violence causes misery in his
own family or tribe, and none for the misery which
he exults in heaping on his human prey. The
moral insensibility and recklessness exhibited
amongst the lost classes of our own population,
might be described in similar terms, and I scarcely
need point to the extinction of remorse, as to many
actions ordinarily reprobated, in the wars of enlightened nations.

Although, for the sake of perspicuity, I have endeavoured to trace the distinct effects of the same
or similar actions under the three predicaments,
separately from each other, I have not been able
to avoid altogether some reference to their reci-
procal influence, and this may now be expressly
taken into view.

Whatever may be the first effects of our moral
experience, it cannot be doubted that when we not
only are subject in our own persons to the actions
of others, but witness similar actions between

indifferent parties, and do them ourselves to our
neighbours, the sentiment prevailing in each case
must be liable to a reflex influence from the other
cases; and that by this influence it will be
strengthened or intensified. Our moral approbation, for example, of a magnanimous action done by
A to B is enlivened and enhanced by a recollection
of having personally performed or personally met
with similar conduct; and the self-condemnation
felt in regard to some unworthy act of our own, is
greatly aggravated by recalling the strong reprobation with which we visited the same fault in a
neighbour; or by reflecting on the universal exe-
cration with which we saw it was assailed. In this
way we come to associate certain intensities of
moral sentiment with certain kinds of action, by
whomsoever or to whomsoever performed.

I may also remark, what indeed I have already
hinted, that although I have considered the modification effected in our moral sentiments according
as actions are done to those we love, those in regard
to whom we are neutral, and those we hate, only
in the case of actions coming under the second
predicament, because in them the modification is
the most remarkable, yet similar effects might be
traced on our feelings in the case of actions coming
under the two other predicaments. It would be
tedious, however, to go through such an exposition;
and what has been said of one set of cases may be
applied *mutatis mutandis* to all. Whether we are

the subjects of actions done by others, or are merely
the spectators of actions between others, or the
doers of actions to others, our sentiments will be
modified by the circumstance of those *others* standing to us in the relation of friends, neutrals, or
enemies.

With the moral sentiments the course of which
I have endeavoured to describe, there is one circumstance necessarily mixed up, and of great influence
in modifying the sentiments themselves, I mean
the outward manifestations of them which actions
call forth from those persons whom they directly
or indirectly affect.

The principal manifestations of this kind are
evidently efforts to gratify the natural desire of
reciprocating pleasure or pain intentionally given.
They are sometimes looks, sometimes gestures,
sometimes tones, sometimes words, sometimes actions.   They embrace the whole range of rewards
and punishments, and their general effect may be
stated to be the satisfaction of that desire for reciprocation just mentioned, and the encouragement
or discouragement of the actions which have called
them forth.   The case of verbal manifestation is
worthy of particular notice.   We have an almost
irresistible impulse to express in language the
pleasure and gratitude we feel at kindness and
beneficence, and our displeasure and resentment at
intentional injury.

These verbal manifestations are almost invariably

employed whether they are accompanied by other
actions or not. Other means may be wanting to
show our gratitude and resentment, but these are
always at hand: they are at once a relief to our
feelings, and gratify or annoy the persons to whom
they are directed, and by whom they are often
deeply felt, constituting in fact a powerful instrument of reward and punishment. In regard to
extensive classes of virtues and vices, they are the
only direct means of encouragement and discouragement within our reach, and in certain states of
society they exert a pervading control. They give
to moral sentiments greater precision, and operate
on the conduct with the effect of authoritative
precepts.

The influence of the moral approbation and disapprobation of our fellow creatures as manifested
in words, attains its highest degree (in civilized
communities at least) when the expression of those
sentiments proceeds from bodies of men or communities. Doubtless this influence is greatly enhanced
by an apprehension of the material consequences
to which the verbal manifestations lead, or with
which they are frequently united — consequences
to property, reputation, liberty, and life; but
taking the expressed sentiments alone (however
they may have been formed), their sway over the
mind, when proceeding from large numbers or
masses of men, is remarkable, prompting on the
one hand to deeds of moral heroism, and on the

other warning from all that is base in general
estimation and aggravating the remorse of guilt.

There is one objection which I foresee may be
taken to the prominence I have given to resentment in my account of the moral constitution of
man. I have represented it (in the usual narrow
sense) as an essential ingredient in moral disapprobation, and consequently as a wholesome and
laudable feeling, while it is generally regarded as a
passion to be repressed and extirpated. To this it
may be sufficient to reply that I am only taking
human nature as it is, and showing the original
elements of moral sentiment amongst which the
desire for reciprocation always appears. Like other
principles within us, it has, of course, its appropriate limits and is not to be indefinitely gratified;
but it is so indispensable to the conservation of
morals that society could not exist without it.
The question is one of those, perhaps, in which
authority may prevail with some better than argument, and I may refer the objectors to Bishop
Butler, in whose writings, indeed, they may find
both, and who has left us the best explanation and
vindication of resentment that I can at present
call to mind.

"The good influence," he says, "which this
passion has, in fact, upon the affairs of the world,
is obvious to every one's notice. Men are plainly
restrained from injuring their fellow-creatures by
fear of their resentment; and it is very happy that

they are so."   Again, " That passion, from whence
men take occasion to run into the dreadful vices
of malice and revenge; even that passion, as im-
planted in our nature by God, is not only innocent,
but a generous movement of mind.   It is in itself,
and in its original, no more than indignation against
injury and wickedness." *

* Sermon upon Resentment.

LETTER XV.

MORAL SENTIMENTS (*in continuation*).

In the preceding letter I have shown, or endeavoured to show, that when actions which intentionally produce pleasure or pain are done by human beings to each other, and the effects of such actions as well as the intention are felt or discerned, they generate respectively moral approbation and disapprobation, varied in intensity according to the circumstances in which the actions take place.

If this feeling or discernment of consequences were perfect, and no other principles came into play, we should undoubtedly apportion our moral approbation and disapprobation according to the real tendencies of actions, and this would be the perfection of moral sentiment.

It is instructive to inquire how it is that the perfection here described is not attained; why the moral feelings of mankind, so far from conforming to the real effects of human conduct, are not seldom in extreme contrariety with them.

In the first place, it may be observed, that all which is necessary for engendering gratitude or

resentment is that a man should be pleased or displeased with an action, whether his feeling is well
grounded or not.   The action may be sudden and
the feeling equally so.   His pleasure or displeasure
may be prompted by some partial view or momentary thought, or be merely the caprice of his
temper, unaccountable even to himself; but it
exists and may be recurrent on similar occasions.
Hence it will be a mere matter of chance whether
his sentiment regarding the action tallies with its
actual consequences, or is at variance with them.

   In the next place, to take more deliberate cases,
we must bear in mind that effects are not always
plain, simple, and direct; on the contrary, they are
often obscure, complicated, and indirect: and this
is sometimes true in regard to the consequences of
actions, as it is in regard to those of other causes.
Hence a complete appreciation of conduct would
have to take into view not only immediate, unmixed,
and clear, but in some cases remote, confused, and
dim effects, which are for the most part matters of
inference, not of actual cognisance, and concerning
which mankind are exceedingly liable to fall into
various and extraordinary errors, especially when
they take no pains to be right.

   This circumstance is alone sufficient to prevent,
in certain circumstances, an exact adjustment of
moral feeling to real effects.   On the most favour-
able supposition, in the absence of all disturbing
incidents, and even when we have time and ability

to think, we must occasionally mistake the true
tendencies of conduct from sheer incapacity to
follow them out, or from oversights and miscon-
ceptions in trying to do so; and if the thoughtful
portion of mankind run into such errors, it can be
no wonder that moral approbation and disapprobation with the multitude often fall in the wrong
places.   Moreover, the difficulty of ascertaining
consequences, or the necessity of taking even slight
pains to do it, in complicated circumstances and
removed from direct observation by space or time,
affords great room for those eccentricities of personal taste and caprices of imagination already
referred to; whence human conduct is liable to
be approved and disapproved on fantastic and
whimsical grounds, or on no discernible grounds
at all.   Men, instead of rigidly ascertaining, are
apt to save themselves trouble by fancying effects,
and all complication of this kind gives occasion to
error in moral sentiment.   In consonance with
these observations, we find that, as knowledge ad-
vances or retrogrades in a' community, as habits
of thinking and feeling vary, and as modes of
living alter, the general approbation and disapprobation of the people very often change their objects
or shift their direction.   Actions formerly disliked
and reprobated are discovered or imagined to be
useful, or deemed to be agreeable, and are praised;
while others once loaded with commendation in-
sensibly slide out of vogue, or turn out to be

Q

pregnant with evil, and become marks for antipathy and scorn.

In the third place, a fact of no little importance presents itself: our moral sentiments are not all formed from our own discernment or inferences, or even suppositions, of the consequences of actions whether immediate or remote, nor from our own direct likings and dislikings; but they are derived, to a very great extent, from tradition. We are in many cases not left to personal experience, but are taught and trained how to feel towards a given action, long before we can perceive the effects of it for ourselves, or have formed an independent taste to be gratified or offended.

If we suppose, for the sake of illustration, one original family existing in the infancy of the race, although the heads or progenitors of it, limited as they would be to their personal experience, would approve or disapprove actions according to their tendency, or rather as they liked or disliked them, whether according to their true tendency or not; the members of the family under their direction would regard many of the actions of each other with approbation and disapprobation at second-hand. They would so regard them, not from discerning or fancying anything in them of a beneficial or injurious, pleasing or displeasing nature, but simply from being told and trained to believe that the actions were respectively the proper objects of those feelings, and from seeing them treated

as such by the leaders of their little world. The
influence of such impressions would extend itself
(it is easy to see) more and more through successive generations; and if, originally, approbation
and disapprobation had been wrongly applied, the
actual moral sentiments of the community would,
in process of time, be found to diverge widely from
a conformity with the real effects of the conduct
to which they were directed.

In this way mankind derive not only knowledge,
but modes of feeling on particular occasions, from
their forefathers; whence it may be affirmed with
truth that the moral sentiments of any given
people at any given time, have been formed partly
from their own feeling and observation of the
effects of human actions, partly from their whims
and caprices, imaginations and suppositions, and
in a very large proportion from tradition—*i. e.* from
the blind impressions regarding such actions which
have been left on their minds by their predecessors.
We need not, consequently, be surprised at the
numerous inconsistencies between moral sentiment
and the real tendencies of conduct, prevailing in
even civilised communities. It is by no means
unusual to see actions of the most mischievous
character looked upon with the warmest moral
approbation; and, on the other hand, to find
conduct positively calculated to exalt and benefit
the world, treated with profound and intense re-
pugnance; while it is equally common for neutral

actions to be ranked sometimes in one class and sometimes in the other.

In all such cases the sentiments, originally founded on the erroneous impressions of a former generation, may have been associated with the actions they cling to in the minds of its posterity from mere tradition, without the slightest discernment of effects and tendencies, or even the faintest intrusion of any peculiar tastes and fancies on the part of the actual holders. It may be added, to show the power of traditionary impressions, that even in very simple cases, where the immediate effects of an action are personally felt or discerned, tradition sometimes operates to overcome the natural feeling, and inspire us with approbation of that which, if left to ourselves, we should instantly and heartily reprobate. If I should be considered by some of my readers as going too far to assert that tradition can make black appear white, I might be regarded by others as stopping short of the truth to affirm that it can turn it very gray.

Powerful, however, as tradition may be, it is obvious but important to remark that the inherited sentiments of every generation are liable to be extensively modified by a struggle with the influence of circumstances and idiosyncrasies peculiar to itself. Every age, in a progressive country at least, has its own moral and social materials and its own impulses to actuate it in dealing both with them and with the opinions and feelings bequeathed to it.

These traditional modes of regarding actions, or,
as they may be called, derivative moral sentiments,
are frequently impressed on the mind by direct
precepts or commands as well as by example, by
instruction as to the tendency of the actions, by
declarations of liking or aversion, and by other
incidental methods. "You must do this," and
"you must refrain from that," is the language of
the superior to his dependents, often without any
assignment of the grounds on which the injunction
proceeds. The consequence is that actions come
to be approved and disapproved amongst many
people, and to a great extent, not because they are
directly perceived or traditionally held to be beneficial or injurious, but solely because they are
absolutely commanded or prohibited with no reference to any other circumstance or attribute:
and thus morality is doubtless simplified to the
multitude, who grow into the habit of only looking
at rules without troubling themselves with effects
and tendencies, except such as make their presence
immediately felt. The readiest appeal is always to
a recognised law or maxim. Indeed, some arrangement of acts under things to be done and things
not to be done, simply as such, seems unavoidable;
for in the absence of all constituted authority (were
such a state of affairs possible for a permanence),
the necessities of society would shape the mutual
sentiments and conduct of men into a conformity
with certain manifest requirements which, in the

course of time, would acquire the character of
authoritative rules, and which would be appealed to
as decisive in many cases without a fresh estimate
of consequences or any other special considerations.
In all this, although there is not of necessity any
perversion of moral sentiment, which is the subject
I am seeking to elucidate, there is no security that
the actions approved or reprobated are beneficial
or injurious, and the sentiments regarding them
being mere prejudices stand little chance of being
modified.   If wrong, they will, in all likelihood,
long remain so.

I have not hitherto particularly adverted to the
influence of superstition in perverting moral sentiment, because it is, in truth, included in my account
of the general causes operating to produce that evil
result; and although from its importance it deserves not only a separate consideration, but a
treatise to itself, I can here only touch upon it in
passing.   It is, a marvellous problem how the
minute and multitudinous rules and rites, and
ceremonies and doctrines, originated and established
themselves in some of the existing systems of superstition;* but whatever may have been their
sources, the grand instrument of perpetuating
them, as well as their unhappy bearing on morality,
has obviously been tradition.   It is probable, or

* The rise and establishment of the Mormons in our own
day, within the very bosom of modern civilisation, is worth
studying in this view.

possible at least, that in most cases they sprung to birth through the idiosyncrasies of individual human beings, men of more ardent minds, more vigorous thoughts, more exalted feelings, more ambitious desires, than their fellows, and who, finding themselves completely at sea in their aspirations and efforts after knowledge, imagined what they could not discover, and transmuting their own fancies into real events, gave them forth as mysterious and divine.

What, however, belongs to my present subject is a remarkable feature in most of these systems of superstition; their influence has operated not so much to pervert moral approbation and disapprobation in their application to the ordinary actions of life (although in that province it has largely and mischievously intermeddled), as to create false virtues and false vices and crimes, which it has foisted upon mankind by the alleged authority of supernatural beings equally fictitious. Nothing, perhaps, has done more to strip moral sentiment of its beneficial influence on society, or has entailed more positive misery on the human race, than these counterfeit virtues and vices, the profuse offspring of ignorance and imposture. It unhappily cannot be affirmed that they have disappeared before modern cultivation.

The account of the reasons which I have now assigned why our moral sentiments do not always conform to the real tendencies of actions, points

also to an analogous explanation of the differences
in moral sentiment between one nation, one tribe,
or one community, and another.

When surveying the condition of mankind in
the various countries of which accounts have come
down to us, or which have been visited and described in our own age, no one can help being
struck with the great discrepancies existing
amongst such nations as well in moral theory
as in moral practice. I have already adverted
to some of these discrepancies, and for my present purpose it is not needful to do more than
touch on two or three further examples.

In one country the vice of lying is universal
and venial; in another it is despised and scouted:
one nation is licentious without shame, another
enforces comparatively strict laws of chastity:
there are tribes among whom stealing, and especially adroit stealing, is highly extolled; and there
are others where, whether dexterously accomplished or not, it puts the perpetrator out of the
pale of society; with some, cheating is a clever
feat; with others, it sinks the man convicted of it
into abject disgrace. Even the crime of murder,
which is looked upon in some civilized countries
with all the horror of which human nature is susceptible, draws little odium on the guilty in communities debased by ignorance and superstition.[*]

* Mr. Mill puts the case well and forcibly: " But where
are these unanimously recognised vices and virtues to be

To anyone speculating on moral discrepancies such as these, it would necessarily appear an impossible feat, were it attempted, to take the peculiarities of every nation, or even of any one nation, as they exist, and trace them with precision to their several sources. But on the principles which I have explained, we shall be at no loss to discern generally how they may have arisen; or, at all events, we shall not feel much difficulty in seeing that the growth of great and even extreme discrepancies is unavoidable.

In a preceding page, in order to elucidate the divergence of moral sentiment in a community from the real tendency of actions, I supposed the case of a single insulated family: at present, in order to elucidate the discrepancies in moral sentiment subsisting between different communities, I will take the hypothetical case of two families.

Suppose two original families or tribes to be endowed with the qualities I have described (without which they could scarcely, indeed, be called human)—namely, the sensibility to pleasure and pain; the liking and disliking of the causes of such feelings; the propensity to reciprocate good

found? Practices the most revolting to the moral feelings of some ages and nations, do not incur the smallest censure from others; and it is doubtful whether there is a single virtue, which is held to be a virtue by all nations in the same sense and with the same reservations."—Dissertations and Discussions, by J. S. Mill, vol. ii. p. 498.

and evil received from other sensitive beings; the
anticipation of similar reciprocity from them; and
a certain measure of sympathy with all: suppose
further the families so endowed to be severally
placed in different climates, in different soils, at
different elevations, with different kinds of animals
and vegetables around them; and whatever moral
similarity there may have been at the outset, they
will in no long time inevitably diverge into different moral codes and practices merely from the
operation of dissimilar surrounding circumstances;
i. e. from different motives and courses of conduct
being presented to their minds. But to these
sources of discrepancy must be added the idiosyncrasies of each family, and especially of their
chiefs.   In no case can two men be constituted
exactly alike, but they may be very widely dissimilar; and the personal tastes, propensities, passions, and aptitudes of our two hypothetical
leaders, being left free to expand in the exercise
of uncontrolled authority, will inevitably exert
great influence, and in each case a diverse influence, on the minds and actions of their followers,
who will also respectively contribute the play of
their own idiosyncrasies to the general result.

Thus dissimilar physical conditions co-operating
with dissimilar personal idiosyncrasies, will, in the
lapse of time, place the two families under such
different social regulations, and create such different moral feelings, that few points of complete

analogy will be likely to exist after the first stage of their career or in the next generation: and inasmuch as in every subsequent generation fresh idiosyncrasies, novel circumstances, and new results of experience, will mingle their influence, a few ages will probably suffice to produce two races exceedingly unlike in physical conformation, in customs, arts, manners, modes of thinking, and moral sentiments.

The discrepancies thus unavoidably resulting from the action of different circumstances on human beings who are alike in some qualities but unlike in others, serve to show how necessary it is to be extremely careful in our moral generalizations. For example, notwithstanding such striking discrepancies in moral sentiment as have been brought to view in the preceding exposition, it has been said by a great authority, where human feelings are concerned, that "one touch of nature makes the whole world kin." The saying is true enough, doubtless, of a very circumscribed world; true enough if applied to a multitude of men with similar culture or in a state of similar civilization: but there are many touches of nature extremely powerful in their effect on the sympathies of one community of human beings, which would not ruffle those of another community in the faintest degree.

Nothing perhaps warms the heart of an Englishman more than the heroism of a brave man rushing into the water, at the hazard of his life, to save a drowning fellow-creature whom every spectator shows himself earnestly anxious to rescue: and it might be readily supposed that such sentiments of admiration at disinterested magnanimity and of anxiety for the preservation of human life, were · indigenous to the race, and would be felt by every being in a human form.

Let us see, however, the effect of such an incident on the minds of a people trained under a totally different system of thought and feeling.

"As myself and a friend," says a traveller in Burmah from whose pages I have before quoted, "were enjoying a morning ride by the lake-side at Kemmendine, our attention was attracted by a noise which proceeded from the opposite shore. We saw a man struggling in the water, and a number of Burmese (male and female) standing by, looking on, apparently unmoved by any feeling save that of amused curiosity. No one, judging from the attitudes of the spectators, would have thought for a moment that anything serious was the matter, especially as the sound of occasional shouts resembling laughter, was borne by the breeze across the water to where we were riding. It occurred, however, to my friend that the man in the water might possibly be in some peril, especially as he appeared to be a considerable distance from the shore. We accordingly spurred our horses on the instant, and soon reached the spot

where the spectators had congregated. It was as
we conjectured might be the case. The struggling
wretch was frantically endeavouring to reach terra
firma, but had become exhausted by his efforts,
and he sank immediately before our arrival. My
friend (a good swimmer) instantly threw off his
coat, plunged into the lake, made his way to the
place where he had seen the drowning man disappear, and made several efforts to find him. In
these, unfortunately, he was unsuccessful, the bottom being so foul as to render it impossible for
him to effect his purpose. All this time the people on the bank were looking on, and repeatedly
manifested their amusement at the several incidents of the scene in unequivocal bursts of
merriment. My friend (a member of the Pegu
Commission) rebuked them for their unseemly
behaviour in pretty strong terms. They were,
however, evidently but little concerned, although
they listened to his reproaches with the respect
which is due to authority; and as the last act
of the pleasant little comedy had terminated, they
very soon dispersed."*

Incidents of this kind (and the example might
be easily paralleled from other nations) serve to
show that when we ascribe certain sentiments to
human nature or to men universally on given
occasions, because they exist amongst ourselves on

* Four Years in Burmah, by W. H. Marshall, quoted in the
Athenæum.

those occasions, it is by no means a safe inference: we cannot safely ascribe them except to men under analogous circumstances of knowledge and civilization.

We may attribute with confidence to most men and to most races of men, the rudimentary feelings which I have shown to originate and to constitute moral sentiment; and some of them with equal confidence to all men: namely, sensibility to corporeal pleasure and pain; liking the causes of one and disliking the causes of the other; the propensity to reciprocate both good and evil; the expectation of the same reciprocation; and more or less sympathy with other sensitive beings; but the direction and intensity of these emotions respectively it is often difficult and even impossible to assign: there are so many causes at work to counteract, or modify, or suppress such of these common susceptibilities as can be counteracted, or modified, or suppressed — to call them forth or to keep them in, that, unfurnished with precise knowledge of national and social circumstances, we cannot predict with confidence how they will manifest themselves on particular occasions. Without specific information of this kind we cannot safely pronounce that the people of rude or distant and imperfectly explored countries would, under given circumstances, share in those affections and moral sentiments which it seems contrary to our own very nature, under such circumstances, not to have.

Our general propositions regarding human nature, with the exceptions intimated and possibly a few others, should be limited to those nations and races which we have had an opportunity of knowing.

How feebly some of even the rudimentary affections enumerated exist in certain cases, has already been illustrated, and may be seen strikingly exhibited in various other Eastern tribes and nations besides those cited, whose style of civilization (if they may be called civilized) is thoroughly different from ours. The Rajpoots, for example, have, we are told, little sensibility, little compassion, scarcely any disposition to relieve suffering, or to resent wrong done to themselves or others. The feeble resentment of personal injury is ah extraordinary trait in the picture and must not be mistaken for an indication of high culture. To have it deficient in strength below a certain point, is, in truth, a mark of moral inferiority.

Even in our own country we cannot always infer the feelings of one set of its inhabitants from those of another. Extreme diversities of moral sentiment (as extreme almost as those which characterise respectively Eastern and Western civilizations) are found in close neighbourhood. Take, for example, the latest questions of morality which have arisen amongst us—those, namely, which have reference to the process of thinking itself. While the man of highest culture sees clearly that opinions, whether theological or anthropological, or geological or physiological, cannot be the proper ground of ascribing either merit or demerit, praise or blame, to the holder,* there are thousands around him who feel the deadliest rancour against every dissentient from their traditional creed, and deem heresy from their own faith the blackest and most unpardonable of offences.

These are real moral sentiments, precisely parallel to those manifested by the Mahommedan in his savage animosity against the Christian unbeliever in the prophet of Mecca.

* I am sorry to find that in this estimate of the present sentiments of cultivated minds, I am not altogether correct. That men reputed to be of high culture, and writing in our own day, still differ *toto cælo* on the important point mentioned in the text, is shown by the two following extracts, the antagonism between which needs no comment from me. "It is," says Dr. Tulloch, "the strangest and most saddening of all spectacles to contemplate the slow and painful process by which the human mind has emancipated itself from *the dark delusion* that intellectual error is a subject of moral offence and punishment."—*Leaders of the Reformation.*

"Men are blameable," says Dr. Whewell, "In disbelieving truths after they have been promulgated, though they are ignorant without blame before the promulgation;" and again the same moralist tells us, that it is man's "duty to think rationally." I am not the writer to quarrel with Mr. Mill (to whose "Discussions," vol. ii. p. 508, I am indebted for a knowledge of these most extraordinary declarations) when he designates them as "the very essence of religious intolerance." It seems I was as premature as Dr. Tulloch in thinking that such sentiments had vanished from cultivated minds. In the second extract how quietly, and unconsciously to all appearance, is infallibility assumed! For another point in literary morals, see Note D.

Such a review as I have now taken of the origin of our moral sentiments, and of the circumstances which cause those great discrepancies that undeniably exist between the moral sentiments of different nations, and even of different classes and individuals of the same nation, prepares the way for a further most momentous inquiry.

We see what the moral sentiments of nations are, how discrepant and contradictory; we look around us, and mark even in our neighbours how widely they vary; and we are unavoidably led to ask, Are all these diverse sentiments right by the very fact of their existence? or if this cannot for a moment be supposed, is there some way of determining amongst them which are right and which are wrong? Is there some test or criterion by which to decide points of so much vital importance? To the substance of these inquiries I purpose to address myself in the ensuing letter.

LETTER XVI.

MORAL SENTIMENTS (*in continuation*).

TAKE any man you choose and you will find that his moral sentiments have arisen in various ways, such as I have already described; some from tradition, some from the commands of his superiors, some from his own direct likings and dislikings, some from the proclaimed likings and dislikings of others; while in many, if not all, of them, he may materially differ from his neighbour; or to place the matter, if he is an Englishman, beyond all doubt, from a Burman or a native of the Celestial Empire.

Now what security is there, what assurance can he feel, or how can he prove to his own satisfaction, or to the conviction of anybody else, that in any one important sentiment he is right, and the man who entirely differs from him is wrong?

The mere fact of his feeling the sentiment to be right, or of his being assured that it is in consonance with some injunction of his superiors, or of his believing that other persons feel the same, can be of no avail in proving its rectitude, because the man who entertains a totally different sentiment may adduce the same or similar allegations in support of his own.

Amidst such contending claims and discordant appreciations, how shall we discriminate the right and the wrong? Is there any test, any quality or set of qualities, any method or expedient, by which the question can be determined?

Of this problem in Moral Philosophy which, in some shape or other, has, over and over again, been explained and discussed, the preceding account of the rise of our moral sentiments may perhaps help us to a solution as simple and direct as we can obtain from any other source.

If, as the foregoing review of their *genesis* has shown, moral sentiments primarily arise from our likings and dislikings of the actions of our fellow-creatures because they give us pleasure and pain, contribute to our happiness or our misery, or because we apprehend that they do so or tend to do so, it is evidently of the first importance to our well-being to take care that our likings and dislikings are well-founded — *i.e.* that the actions have really the several effects and tendencies ascribed to them; and although some cases in which our sensibility is directly affected, are so plain as to preclude doubt or hesitation, other cases, as we have seen, are more or less uncertain, or difficult, or complicated, so that some attention and discrimination are required to trace the real effects produced.

Such an examination whether our likings and dislikings are well-grounded seems to be, in all dubious cases, not only the right, but the only course that can be pursued in order to determine whether our moral approbation and disapprobation are correctly applied; and it is, indeed, the natural test resorted to (with more or less irregularity and inconsistency I admit) by men in general when their prejudices are not in the way to bar inquiry; while it is also that which the maturest wisdom would prescribe from a view of the consequences of applying it.

The end or use of moral approbation and disapprobation can be no other than to promote or prevent those actions to which they are respectively applied: and it is manifest that if the sentiments so named could be always directed and proportioned to the real tendency of conduct, we should attain the good in view in the fullest measure. Unless moral sentiments have no influence on the actions of mankind, they would then bear with their whole weight on the encouragement of such as contribute to the happiness of society, and on the repression of such as are inimical to it. Good actions would be multiplied, and the number of bad actions reduced.

It is remarkable that although the principle of trying actions by their consequences and approving or disapproving them according to the goodness or badness of those consequences, has been denounced in various ways as being inadmissible; yet, on occasion, almost all moralists virtually adopt it, often unconscious of what they are about, especially when any new case presents itself " for which the file affords no precedent," * and which is consequently not encumbered by prejudices; or when they fall into momentary forgetfulness that they have a theory to maintain. While sitting in judgment even on what, for shortness, has been called the greatest-happiness principle, it is not uncommon for ethical writers to shake their heads in grave disapprobation, and pronounce it to be a mischievous doctrine; unconsciously applying to a theory the very test they in the same breath condemn when applied to an action.

The difficulty of applying such a criterion has been sometimes urged. The obstacles that lie in the way of tracing all the consequences of an action, have been alleged as depriving the test of practical utility. But the difficulty, whatever it may be, is only the same as we meet with in other inquiries, and other endeavours to form just estimates. We have nothing more arduous to do in determining the beneficial or injurious qualities of conduct, than what we have to do in ascertaining the wholesome or deleterious properties of food, or

* Burke.

in tracing the good or bad influence of a statute.
In each of these cases, subject as we are to error
alike in all of them, we have to follow effects as
far as we can; and it is by its ascertainable, not by
its unascertainable consequences, that we pronounce an action, as we pronounce an article of
sustenance, or a legislative enactment, to be good or
bad, to be worthy of approval or of condemnation.
The residuum of unknown effects, if any there is,
must necessarily be left out of the question in all
the three instances alike.

Of a great number of the most important actions
of mankind, the main consequences to human
happiness are, in civilized communities at least,
plain and manifest to the parties interested in
them; and of another large class, the main effects
may be ascertained by a well-directed and diligent
inquiry, leaving a comparatively few doubtful or
indeterminate, except to the careless and the
ignorant; and it is to this remnant alone, which
can never be of great moment in any enlightened
society, that the supposed objection can be
applicable, while even then it is worthless.   So
far as the consequences of an action to human
happiness are beyond the power of man to ascertain
them, they are of no value; and if none of them
are ascertainable, the action itself must be neutral
or indifferent, neither good nor bad.

The criterion in question, for the reasons here
assigned, is, I venture to think, not only excellent

in itself, but as readily available as analogous tests
in other cases. If it were generally adopted and
honestly applied, ethical discrepancies might still
exist, but they would gradually disappear as
knowledge advanced, and the moral sentiments
would alight more and more upon their proper
objects.

Another objection is sometimes urged of this
tenour: " The criterion you advocate is good as far
as it goes; it may be admitted that actions productive of happiness are rightly or wisely approved,
and those by which it is injured are rightly or
wisely condemned: but this is only a part of the
matter; there are other *criteria* of right and
wrong which the advocates of the happiness-test
overlook. We continually put actions upon their trial
by examining whether they are just or generous,
or disinterested or benevolent, or the contrary; and
we then approve or disapprove without reference to
the happiness or the unhappiness which may flow
from them; so that there are other tests perfectly
distinct from the production of pleasure and pain,
happiness and unhappiness, according to which
actions are, and ought to be, morally approved or
disapproved."

In order to simplify the examination of this
argument, let us take one of the qualities enumerated, since what will apply to one will apply to
all. We cannot do better than select the great
moral attribute *justice*. If we make justice a test

of certain actions independent of everything else,
we must unavoidably proceed on the grounds that
it is in itself peculiarly pleasant or agreeable to us,
irrespective of its other effects, which, by the
hypothesis, are not to be taken into account; and
that it obtains our moral approbation at once by
that bare circumstance: for we cannot on any
theory dissociate pleasantness or agreeableness
from moral approbation, which it must precede.

So much being premised, I think it will be
possible to show that the alleged test would be in
perfect accordance with that proposed in the
present letter, if it would not be identical with it.

Happiness, we must recollect, does not denote
one homogeneous thing like air or water, but is a
general appellation comprehending a great variety
of feelings; all the agreeable affections of our
nature, every kind of joy and pleasantness that
we experience. Conduct which gives rise to any
of these, makes the subject of them so far happy.

Happiness may, in fact, be considered as the
genus, and all these pleasurable emotions as species
under it; and when we would determine that a
given action is a proper object of approbation on
account of its producing happiness, we can do so
only by ascertaining that it occasions some particular kind of pleasant or agreeable feeling.

There is no such thing as happiness in general,
as there is no such thing as an animal in general.
Happiness cannot exist except in the shape of

some agreeable emotion or combinations of agreeable emotions, any more than an animal can exist
except in the form of an individual organism.

Hence if justice, as the objection alleges, is a
quality naturally and directly giving a peculiar
kind of pleasure independent of any other consequences, it follows that when any action which
has to be tested by this standard, is determined to
be just, and consequently worthy of moral approbation, the proceeding is precisely similar to that
of the moralist who applies the criterion of the
production of happiness. It is doing as he does —
namely, assigning a quality which gives a peculiar
pleasure, as the ground of moral approbation.
Pronouncing it to be morally commendable according to the hypothesis, solely because it is just,
is pronouncing it to be morally commendable
because it produces one species of those pleasant
states of mind which are arranged under the
genus happiness.

I scarcely need add, however, that the mode in
which a just action affects us, is altogether different
from that which this objection would represent it
to be. Whatever association may subsequently
effect, a discernment of the conditions requisite to
make an action just, must originally precede any
pleasurable emotion and any approbation which it
may excite, and this discernment involves a view,
more or less complete, of consequences.

There can be no objection, nevertheless, with any moralist to making justice itself a criterion of actions; but why? Simply because that quality has already been determined, over and over again, to be one of the most beneficial principles which can enter into the conduct of man, and has established itself in our minds with a thousand subsidiary associations. This is, in effect, to say that it has already been tried by its consequences, and having triumphantly passed the ordeal, has become one of those intermediate principles which are found so useful and even necessary in practice. In every walk of life and department of knowledge, such intermediate aids are employed without recurrence to the principal. standard. It is not requisite to measure an arc of the meridian every time it is wished to adjust the boundaries of a kingdom or ascertain the dimensions of an estate.

What sometimes seems to disguise our moral sentiments of praise and blame, is a class of feelings often mixed up with them, but of a distinct character. Such are pity, wonder, awe, admiration, the sense of the ludicrous, and other emotions, which, being dependent on variable circumstances connected with an action, may or may not accompany the moral approbation or disapprobation excited by it; but which, when they are present, may any of them give respectively to those sentiments a peculiar momentary character.

We may, for example, strongly approve of an action while we are greatly awed by it, and we may also as strongly condemn one, although it fills us with the same emotion. So we may look with decided approbation on a good act, while we cannot repress some degree of contempt for the intellectual weakness displayed at the same time by the agent: and we may reprobate vicious conduct, while we feel pity for the man who is guilty of it, or laugh at its ludicrous absurdity.

These, it is obvious, are accidental not necessary connexions, since the feelings described and the sentiments of moral approbation and disapprobation may exist detached from each other, and the former may some of them be occasioned even by material objects and physical events.

It would be a grave omission on my part in treating this portion of the subject, were I not to bestow some notice on a word which has made a conspicuous figure in many dissertations upon it, and the employment of which I have hitherto, as far as possible, purposely avoided — I mean *utility*. The question as to the criterion of morality in actions, has been frequently answered by this one word ; and the answer, properly understood, comes to the same thing, in effect, as that which I have given in the preceding exposition. But utility in this connexion and for this purpose, is, I conceive, an objectionable term on several accounts. The epithet useful is not employed in common language to indicate what is directly productive of happiness, but only that which is instrumental in its production, and in most cases customarily or recurrently instrumental. Although a blanket is of continual utility to the poor wretch who is starving through a severe winter, the benevolent act of the donor is not termed useful inasmuch as it confers the benefit and ceases. On the other hand, diligence in a man's calling is equally a virtuous quality; but since it can manifest itself only in a course of conduct, it can scarcely be said to confer happiness directly at any one point: it is the means of good; and utility may be appropriately predicated of it, although it could not be so predicated of benevolence.

Utility is thus too narrow a word to comprehend all the actions which are entitled to our approbation. We have not, indeed, in the English language, as far as I am aware, an uncompounded substantive which is capable by itself of expressing the two attributes of *conferring* and *conducing to* happiness. Perhaps for a descriptive phrase, *producing* happiness is as succinct as any, and comes the nearest to what is wanted; but still it is a circumlocution, and does not supply us with the desiderated noun.

Besides this objection to the word utility and its kindred phrases, there is another which has probably had some part in creating the distaste manifested towards the theory in which they are employed. The term useful is so frequently fated to designate what is serviceable in the objects and affairs of common life, that in the minds of people in general it carries with it many homely associations, which, to the fastidious at least, cast upon it a degree of incongruousness with the higher parts of moral thought and feeling. Who, they ask, would tolerate the application of the epithet useful, to the heroic devotion of a great man to a great cause?

Hence the philosophical doctrine which erects utility as its banner, is apt to be deemed by the unthinking, low, mean, and derogatory to human nature and human aspirations, notwithstanding that the real import of the doctrine is wholly free from such a reproach.

Although the phrase is doubtless compendious and exceedingly convenient in default of a better, yet being thus liable to misconstruction and disparaging associations, it may be advisable to avoid the systematic employment of it in the exposition of the principles of morality, and especially to forbear placing it in the front of a theory.

Most of the trite objections to the true doctrine of morals, appear to me to turn on the narrowest acceptations of this term; and since the associations connected with it are not easily eradicated, the best way of dealing with the subject is, I conceive, to shun the language to which they attach themselves.

My account of the rise and formation of our

moral sentiments, also leads to the ready solution
of another difficulty which has occasioned much
discussion.

I allude to the question (whatever form it may
be thrown into) " whether our moral sentiments
have their origin in Reason or in a separate power
called the Moral Sense?"

According to the view of man's sensitive and
intellectual nature taken in the present treatise,
this inquiry, which is generally rather vague in
its terms, is soon disposed of.

We have seen that our moral sentiments in their
rudimentary state, comprise sensibility to pleasure
and pain; respectively liking and disliking their
causes; consequent gratitude and resentment;
expectation that these sentiments will be reciprocated; joy and sorrow for ourselves, and sympathy
with the pleasure and pain of other beings. If
you call these feelings collectively, or any part of
them, a moral sense, or attribute them to the
action of a moral sense, you may be doing no
great harm, but you are only employing an additional term without at all elucidating the real facts
which you seek to designate. We have not the
various feelings described, and *also* a moral sense:
take them away, and you have nothing left to
constitute it. If you say that such feelings are
the operations of the moral sense, you do not
thereby enlarge the phenomena, or improve the
classification: you are only creating a fictitious

entity which can furnish you, at the best, with no
assistance, no guiding light, but may prove an
ignis fatuus to lead you astray. The feelings in
question (rest assured) are not the feelings of any
sense, or power, or faculty, but they are *bonâ fide*
your own—the feelings of the man.

Further : the feelings described cannot take
place without your observing a number of circumstances attending them; such as the causes of the
pleasure and the pain; nor without your inferring
the intentions of the agents; nor yet (where intellectual discernment is not superseded by personal
feeling) without noting the effects which the
actions produce. Unless, in truth, these intellectual
operations took place, no moral sentiments would
rise up.

You may, if you like, ascribe such discerning
and inferring, which are directly your own intellectual acts, to an imaginary power called Reason;
and adopting a phraseology which I myself avoid,
you may assert moral sentiments to be the joint
product of reason and the moral sense. Such phraseology, however, is, in my opinion, eminently
useless, and tends to obscure the truth. It is clear
enough to any one capable of reflection, that the
emotions I have already enumerated, the feelings
of pleasure and pain, liking and disliking, gratitude
and resentment, sympathy and antipathy, although
they may rise simultaneously with intellectual
states, differ, as mental phenomena, from the acts of

discerning and inferring their causes, their circumstances, and their effects; but it seems not only
superfluous, but calculated to lead us into a wrong
classification and a confusion of fact with fiction,
to marshal these two sets of phenomena respectively under the appellations of moral sense and
reason, when we have such excellent general
names as *feeling*, and *discerning*, and *inferring*, for
the described affections and operations ; names
which are simple and direct, and which, while
they answer every purpose of philosophical thought
and communication, have no tendency to mislead
our imaginations, or vitiate our conclusions.

If, however, I were to answer the question
before us in the conventional language in which it
is put, I should unavoidably say that every moral
sentiment (except perhaps such as may be acquired
by mere rote) implies both an act of reason and an
operation of the moral sense, inasmuch as in every
case of the kind we discern, and we infer, and
we feel.

The term *conscience* has sometimes been considered to be synonymous with moral sense.

Bishop Butler, in one place, speaks of it, not
only as denoting the same thing as reflection, but
as equivalent to "an approbation of some principles
or actions, and disapprobation of others."* The
word, however, is more properly restricted, as

* Fifteen Sermons at the Rolls' Chapel, p. 13.

Butler himself afterwards limits it, to the sensibility which every human being has, in regard to the moral qualities of his own mind and conduct.

As to the identification of *conscience* and *reflection*, I will pass it by with the remark that although reflection may doubtless accompany, for the most part, the feelings indicated by the former, yet there is obviously much reflection (however the phrase may be construed) which has nothing to do with self-approbation or self-condemnation; and therefore to identify the two words in question is plainly inexpedient.

The preceding exposition has facilitated the clearing up of any mystery or misapprehension which may surround the personification passing under this name of conscience. We have seen how our feelings in regard to our own conduct arise first from our necessarily looking upon our personal actions in the same light and with the same associations (modified to a certain extent) which invest actions done by others; and secondly, from our being at the same time the subjects on the one hand of regret and fear of consequences, and on the other of self-complacency and hope, as the nature of the action may be.

You may in this case, as in the other cases, create a fictitious entity and call it conscience: you may talk of its smiles and its frowns, its satisfaction and its violation, its stings and its

8

dictates, and its supremacy; but by so doing you
only get an additional name in your moral
vocabulary, with a crowd of figurative events
which can do nothing else than embarrass your
progress: you do not acquire an additional truth,
or even an additional aid in your investigations.
The man who has been guilty of some offence
which he would condemn in another, and in
regard to which he feels contrition together with
a strong apprehension of resentment, reprobation,
and reprisals from his fellow-men, and punishment
perhaps from a Supernal Ruler, has not these
feelings, so combined and mutually aggravated,
plus the stings of conscience.   The imaginary
power with its figurative weapons and metaphysical punctures, serves only to obscure and perplex
the actual facts which stand out by themselves
with perfect clearness.   It is a mere impersonation,
convenient in common discourse or rhetorical de-
clamation as a brief summary of mental events, but
detrimental in close thinking or scientific inquiry.

So much misrepresentation of philosophical doctrines abounds, that I probably may be charged
with denying man's moral nature, because I dis-
pute the propriety, or rather scientific utility, of
a personification; but it will be understood by
any one of ordinary intelligence that I am only
trying to put aside the verbal mask behind which
moral facts, in themselves undeniable, are wholly
or partially hid.

NOTES AND ILLUSTRATIONS.

261

NOTE A. — Page 2.

Extract from Comte's " Philosophie Positive." — Tome I. p. 35.

" Ils ont imaginé, dans ces derniers temps, de distinguer, par une subtilité fort singulière, deux sortes d'observations d'égale importance, l'une extérieure, l'autre intérieure, et dont la dernière est uniquement destinée à l'étude des phénomènes intellectuels. Ce n'est point ici le lieu d'entrer dans la discussion spéciale de ce sophisme fondamental. Je dois me borner à indiquer la considération principale qui prouve clairement que cette prétendue contemplation directe de l'esprit par lui-même est une pure illusion.

" On croyait, il y a encore peu de temps, avoir expliqué la vision, en disant que l'action lumineuse des corps détermine sur la rétine des tableaux représentatifs des formes et des couleurs extérieures. À cela les physiologistes ont objecté avec raison, que, si c'était comme *images* qu'agissaient les impressions lumineuses, il faudrait un autre œil pour les regarder. N'en est-il pas encore plus fortement de même dans le cas présent ?

" Il est sensible, en effet, que, par une nécessité invincible, l'esprit humain peut observer directement tous les phénomènes, excepté les siens propres. Car, par qui serait faite l'observation ? On conçoit, relativement aux phénomènes moraux, que l'homme puisse s'observer lui-même sous le rapport des passions qui l'animent, par cette raison anatomique, que les organes qui en sont le siége sont distincts de ceux destinés aux fonctions observatrices. Encore même que chacun ait eu occasion de faire sur lui de telles remarques, elles ne sauraient évidemment avoir jamais une grande importance scientifique, et le meilleur moyen de connaître les passions sera-t-il toujours de les observer

en dehors ; car tout état de passion très-prononcé, c'est à dire
précisement celui qu'il serait le plus essentiel d'examiner,
est nécessairement incompatible avec l'état d'observation.
Mais, quant à observer de la même manière les phénomènes
intellectuels pendant qu'ils s'exécutent, il y a impossibilité
manifeste. L'individu pensant ne saurait se partager en
deux, dont l'un raisonnerait, tandis que l'autre regarderait
raisonner. L'organe observé et l'organe observateur étant,
dans ce cas, identiques, comment l'observation pourrait-elle
avoir lieu ? "

Note B. — Page 105.

Of the incapacity to write good English frequently manifested by eminent classical scholars, whether from sheer
carelessness or want of specific training, the celebrated
Dr. Bentley is an acknowledged instance; but I have never
seen it remarked that his biographer, Dr. Monk, is open to
the same criticism, although not, it may be, to an equal
extent. For example, the learned biographer writes as
follows: "These various pieces were entirely eclipsed by
Middleton's 'Further Remarks,' in which it was generally
conceived that *he* had obtained a complete victory over
Bentley, and that the certain consequence would be the
abandonment of *his* scheme of a new edition : and when it
was found that the publication was suspended, the *cause*
was universally *attributed* to the *irrecoverable* blow experienced from *his* adversary's publication." If this passage,
which would certainly discredit a schoolboy, does not show
any transplantation of classical idioms into English, it shows
a carelessness of composition which could hardly have proceeded from a trained English scholar. It will be observed
that by the construction of the sentence the "he" and the
"his" ought to refer to the same person, which they do not,
— a confusion of antecedents more easily made in English

than in Latin, which fortunately possesses more distinctive
pronouns. By care and skill, nevertheless, the grammatical
disadvantage in our idiom may always be remedied.   The
error of speaking of a *cause* being *attributed* to a blow, is
rather logical than grammatical, and is a strange oversight
in any one accustomed to the orderly arrangement of his
thoughts, although it is not uncommon in the casual
writings of uneducated men. No reader needs to be told
that we attribute effects to causes, not causes to themselves.
Dr. Monk meant, but failed to say, that the effect — the
suspension of the publication — was attributed to the blow
as its cause.   Even the expression "irrecoverable blow"
is a solecism.   The writer doubtless meant a blow from
the consequences of which Bentley could not recover. We
may say elliptically that a person *recovers from* a blow
(meaning from the effects of the blow), not that he *recovers*
a blow, and therefore we cannot speak of a "recoverable
blow;" the nearest approach to it would be a "blow recoverable from," which, barbarous as it is, would be correct.
A similar remark, by the way, (with no reference to Bentley
or his biographer) may be made as to the word *reliable*, now
creeping into use without its preposition. "Aid to be
relied upon," or "reliable upon," is shortened into "reliable
aid." De Quincey, who charges Coleridge with the coinage
of this word, suggests *relyuponable* as more correct English*;
a form which few if any will be hardy enough to adopt.

But to return to Dr. Monk. These instances of bad
writing in the biography, are not merely accidental. The
same inaccuracy prevails more or less throughout. We
are told farther on that Dean Hare "saw that the fruits of
his own labour were at once driven out of the field," which,
indeed, is perfectly grammatical; but as we cannot suppose
any allusion to harvest-home to be intended, it is clearly
a rhetorical lapse: and in another place we are informed

* Critical Suggestions on Style and Rhetoric, p. 244.

that Dr. Voss "was then recently dead." On one occasion the author writes "it would have been impossible *to have given*;" on other occasions he misplaces such phrases as *not only*; and repeatedly confuses the sense of his periods with stray pronouns, unable, like lost children, to tell to whom or to what they belong. If it be objected that such errors in Bentley and Monk are not ascribable to the classical pursuits and proficiency of the writers, they must at all events be allowed to prove that a lame and incorrect English style is compatible with eminent attainments in the learned languages; and they proclaim a truth too often neglected, that accuracy and purity of composition in our native tongue, must be attained by the same means which secure excellence in other accomplishments—special devotion to the object—and will not come by attending to anything else. Modern English is too often disgracefully loose and inaccurate, partly perhaps from a foolish contempt of verbal criticism—a reaction from the age of Kames and Blair.

The reader who wishes to prosecute the subject, and to see how negligent English composition is, even in some of our first writers, may consult such works as "The Rise, Progress, and Present Structure of the English Language," by the Rev. Matthew Harrison; "Modern English Literature," by Henry H. Breen; and "A System of English Grammar," by C. W. Connon. The last-mentioned author, who is an acute critic and master of his subject, computes the grammatical errors in Hallam's "Introduction to the Literature of Europe," to be about five hundred; and those in Alison's "History of Europe" to amount to the prodigious number of about fifteen hundred.* Even such correct writers as Arnold and Macaulay furnish instances of careless composition in their best works. De Quincey roundly asserts that he had never seen the writer who had

---

* Grammar, p. 106.

not violated English grammar.*   "It is remarkable," he
says in another place, "that grammatical inaccuracies so
common among ourselves, and common even amongst our
literary people, are almost unknown amongst the educated
French."† Why should such a reproach continue? Why
should not English be written as accurately as French?
To those who would disparage attention to these things as
trifling or pedantic, I would recommend what the same
author subsequently observes, that a sentence, even when
insulated and viewed apart for itself, is a subject for complex art, and capable of multiform beauty. He adds that
it is "liable to a whole nosology of mal-conformations."
And further on in the same treatise, he maintains that
style, or the management of language, ranks among the fine
arts, and is able therefore to yield a separate intellectual
pleasure quite apart from the interest of the subject
treated.‡ But the weightiest consideration of all is the
inseparable connection between thoughts and words. Inexact writing and precise thinking, in men at least who are
accustomed to composition, are incompatible. The fear
sometimes entertained that pedantic formality or stiffness
would result from rigid accuracy, is wholly groundless.
Accuracy when habitual is just as *lithe* as inaccuracy. It is
a mistake to suppose that there are ease and grace in laxity
and incorrectness. I will further support these views of
the importance of the subject by two or three brief extracts
from an excellent article in the "Quarterly Review" of April
1861 (p. 380). "To attain a power of exact expression,"
says the writer, "is the one end of true literary discipline."
Again, "spoken language has eyes, hands, every movement
on the face, every gesture of the body, every tone of the
speaker's voice, to illustrate it as it flows. To written

* Critical Suggestions on Style and Rhetoric, p. 108.
† Leaders in Literature, p. 91.
‡ Ibid. p. 93.

language all these aids are wanting, and the want of all
must be supplied by special care for the right use of words.
. . . It is the strength of exact fitness that has to be
sought."

Note C. — Page 177.

Art, both poetically and transcendentally, is sometimes
comprehended in Nature; but so long as Nature and Art
continue to be compared and contrasted — an antithesis
conspicuously pervading our literature — the philosopher,
at least, should consistently keep to the distinction between
them. The poetical amalgamation of the two may be seen
in the following lines by as genuine a poet as ever sang:—

> "'Thou lov'st the woods, the rocks, the quiet fields!'
> But tell me, if thou canst, enthusiast wan!
> Why the broad town to thee no gladness yields?
> If thou lov'st Nature, sympathise with man,
> For he, and his, are part of Nature's plan.
> But can'st thou love her, if she love not thee?
> She will be wholly lov'd, or not at all.
> Thou lov'st her streams, her flowers; thou lov'st to see
> The gorgeous halcyon strike the bullrush tall;
> Thou lov'st to feel the veil of evening fall,
> Like gentlest slumber on a happy bride;
> For these are Nature's. — Art not thou hers too?
> A portion of her pageantry and pride,
> In all thy passions, all thou seek'st to do,
> And all thou dost?"*

* "Steam at Sheffield," by Ebenezer Elliott.

Note D. — Page 240.

Although it is to be regretted that correct moral sentiments in regard to opinions and to the free communication of thought, are not yet, as we see in the extracts given in page 240, universal among even cultivated men, there is scarcely room to doubt that they will eventually become so.

The other point of literary morality (if I may apply that phrase to both cases) alluded to in the same page, and in which future improvement may be equally looked for, is the moral sentiments of the community in relation to public criticism. It is by no means generally felt at present, that the man who takes upon himself the office of public critic, takes upon himself also the same responsibilities as those which devolve upon the judge in a court of law. Impartiality in the reception of evidence, anxiety to understand the cause, patience in mastering details, conscientiousness in the decision, and, what these imply, exemption from bias, freedom from private motives whether of favour or of hostility, are just as incumbent on the critic as on the judge. No one who does not sincerely and earnestly strive after these qualities is fit for either function.

It is a subject for rejoicing that an improvement in moral sentiment on this point, at least in the higher regions of criticism, has taken place, since the days when Scott declared *, apparently without a blush, that in one of his reviews he was governed by other motives than the desire

---

* See his account of writing an article on the Curse of Kehama for the "Quarterly Review," in which he confesses he gave as much weight as possible to the beautiful passages, and slurred over the absurdities, adding, that if the order of the day had been to tear it in pieces, he would have made a very different hand of it indeed.—*Memoirs of Sir Walter Scott*, Vol. II. p. 302.

to do justice to the author and the public; when Southey
wrote articles marked with such undue asperity as to draw
from him an acknowledgment of repentance*; when Jeffrey
could commence a criticism on a volume of genuine poetry
by the contemptuous expression, "This will never do," or
something equivalent to it; and when the same critic
wantonly held up to derision a man of real genius and
modesty, of whose personal character and habits he knew
nothing, by representing him as intoxicated with weak tea
and the praises of sentimental ensigns.

With the great critics of our own day such unprincipled
criticism and insulting language are, it is to be hoped, impossible; and if they may still be occasionally met with in
the lower walks of literature, we must recollect that moral
meliorations of this nature spread but slowly downward.
The time, however, will most assuredly come, although
we of this generation may not live to see it, when the
public critic will be required by the voice of the community
to be as scrupulous in his decisions as the judge on the
bench; and when it will be generally questioned whether,
with the view of attaining that end, the former functionary
ought not to be placed like the latter under the salutary

---

* If we may trust Southey's own account of the state of criticism
in his day (and he lived in the very midst of the turmoil), it was
deplorable enough. "For one competent critic—one equitable one—
there are twenty coxcombs who would blast the fortunes of an author
for the sake of raising a laugh at his expense."—*Life by his Son*,
Vol. IV. p. 351. The confession made by himself is, "Of all my literary
misdeeds, the only ones of which I have repented have been those
reviewals which were written with undue asperity, so as to give unnecessary pain."—*Ibid.* Vol. III. p. 222. Coleridge, writing about the
same time, or earlier, may be cited as confirming Southey's representation in the first of the above extracts. "Books," he says, "at
present seem degraded into culprits, to hold up their hands at the
bar of every self-elected, yet not the less peremptory judge."—
Biographia Literaria, Vol. I. p. 59.

chock of publicity, *i. e.* of boing personally known as tho dispensor of tho award.

The point even now is sometimes mooted, whether it is right that individuals who assume the offico of issuing public vordicts affecting, often decply, the woll-being of their fellow-men, should pronounce those verdicts behind an impenetrablo screon.

14 LYDGATE HILL, E.C.
(During the rebuilding of the Premises in Paternoster Row)
LONDON, *December* 1862.

GENERAL LIST OF WORKS,

NEW BOOKS AND NEW EDITIONS,

PUBLISHED BY

Messrs. LONGMAN, GREEN, LONGMAN, ROBERTS, and GREEN.

—————

THE CAPITAL OF THE TYCOON: A Narrative of a Three Years' Residence in Japan. By Sir RUTHERFORD ALCOCK, K.C.B., Her Majesty's Envoy Extraordinary and Minister Plenipotentiary in Japan. 2 vols. 8vo. with Maps and above 100 Illustrations. [*Just ready.*

THE LIFE OF SIR JOHN ELIOT. By JOHN FORSTER. With Two Portraits, from original Paintings at Port Eliot. 2 vols. post 8vo. uniform with 'The Arrest of the Five Members,' by the same Author. [*Just ready.*

HISTORY OF THE REFORMATION IN EUROPE IN THE TIME OF CALVIN. By J. H. MERLE D'AUBIGNÉ, D.D., President of the Theological School of Geneva, and Vice-President of the Société Evangélique; Author of *History of the Reformation of the Sixteenth Century.* VOLS. I. and II. 8vo. [*Just ready.*

THE PENTATEUCH AND BOOK OF JOSHUA, Critically Examined. PART I. the Pentateuch Examined as an Historical Narrative. By the Right Rev. JOHN WILLIAM COLENSO, D.D., BISHOP of NATAL. Second Edition, revised. 8vo. 6s. PART II. *the Age and Authorship of the Pentateuch Considered,* is nearly ready.

THE STORY OF A SIBERIAN EXILE. By M. RUFIN PIETROWSKI. Followed by a Narrative of Recent Events in Poland. Translated from the French. Post 8vo. [*Nearly ready.*

A

REMINISCENCES OF THE LIFE AND CHARACTER OF COUNT CAVOUR. By WILLIAM DE LA RIVE. Translated from the French by EDWARD ROMILLY. 8vo. 8s. 6d.

JEFFERSON AND THE AMERICAN DEMOCRACY : An Historical Study. By CORNÉLIS DE WITT. Translated, with the Author's permission, by R. S. H. CHURCH. 8vo. 14s.

DEMOCRACY IN AMERICA. By ALEXIS DE TOCQUEVILLE. Translated by HENRY REEVE, Esq. New Edition, with an Introductory Notice by the Translator. 2 vols. 8vo. 21s.

AUTOBIOGRAPHY OF THE EMPEROR CHARLES V. Recently Discovered in the Portuguese Language by Baron Kervyn De Lettenhove, Member of the Royal Academy of Belgium. Translated by LEONARD FRANCIS SIMPSON, M.R.S.L. Post 8vo. 6s. 6d.

THE LAW OF NATIONS CONSIDERED AS INDE-PENDENT POLITICAL COMMUNITIES. By TRAVERS TWISS, D.C.L., Regius Professor of Civil Law in the University of Oxford, and one of Her Majesty's Counsel. PART I. *The Right and Duties of Nations in Time of Peace.* 8vo. 12s.

> PART II. *The Right and Duties of Nations in Time of War,* is in preparation.

THE CONSTITUTIONAL HISTORY OF ENGLAND, since the Accession of George III. 1760—1860. By THOMAS ERSKINE MAY, C.B. In Two Volumes. VOL. I. 8vo. 16s. VOL. II. in preparation.

THE PRINCE CONSORT'S FARMS; An Agricultural Memoir of H. R. H. the late PRINCE CONSORT. Prepared, with the sanction and permission of Her Majesty the QUEEN. By J. C. MORTON. 4to. with 30 pages of Illustrations, comprising Maps of Estates, Plans, Sketches, and Views in Perspective of Farm Buildings and Cottages.

[*Nearly ready.*]

THE HISTORY OF ENGLAND, from the Accession of
James II. By the Right Hon. LORD MACAULAY. Library Edition.
5 vols. 8vo. £4.

LORD MACAULAY'S HISTORY OF ENGLAND, from the
Accession of James II. New Edition, revised and corrected, with
Portrait and brief Memoir. 8 vols. post 8vo. 48s.

THE HISTORY OF FRANCE. (An entirely new Work,
in Four Volumes.) By EYRE EVANS CROWE, Author of the 'History
of France,' in the *Cabinet Cyclopædia.* 8vo. VOL. I. 14s.; VOL. II. 15s.
*** The THIRD VOLUME is in the press.

A HISTORY OF THE ROMANS UNDER THE EMPIRE.
By the Rev. CHARLES MERIVALE, B.D., late Fellow of St. John's College,
Cambridge. 7 vols. 8vo. with Maps, £5 6s.

By the same Author.
THE FALL OF THE ROMAN REPUBLIC: A Short
History of the Last Century of the Commonwealth. 12mo. 7s. 6d.

A CRITICAL HISTORY OF THE LANGUAGE AND
LITERATURE OF ANCIENT GREECE. By WILLIAM MURE, M.P.,
of Caldwell. 5 vols. 8vo. £3. 9s.

THE HISTORY OF GREECE. By the Right Rev. the
LORD BISHOP OF ST. DAVID'S (the Rev. Connop Thirlwall). 8 vols. 8vo.
with Maps, £3; an Edition in 8 vols. fcp. 8vo. 28s.

HISTORICAL AND CHRONOLOGICAL ENCYCLOPÆDIA,
presenting in a brief and convenient form Chronological Notices of all
the Great Events of Universal History; including Treaties, Alliances,
Wars, Battles, &c.; Incidents in the Lives of Great and Distinguished
Men and their Works; Scientific and Geographical Discoveries;
Mechanical Inventions, and Social, Domestic, and Economical Improve-
ments. By B. B. WOODWARD, F.S.A., Librarian to the Queen. 8vo.
[*In the press.*

THE ANGLO-SAXON HOME: a History of the Domestic Institutions and Customs of England, from the Fifth to the Eleventh Century. By JOHN THRUPP. 8vo. 12s.

LIVES OF THE QUEENS OF ENGLAND. By AGNES STRICKLAND. Dedicated, by permission, to Her Majesty; embellished with Portraits of every Queen. 8 vols. post 8vo. 60s.

LIVES OF THE PRINCESSES OF ENGLAND. By Mrs. MARY ANNE EVERETT GREEN. With numerous Portraits, 6 vols. post 8vo. 63s.

LORD BACON'S WORKS. A New Edition, collected and edited by R. L. ELLIS, M.A.; J. SPEDDING, M.A.; and D. D. HEATH, Esq. VOLS. I. to V., comprising the Division of *Philosophical Works.* 5 vols. 8vo. £4. 6s. VOLS. VI. and VII., comprising the Division of *Literary and Professional Works.* 2 vols. 8vo. £1. 16s.

THE LETTERS AND LIFE OF FRANCIS BACON, including all his Occasional Works and Writings not already printed among his *Philosophical, Literary*, or *Professional Works.* Collected and chronologically arranged, with a Commentary, biographical and historical, by J. SPEDDING, Trin. Col. Cam. Vols. I and II. 8vo. 24s.

MEMOIR OF THE LIFE OF SIR M. I. BRUNEL, Civil Engineer, &c. By RICHARD BEAMISH, F.R.S. *Second Edition*, revised; with a Portrait, and 16 Illustrations. 8vo. 14s.

LIFE OF ROBERT STEPHENSON, F.R.S., late President of the Institution of Civil Engineers. By JOHN CORDY JEAFFRESON, Barrister-at-Law; and WILLIAM POLE, Member of the Institution of Civil Engineers. With Portrait and Illustrations. 2 vols. 8vo.
[*In the press.*

THE LIFE OF SIR PHILIP SIDNEY. By the Rev. JULIUS LLOYD, M.A. Post 8vo. 7s. 6d.

27

THE ROLL OF THE ROYAL COLLEGE OF PHYSICIANS

OF LONDON; compiled from the Annals of the College, and from other Authentic Sources. By WILLIAM MUNK, M.D., Fellow of the College, &c. VOLS. I. and II. 8vo. 12s. each.

28

THE HISTORY OF MEDICINE: Comprising a Narrative

of its Progress, from the Earliest Ages to the Present Time, and of the Delusions incidental to its advance from Empiricism to the dignity of a Science. By EDWARD MERYON, M.D., F.G.S., Fellow of the Royal College of Physicians, &c. VOL. I. 8vo. 12s. 6d.

29

MATERIALS FOR A HISTORY OF OIL PAINTING.

By Sir CHARLES L. EASTLAKE, R.A. 8vo. 16s.

30

HISTORY OF THE ROYAL ACADEMY OF ARTS.

From its Foundation in 1768 to the Present Time: With Biographical Notices of all the Members. By WILLIAM SANDBY. With 14 Illustrations. 2 vols. 8vo. 30s.

31

HALF-HOUR LECTURES ON THE HISTORY AND

PRACTICE of the FINE and ORNAMENTAL ARTS. By WILLIAM B. SCOTT, Head Master of the Government School of Design, Newcastle-on-Tyne. 16mo. with 50 Woodcuts, 8s. 6d.

32

SAVONAROLA AND HIS TIMES. By PASQUALE VILLARI,

Professor of History in the University of Pisa; accompanied by new Documents. Translated from the Italian by LEONARD HORNER, Esq., F.R.S., with the co-operation of the Author. 8vo. [*Nearly ready.*

33

LIFE OF RICHARD PORSON, M.A., Professor of Greek

in the University of Cambridge from 1792 to 1808. By the Rev. J. S. WATSON, M.A. With Portrait and 2 Facsimiles. 8vo. 14s.

By the same Author, nearly ready.

LIFE OF BISHOP WARBURTON.

BIOGRAPHIES OF DISTINGUISHED SCIENTIFIC MEN.
By FRANÇOIS ARAGO. Translated by Admiral W. H. SMYTH, D.C.L.,
F.R.S., &c.; the Rev. B. POWELL, M.A.; and R. GRANT, M.A., F.R.A.S.
8vo. 18s.

By the same Author.

METEOROLOGICAL ESSAYS. With an Introduction by
Baron HUMBOLDT. Translated under the superintendence of Major-
General E. SABINE, R.A., V.P.R.S. 8vo. 18s.

POPULAR ASTRONOMY. Translated and edited by
Admiral W. H. SMYTH, D.C.L., F.R.S.; and R. GRANT, M.A., F.R.A.S.
With 25 Plates and 358 Woodcuts. 2 vols. 8vo. £2. 5s.

TREATISE ON COMETS, from the above, price 5s.

LIFE OF THE DUKE OF WELLINGTON, partly from
the French of M. BRIALMONT; partly from Original Documents. By
the Rev. G. R. GLEIG, M.A., Chaplain-General to H.M. Forces. *New
Edition*, in One Volume, with PLANS, MAPS, and a PORTRAIT. 8vo. 15s.

MEMOIRS OF SIR HENRY HAVELOCK, Major-
General, K.C.B. By JOHN CLARK MARSHMAN. With Portrait, Map,
and 2 Plans. 8vo. 12s. 6d.

**MEMOIRS OF ADMIRAL PARRY, THE ARCTIC
NAVIGATOR.** By his Son, the Rev. E. PARRY, M.A. Seventh
Edition; with Portrait and coloured Chart. Fcp. 8vo. 5s.

VICISSITUDES OF FAMILIES. By Sir BERNARD BURKE,
Ulster King of Arms. FIRST, SECOND, and THIRD SERIES. 3 vols.
crown 8vo. price 12s. 6d. each.

**GREEK HISTORY FROM THEMISTOCLES TO ALEX-
ANDER,** in a Series of Lives from Plutarch. Revised and arranged by
A. H. CLOUGH, sometime Fellow of Oriel College, Oxford. With 44
Woodcuts. Fcp. 8vo. 6s.

TALES FROM GREEK MYTHOLOGY. By the Rev. G. W. Cox, M.A., late Scholar of Trinity College, Oxford. Square 16mo. price 3s. 6d.

By the same Author.

TALES OF THE GODS AND HEROES. With 6 Landscape Illustrations from Drawings by the Author. Fcp. 8vo. 5s.

THE TALE OF THE GREAT PERSIAN WAR, from the Histories of *Herodotus.* With 12 Woodcuts. Fcp. 8vo. 7s. 6d.

A DICTIONARY OF ROMAN AND GREEK ANTI-QUITIES, with nearly 2,000 Wood Engravings, representing Objects from the Antique, illustrative of the Industrial Arts and Social Life of the Greeks and Romans. Being the Second Edition of the *Illustrated Companion to the Latin Dictionary and Greek Lexicon.* By ANTHONY RICH, Jun., B.A. Post 8vo. 12s. 6d.

ANCIENT HISTORY OF EGYPT, ASSYRIA, AND BABYLONIA. By ELIZABETH M. SEWELL, Author of ' Amy Herbert,' &c. With Two Maps. Fcp. 8vo. 6s.

By the same Author.

HISTORY OF THE EARLY CHURCH, from the First Preaching of the Gospel to the Council of Nicæa, A.D. 325. *Second Edition.* Fcp. 8vo. 4s. 6d.

MEMOIR OF THE REV. SYDNEY SMITH. By his Daughter, LADY HOLLAND. With a Selection from his Letters, edited by MRS. AUSTIN. 2 vols. 8vo. 28s.

THOMAS MOORE'S MEMOIRS, JOURNAL, AND COR-RESPONDENCE. People's Edition. With 8 Portraits and 2 Vignettes. Edited and abridged from the First Edition by the Right Hon. EARL RUSSELL. Square crown 8vo. 12s. 6d.

SPEECHES OF THE RIGHT HON. LORD MACAULAY, Corrected by HIMSELF. *New Edition.* 8vo. 12s.

LORD MACAULAY'S SPEECHES ON PARLIAMENTARY REFORM IN 1831 AND 1832. Reprinted in the TRAVELLER'S LIBRARY. 16mo. 1s.

SOUTHEY'S LIFE OF WESLEY, AND RISE AND PROGRESS OF METHODISM. Fourth Edition, with Notes and Additions. Edited by the Rev. C. C. SOUTHEY, M.A. 2 vols. crown 8vo. 12s.

THE HISTORY OF WESLEYAN METHODISM. By GEORGE SMITH, F.A.S., Member of the Royal Asiatic Society, &c. 3 vols. crown 8vo. 31s. 6d.

THE VOYAGE AND SHIPWRECK OF ST. PAUL: With Dissertations on the Life and Writings of St. Luke, and the Ships and Navigation of the Ancients. By JAMES SMITH, of Jordanhill, Esq., F.R.S. *Second Edition*; with Charts, &c. Crown 8vo. 8s. 6d.

THE LIFE AND EPISTLES OF ST. PAUL. By the Rev. W. J. CONYBEARE, M.A., late Fellow of Trinity College, Cambridge; and the Rev. J. S. HOWSON, D.D., Principal of the Collegiate Institution, Liverpool. *People's Edition*, condensed; with 46 Illustrations and Maps. 2 vols. crown 8vo. 12s.

CONYBEARE AND HOWSON'S LIFE AND EPISTLES OF ST. PAUL. New Edition of the Intermediate Edition; with a Selection of Maps, Plates, and Wood Engravings. 2 vols. square crown 8vo. 31s. 6d.

CONYBEARE AND HOWSON'S LIFE AND EPISTLES OF ST. PAUL. The Original Library Edition, with more numerous Illustrations. 2 vols. 4to. 48s.

THE GENTILE AND THE JEW IN THE COURTS OF THE TEMPLE OF CHRIST. An Introduction to the History of Christianity. From the German of Professor DÖLLINGER, by the Rev. N. DARNELL, M.A., late Fellow of New College, Oxford. 2 vols. 8vo. 21s.

PORT-ROYAL; A Contribution to the History of Religion and Literature in France. By CHARLES BEARD, B.A. 2 vols. post 8vo. price 24s.

HIPPOLYTUS AND HIS AGE; or, the Beginnings and Prospects of Christianity. By C. C. J. BUNSEN, D.D., D.C.L., D.Ph. 2 vols. 8vo. 30s.

By the same Author.

OUTLINES OF THE PHILOSOPHY OF UNIVERSAL HISTORY, applied to Language and Religion: Containing an Account of the Alphabetical Conferences. 2 vols. 8vo. 33s.

ANALECTA ANTE-NICÆNA. 3 vols. 8vo. 42s.

EGYPT'S PLACE IN UNIVERSAL HISTORY: An Historical Investigation, in Five Books. Translated from the German by C. H. COTTRELL, M.A. With many Illustrations. 4 vols. 8vo £5. 8s. VOL. V., completing the work, is in preparation.

A NEW LATIN-ENGLISH DICTIONARY. By the Rev. J. T. WHITE, M.A., of Corpus Christi College, Oxford; and the Rev. J. E. RIDDLE, M.A., of St. Edmund Hall, Oxford. Imperial 8vo. 42s.

A GREEK-ENGLISH LEXICON. Compiled by HENRY GEO. LIDDELL, D.D., Dean of Christ Church; and ROBERT SCOTT, D.D., Master of Balliol. *Fifth Edition*, revised and augmented. Crown 4to. price 31s. 6d.

A LEXICON, GREEK AND ENGLISH, abridged from LIDDELL and SCOTT's *Greek-English Lexicon*. Ninth Edition, revised and compared throughout with the Original. Square 12mo. 7s. 6d.

A NEW ENGLISH-GREEK LEXICON, Containing all the Greek Words used by Writers of good authority. By CHARLES DUKE YONGE, B.A. *Second Edition*, thoroughly revised. 4to. 21s.

JOHNSON'S DICTIONARY OF THE ENGLISH LANGUAGE. A New Edition, founded on that of 1773, the last published in Dr. Johnson's lifetime: with numerous Emendations and Additions. By R. G. LATHAM, M.D., F.R.S. 2 vols. 4to. to be published in Monthly Parts. PART I. early in 1863.

THESAURUS OF ENGLISH WORDS AND PHRASES, classified and arranged so as to facilitate the Expression of Ideas, and assist in Literary Composition. By P. M. ROGET, M.D., F.R.S., &c. *Twelfth Edition*, revised and improved. Crown 8vo. 10s. 6d.

A PRACTICAL DICTIONARY OF THE FRENCH AND ENGLISH LANGUAGES.
By Léon Contanseau, lately Professor of the French Language and Literature in the Royal Indian Military College, Addiscombe (now dissolved); and Examiner for Military Appointments. *Fifth Edition*, with Corrections. Post 8vo. 10s. 6d.

By the same Author.

A POCKET DICTIONARY OF THE FRENCH AND ENGLISH LANGUAGES;
being a careful abridgment of the above, preserving all the most useful features of the original work, condensed into a Pocket Volume for the convenience of Tourists, Travellers, and English Readers or Students to whom portability of size is a requisite. Square 18mo. 5s.

LECTURES ON THE SCIENCE OF LANGUAGE,
delivered at the Royal Institution of Great Britain. By Max Müller, M.A., Fellow of All Souls College, Oxford. *Third Edition*, revised. 8vo. 12s.

THE STUDENT'S HANDBOOK OF COMPARATIVE GRAMMAR,
applied to the Sanskrit, Zend, Greek, Latin, Gothic, Anglo-Saxon, and English Languages. By the Rev. Thomas Clark, M.A. Crown 8vo. 7s. 6d.

THE DEBATER: A Series of Complete Debates, Outlines
of Debates, and Questions for Discussion; with ample References to the best Sources of Information. By F. Rowton. Fcp. 8vo. 6s.

THE ENGLISH LANGUAGE. By R. G. Latham, M.A.,
M.D., F.R.S., late Fellow of King's College, Cambridge. *Fifth Edition*, revised and enlarged. 8vo. 18s.

By the same Author.

HANDBOOK OF THE ENGLISH LANGUAGE, for the
Use of Students of the Universities and Higher Classes of Schools. Fourth Edition. Crown 8vo. 7s. 6d.

ELEMENTS OF COMPARATIVE PHILOLOGY. 8vo. 21s.

MANUAL OF ENGLISH LITERATURE, HISTORICAL AND CRITICAL; With a Chapter on English Metres. For the use of Schools and Colleges. By THOMAS ARNOLD, B.A., Professor of English Literature, Cath. Univ. Ireland. Post 8vo. 10s. 6d.

ON TRANSLATING HOMER: Three Lectures given at Oxford. By MATTHEW ARNOLD, M.A., Professor of Poetry in the University of Oxford, and formerly Fellow of Oriel College. Crown 8vo. 3s. 6d.— MR. ARNOLD's *Last Words on Translating Homer*, price 3s. 6d.

JERUSALEM: A Sketch of the City and Temple, from the Earliest Times to the Siege by Titus. By THOMAS LEWIN, M.A. With Map and Illustrations. 8vo. 10s.

PEAKS, PASSES, AND GLACIERS: a Series of Excursions by Members of the Alpine Club. Edited by J. BALL, M.R.I.A., F.L.S. Fourth Edition; with Maps, Illustrations, and Woodcuts. Square crown 8vo. 21s.— TRAVELLERS' EDITION, condensed, 16mo. 5s. 6d.

SECOND SERIES OF PEAKS, PASSES, AND GLACIERS. Edited by E. S. KENNEDY, M.A., F.R.G.S., President of the Alpine Club. With 4 Double Maps and 10 Single Maps by E. WELLER, F.R.G.S.; and 51 Illustrations on Wood by E. WHYMPER and G. PEARSON. 2 vols. square crown 8vo. 42s.

NINETEEN MAPS OF THE ALPINE DISTRICTS, from the First and Second Series of *Peaks, Passes, and Glaciers*. Square crown 8vo. 7s. 6d.

MOUNTAINEERING IN 1861; a Vacation Tour. By JOHN TYNDALL, F.R.S., Professor of Natural Philosophy in the Royal Institution of Great Britain. Square crown 8vo. with 2 Views, 7s. 6d.

A SUMMER TOUR IN THE GRISONS AND ITALIAN VALLEYS OF THE BERNINA. By MRS. HENRY FRESHFIELD. With 2 coloured Maps and 4 Views. Post 8vo. 10s. 6d.

By the same Author.

ALPINE BYWAYS; or, Light Leaves gathered in 1859 and 1860. With 8 Illustrations and 4 Route Maps. Post 8vo. 10s. 6d.

A LADY'S TOUR ROUND MONTE ROSA; including Visits to the Italian Valleys of Anzasca, Mastalone, Camasco, Sesia, Lys, Challant, Aosta, and Cogne. With Map and Illustrations. Post 8vo. 14s.

THE ALPS; or, Sketches of Life and Nature in the Mountains. By Baron H. Von Berlepsch. Translated by the Rev. Leslie Stephen, M.A. With 17 Tinted Illustrations. 8vo. 15s.

THEBES, ITS TOMBS AND THEIR TENANTS, Ancient and Modern; including a Record of Excavations in the Necropolis. By A. Henry Rhind, F.S.A. With 17 Illustrations, including a Map. Royal 8vo. 18s.

LETTERS FROM ITALY AND SWITZERLAND. By Felix Mendelssohn-Bartholdy. Translated from the German by Lady Wallace. *Second Edition*, revised. Post 8vo. 9s. 6d.

A GUIDE TO THE PYRENEES; especially intended for the use of Mountaineers. By Charles Packe. With Frontispiece and 3 Maps. Fcp. 8vo. 6s.

    The Map of the *Central Pyrenees* separately, price 3s. 6d.

HERZEGOVINA, or, Omer Pacha and the Christian Rebels: With a Brief Account of Servia, its Social, Political, and Financial Condition. By Lieut. G. Arbuthnot, R.H.A., F.R.G.S. Post 8vo, Frontispiece and Map, 10s. 6d.

CANADA AND THE CRIMEA; or, Sketches of a Soldier's Life, from the Journals and Correspondence of the late Major Ranken, R.E. Edited by his Brother, W. B. Ranken. Post 8vo. with Portrait, price 7s. 6d.

NOTES ON MEXICO IN 1861 AND 1862, Politically and Socially considered. By Charles Lempriere, D.C.L. of the Inner Temple, and Law Fellow of St. John's College, Oxford. With Map and 10 Woodcuts. Post 8vo. 12s. 6d.

EXPLORATIONS IN LABRADOR : The Country of the
Montagnais and Nasquapee Indiana. By HENRY YOULE HIND, M.A.,
F.R.G.S., Professor of Chemistry and Geology in the University of
Trinity College, Toronto. 2 vols.   [*Just ready.*

By the same Author.

**NARRATIVE OF THE CANADIAN RED RIVER
EXPLORING EXPEDITION OF 1857;** and of the **ASSINNIBOINE
AND SASKATCHEWAN EXPLORING EXPEDITION OF 1858.**
With several Coloured Maps and Plans, numerous Woodcuts, and 20
Chromoxylographic Engravings. 2 vols. 8vo. 42s.

HAWAII ; the Past, Present, and Future of its Island-
kingdom : An Historical Account of the Sandwich Islands (Polynesia).
By MANLEY HOPKINS, Hawaiian Consul-General. Post 8vo. Map and
Illustrations, 12s. 6d.

WILD LIFE ON THE FJELDS OF NORWAY. By
FRANCIS M. WYNDHAM. With Maps and Woodcuts. Post 8vo. 10s. 6d.

SOCIAL LIFE AND MANNERS IN AUSTRALIA ; Being
the Notes of Eight Years' Experience. By a RESIDENT. Post 8vo. 5s.

IMPRESSIONS OF ROME, FLORENCE, AND TURIN.
By the Author of *Amy Herbert.* Crown 8vo. 7s. 6d.

THE LAKE REGIONS OF CENTRAL AFRICA : A
Picture of Exploration. By RICHARD F. BURTON, Captain H.M. Indian
Army. 2 vols. 8vo. Map and Illustrations, 31s. 6d.

By the same Author.

FIRST FOOTSTEPS IN EAST AFRICA ; or, An Exploration of Harar. With Maps and coloured Illustrations. 8vo. 18s.

**PERSONAL NARRATIVE OF A PILGRIMAGE TO EL
MEDINAH AND MECCAH.** *Second Edition ;* with numerous Illustrations. 2 vols. crown 8vo. 24s.

THE CITY OF THE SAINTS ; and Across the Rocky
Mountains to California. *Second Edition ;* with Maps and Illustrations.
8vo. 18s.

THE AFRICANS AT HOME: A Popular Description of Africa and the Africans, condensed from the Accounts of African Travellers from the time of Mungo Park to the Present Day. By the Rev. R. M. MacBraie, M.A. Fcp. 8vo. Map and 70 Woodcuts, 7s. 6d.

LOWER BRITTANY AND THE BIBLE; its Priests and People: with Notes on Religious and Civil Liberty in France. By James Bromfield, Author of 'Brittany and the Bible,' 'The Chase in Brittany,' &c. Post 8vo. [*Just ready.*

AN AGRICULTURAL TOUR IN BELGIUM, HOLLAND, AND ON THE RHINE; With Practical Notes on the Peculiarities of Flemish Husbandry. By Robert Scott Burn. Post 8vo. with 43 Woodcuts, 7s.

A WEEK AT THE LAND'S END. By J. T. Blight; assisted by E. H. Rodd, R. Q. Couch, and J. Ralfs. With Map and 96 Woodcuts by the Author. Fcp. 8vo. 6s. 6d.

VISITS TO REMARKABLE PLACES: Old Halls, Battle-Fields, and Scenes illustrative of Striking Passages in English History and Poetry. By William Howitt. With about 80 Wood Engravings. 2 vols. square crown 8vo. 25s.

By the same Author.
THE RURAL LIFE OF ENGLAND. Cheaper Edition. With Woodcuts by Bewick and Williams. Medium 8vo. 12s. 6d.

ESSAYS ON SCIENTIFIC AND OTHER SUBJECTS, contributed to the *Edinburgh* and *Quarterly Reviews.* By Sir Henry Holland, Bart., M.D., F.R.S., &c., Physician-in-Ordinary to the Queen. *Second Edition.* 8vo. 14s.

By the same Author.
MEDICAL NOTES AND REFLECTIONS. *Third Edition,* revised, with some Additions. 8vo. 18s.

CHAPTERS ON MENTAL PHYSIOLOGY; founded chiefly on Chapters contained in *Medical Notes and Reflections.* *Second Edition.* Post 8vo. 8s. 6d.

PSYCHOLOGICAL INQUIRIES: in a Series of Essays intended to illustrate the Influence of the Physical Organisation on the Mental Faculties. By Sir BENJAMIN C. BRODIE, Bart., &c. Fcp. 8vo. 5s. PART II. Essays intended to illustrate some Points in the Physical and Moral History of Man. 5s.

AN INTRODUCTION TO MENTAL PHILOSOPHY, on the Inductive Method. By J. D. MORELL, M.A., LL.D. 8vo. 12s.

By the same Author.

ELEMENTS OF PSYCHOLOGY: Part I., containing the Analysis of the Intellectual Powers. Post 8vo. 7s. 6d.

OUTLINE OF THE NECESSARY LAWS OF THOUGHT: A Treatise on Pure and Applied Logic. By the Right Hon. and Most Rev. WILLIAM THOMSON, D.D., Archbishop-Designate of York. *Fifth Edition.* Post 8vo. 5s. 6d.

THE CYCLOPÆDIA OF ANATOMY AND PHYSIOLOGY Edited by ROBERT B. TODD, M.D., F.R.S. Assisted in the various departments by nearly all the most eminent cultivators of Physiological Science of the present age. 5 vols. 8vo. with 2,853 Woodcuts, price £6. 6s.

A DICTIONARY OF PRACTICAL MEDICINE: Comprising General Pathology, the Nature and Treatment of Diseases, Morbid Structures, and the Disorders especially incidental to Climates, to Sex, and to the different Epochs of Life. By JAMES COPLAND, M.D., F.R.S. 3 vols. 8vo. price £5. 11s.

HEAT CONSIDERED AS A MODE OF MOTION: A Course of Lectures delivered at the Royal Institution of Great Britain. By JOHN TYNDALL, F.R.S., Professor of Natural Philosophy in the Royal Institution. Crown 8vo. with Illustrations. [*Just ready.*

THE EARTH AND ITS MECHANISM; an Account of the various Proofs of the Rotation of the Earth: with a Description of the Instruments used in the Experimental Demonstrations; also the Theory of Foucault's Pendulum and Gyroscope. By HENRY WORMS, F.R.A.S., F.G.S. 8vo. with 31 Woodcuts, price 10s. 6d.

VOLCANOS, the Character of their Phenomena; their Share in the Structure and Composition of the Surface of the Globe; and their Relation to its Internal Forces: including a Descriptive Catalogue of Volcanos and Volcanic Formations. By G. POULETT SCROPE, M.P., F.R.S., F.G.S. *Second Edition*, with Map and Illustrations. 8vo. 15s.

A MANUAL OF CHEMISTRY, Descriptive and Theoretical. By WILLIAM ODLING, M.B., F.R.S., Secretary to the Chemical Society, and Professor of Practical Chemistry in Guy's Hospital. PART I. 8vo. 9s.

A DICTIONARY OF CHEMISTRY, founded on that of the late Dr. URE. By HENRY WATTS, B.A., F.C.S., Editor of the *Quarterly Journal of the Chemical Society*. To be published in Monthly Parts, uniform with the New Edition of Dr. URE's *Dictionary of Arts, Manufactures, and Mines*, recently completed.

HANDBOOK OF CHEMICAL ANALYSIS, adapted to the Unitary System of Notation: Based on the 4th Edition of Dr. H. Wills' *Anleitung zur chemischen Analyse*. By F. T. CONINGTON, M.A., F.C.S. Post 8vo. 7s. 6d.

CONINGTON'S TABLES OF QUALITATIVE ANALYSIS, to accompany in use his Handbook of *Chemical Analysis*. Post 8vo. 2s. 6d.

A HANDBOOK OF VOLUMETRICAL ANALYSIS. By ROBERT H. SCOTT, M.A., T.C.D., Secretary of the Geological Society of Dublin. Post 8vo. 4s. 6d.

A TREATISE ON ELECTRICITY, in Theory and Practice. By A. DE LA RIVE, Professor in the Academy of Geneva. Translated for the Author by C. V. WALKER, F.R.S. With Illustrations. 3 vols. 8vo. £3. 13s.

AN ESSAY ON CLASSIFICATION [The Mutual Relation of Organised Beings]. By LOUIS AGASSIZ. 8vo. 12s.

A DICTIONARY OF SCIENCE, LITERATURE, AND ART: Comprising the History, Description, and Scientific Principles of every Branch of Human Knowledge. Edited by W. T. BRANDE, F.R.S. L. and E. The Fourth Edition, revised and corrected. 8vo. [*In the press.*

104

THE CORRELATION OF PHYSICAL FORCES. By W. R. Grove, Q.C., M.A., V.P.R.S., Corresponding Member of the Academies of Rome, Turin, &c. *Fourth Edition.* 8vo. 7s. 6d.

105

THE ELEMENTS OF PHYSICS. By C. F. Peschel, Principal of the Royal Military College, Dresden. Translated from the German, with Notes, by E. West. 3 vols. fcp. 8vo. 21s.

106

PHILLIPS'S ELEMENTARY INTRODUCTION TO MINE-RALOGY. A New Edition, with extensive Alterations and Additions, by H. J. Brooke, F.R.S., F.G.S.; and W. H. Miller, M.A., F.G.S. With numerous Woodcuts. Post 8vo. 18s.

107

A GLOSSARY OF MINERALOGY. By Henry William Bristow, F.G.S., of the Geological Survey of Great Britain. With 486 Figures on Wood. Crown 8vo. 12s.

108

ELEMENTS OF MATERIA MEDICA AND THERAPEU-TICS. By Jonathan Pereira, M.D. F.R.S. *Third Edition,* enlarged and improved from the Author's Materials. By A. S. Taylor, M.D., and G. O. Rees, M.D. With numerous Woodcuts. Vol. I. 8vo. 28s.; Vol. II. Part I. 21s.; Vol. II. Part II. 26s.

109

OUTLINES OF ASTRONOMY. By Sir J. F. W. Herschel, Bart., M.A. *Fifth Edition,* revised and corrected. With Plates and Woodcuts. 8vo. 18s.

By the same Author.

ESSAYS FROM THE EDINBURGH AND QUARTERLY REVIEWS, with Addresses and other Pieces. 8vo. 18s.

110

CELESTIAL OBJECTS FOR COMMON TELESCOPES. By the Rev. T. W. Webb, M A., F.R.A.S. With Woodcuts and Map of the Moon. 16mo. 7s.

111

A GUIDE TO GEOLOGY. By John Phillips, M A., F.R.S., F.G.S., &c. Fourth Edition. With 4 Plates. Fcp. 8vo. 5s.

112

THE LAW OF STORMS considered in connexion with the ordinary Movements of the Atmosphere. By H. W Dove, F.R.S., Member of the Academies of Moscow, Munich, St. Petersburg, &c. Second Edition, translated, with the Author's sanction, by R. H. Scott, M.A., Trin. Coll. Dublin. With Diagrams and Charts. 8vo. 10s. 6d.

113

THE WEATHER-BOOK; A Manual of Practical Meteorology. By Rear-Admiral Fitzltoy. With 16 Illustrations engraved on Wood. 8vo.

114

ON THE STRENGTH OF MATERIALS; Containing various original and useful Formulæ, specially applied to Tubular Bridges. Wrought-Iron and Cast-Iron Beams, &c. By Thomas Tate, F.R.A.S. 8vo. 5s. 6d.

115

MANUAL OF THE SUB-KINGDOM CŒLENTERATA. By J. Reay Greene, B.A., M.R.I.A. Being the Second of a New Series of Manuals of the *Experimental and Natural Sciences*; edited by the Rev. J. A. Galbraith, M.A., and the Rev. S. Haughton, M.A., F.R.S. Fellows of Trinity College, Dublin. With 39 Woodcuts. Fcp. 8vo. 5s.

By the same Author and Editors.

MANUAL OF PROTOZOA; With a General Introduction on the Principles of Zoology, and 16 Woodcuts: Being the First Manual of the Series. Fcp. 8vo. 2s.

116

THE SEA AND ITS LIVING WONDERS. By Dr. George Hartwig. Translated by the Author from the Fourth German Edition; and embellished with numerous Illustrations from Original Designs. 8vo. 18s.

By the same Author.

THE TROPICAL WORLD: a Popular Scientific Account of the Natural History of the Animal and Vegetable Kingdoms in Equatorial Regions. With 8 Chromoxylographs and 172 Woodcut Illustrations. 8vo. 21s.

117

FOREST CREATURES. By Charles Boner, Author of 'Chamois Hunting in the Mountains of Bavaria,' &c. With 18 Illustrations from Drawings by Guido Hammer. Post 8vo. 10s. 6d.

118

SKETCHES OF THE NATURAL HISTORY OF CEYLON: With Narratives and Anecdotes illustrative of the Habits and Instincts of the Mammalia, Birds, Reptiles, Fishes, Insects, &c., including a Monograph of the Elephant. By Sir J. EMERSON TENNENT, K.C.S., LL.D., &c. With 82 Illustrations on Wood. Post 8vo. 12*s.* 6*d.*

By the same Author.

CEYLON; An Account of the Island, Physical, Historical, and Topographical; with Notices of its Natural History, Antiquities, and Productions. Fifth Edition; with Maps, Plans, and Charts, and 90 Wood Engravings. 2 vols. 8vo. £2. 10*s.*

119

MARVELS AND MYSTERIES OF INSTINCT; or, Curiosities of Animal Life. By G. GARRATT. *Third Edition*, revised and enlarged. Fcp. 8vo. 7*s.*

120

KIRBY AND SPENCE'S INTRODUCTION TO ENTOMOLOGY; or, Elements of the Natural History of Insects: Comprising an Account of Noxious and Useful Insects, of their Metamorphoses, Food, Stratagems, Habitations, Societies, Motions, Noises, Hybernation, Instinct, &c. *Seventh Edition.* Crown 8vo. 5*s.*

121

YOUATT'S WORK ON THE HORSE; Comprising also a Treatise on Draught. With numerous Woodcut Illustrations, chiefly from Designs by W. Harvey. New Edition, revised and enlarged by E. N. GABRIEL, M.R.C.S., C.V.S. 8vo. 10*s.* 6*d.*

By the same Author.

THE DOG. A New Edition; with numerous Engravings, from Designs by W. Harvey. 8vo. 6*s.*

122

THE DOG IN HEALTH AND DISEASE: Comprising the Natural History, Zoological Classification, and Varieties of the Dog, as well as the various modes of Breaking and Using him. By STONEHENGE. With 70 Wood Engravings. Square crown 8vo. 15*s.*

By the same Author.

THE GREYHOUND; A Treatise on the Art of Breeding, Rearing, and Training Greyhounds for Public Running. With many Illustrations. Square crown 8vo. 21*s.*

123

THE ENCYCLOPÆDIA OF RURAL SPORTS; A Complete
Account, Historical, Practical, and Descriptive, of Hunting, Shooting,
Fishing, Racing, &c. By D. P. BLAINE. With above 600 Woodcut
Illustrations, including 20 from Designs by JOHN LEECH. 8vo. 42s.

124

**COL. HAWKER'S INSTRUCTIONS TO YOUNG SPORTS-
MEN** in all that relates to Guns and Shooting. 11th Edition, revised
by the Author's Son; with Portrait and Illustrations. Square crown
8vo. 18s.

125

THE DEAD SHOT, or Sportsman's Complete Guide; A
Treatise on the Use of the Gun, with Lessons in the Art of Shooting
Game of all kinds; Dog-breaking, Pigeon-shooting, &c. By MARKSMAN.
Third Edition; with 6 Plates. Fcp. 8vo. 5s.

126

THE FLY-FISHER'S ENTOMOLOGY. By ALFRED
RONALDS. With coloured Representations of the Natural and Artificial
Insect. *Sixth Edition*, revised by an Experienced Fly-Fisher; with
20 new coloured Plates. 8vo. 14s.

127

THE CHASE OF THE WILD RED DEER in the Counties
of Devon and Somerset. With an APPENDIX descriptive of Remarkable
Runs and Incidents connected with the Chase, from the year 1780 to
the year 1860. By C. P. COLLYNS, Esq. With a Map and numerous
Illustrations. Square crown 8vo. 16s.

128

THE HORSE'S FOOT, AND HOW TO KEEP IT SOUND.
Eighth Edition; with an Appendix on Shoeing and Hunters. 12
Plates and 12 Woodcuts. By W. MILES, Esq. Imperial 8vo. 12s. 6d.

Two Casts or Models of Off Fore Feet—No. 1, *Shod for All Purposes*; No. 2,
Shod with Leather, on Mr. Miles's plan—may be had, price 3s. each.

By the same Author.

A PLAIN TREATISE ON HORSE-SHOEING. With Plates
and Woodcuts. *New Edition*. Post 8vo. 2s.

129

HINTS ON ETIQUETTE AND THE USAGES OF SOCIETY;
With a Glance at Bad Habits. New Edition, revised (with Additions).
By a LADY of RANK. Fcp. 8vo. 2s. 6d.

130

SHORT WHIST; its Rise, Progress, and Laws: With
Observations to make anyone a Whist-player. Containing also the
Laws of Piquet, Cassino, Ecarté, Cribbage, Backgammon. By Major
A. Fcp. 8vo. 3s.

131

TALPA; or, the Chronicles of a Clay Farm: An Agricultural Fragment. By C. W. Hoskyns, Esq. With 24 Woodcuts from
Designs by G. Cruikshank. 16mo. 5s. 6d.

132

THE SAILING-BOAT: A Treatise on English and Foreign
Boats, with Historical Descriptions; also Practical Directions for the
Rigging, Sailing, and Management of Boats, and other Nautical Infor-
mation. By H. C. Folkard, Author of *The Wildfowler*, &c. Third
Edition, enlarged; with numerous Illustrations.   [*Just ready.*

133

ATHLETIC AND GYMNASTIC EXERCISES: Comprising
114 Exercises and Feats of Agility. With a Description of the requisite
Apparatus, and 64 Woodcuts. By John H. Howard. 16mo. 7s. 6d.

134

THE LABORATORY OF CHEMICAL WONDERS: A
Scientific Mélange for the Instruction and Entertainment of Young
People. By G. W. S. Piesse, Analytical Chemist. Crown 8vo. 5s. 6d.

By the same Author.

CHEMICAL, NATURAL, AND PHYSICAL MAGIC, for the
Instruction and Entertainment of Juveniles during the Holiday Vacation. With 90 Woodcuts and an Invisible Portrait. Fcp. 8vo. 3s. 6d.

THE ART OF PERFUMERY; being the History and
Theory of Odours, and the Methods of Extracting the Aromas of Plants,
&c. Third Edition; with numerous additional Recipes and Analyses,
and 53 Woodcuts. Crown 8vo. 10s. 6d.

135

THE CRICKET FIELD; or, the History and the Science of
the Game of Cricket. By the Rev. J. Pycroft, B.A., Trin. Coll.
Oxon. *Fourth Edition*; with 2 Plates. Fcp. 8vo. 5s.

By the same Author.

THE CRICKET TUTOR; a Treatise exclusively Practical,
dedicated to the Captains of Elevens in Public Schools. 18mo. 1s.

THE WARDEN : A Novel. By ANTHONY TROLLOPE. New and cheaper Edition. Crown 8vo. 3s. 6d.

By the same Author.

BARCHESTER TOWERS : A Sequel to the *Warden*. New and cheaper Edition. Crown 8vo. 5s.

ELLICE : A Tale. By L. N. COMYN. Post 8vo. 9s. 6d.

THE LAST OF THE OLD SQUIRES : A Sketch. By the Rev. J. W. WARTER, B.D., Vicar of West Tarring, Sussex. *Second Edition.* Fcp. 8vo. 4s. 6d.

THE ROMANCE OF A DULL LIFE. Second Edition, revised. Post 8vo. 9s. 6d.

By the same Author.

MORNING CLOUDS. Second and cheaper Edition, revised throughout. Fcp. 8vo. 5s.

THE AFTERNOON OF LIFE. Second and cheaper Edition, revised throughout. Fcp. 8vo. 5s.

PROBLEMS IN HUMAN NATURE. Post 8vo. 5s.

THE TALES AND STORIES OF THE AUTHOR OF AMY HERBERT. New and cheaper Edition, in 10 vols. crown 8vo. price £1. 14s. 6d. ; or each work separately, complete in a single volume, as follows :—

AMY HERBERT .... 2s. 6d.	IVORS .... 3s. 6d.
GERTRUDE .... 2s. 6d.	KATHARINE ASHTON . 3s. 6d.
The EARL'S DAUGHTER 2s. 6d.	MARGARET PERCIVAL 5s. 0d.
EXPERIENCE of LIFE... 2s. 6d.	LANETON PARSONAGE 4s. 6d.
CLEVE HALL .... 3s. 6d.	URSULA .... 4s. 6d.

SUNSETS AND SUNSHINE ; or, Varied Aspects of Life. By ERSKINE NEALE, M.A., Vicar of Exning, and Chaplain to the Earl of Huntingdon. Post 8vo. 8s. 6d.

MY LIFE, AND WHAT SHALL I DO WITH IT? A Question for Young Gentlewomen. By an OLD MAID. *Fourth Edition.* Fcp. 8vo. 6s.

DEACONESSES : An Essay on the Official Help of Women in Parochial Work and in Charitable Institutions. By the Rev. J. S. Howson, D.D., Principal of the Collegiate Institution, Liverpool. Fcp. 8vo. 5s.

ESSAYS IN ECCLESIASTICAL BIOGRAPHY. By the Right Hon. Sir JAMES STEPHEN, LL.D. Fourth Edition, with a Biographical Notice of the Author, by his Son. 8vo. 14s.

By the same Author.

LECTURES ON THE HISTORY OF FRANCE. Third Edition. 2 vols. 8vo. 21s.

CRITICAL AND HISTORICAL ESSAYS contributed to The Edinburgh Review. By the Right Hon. Lord MACAULAY. Four Editions, as follows :—

1. LIBRARY EDITION (the *Tenth*), 3 vols. 8vo. 36s.
2. Complete in ONE VOLUME, with Portrait and Vignette. Square crown 8vo. 21s.
3. Another NEW EDITION, in 3 vols. fcp. 8vo. 21s.
4. The PEOPLE'S EDITION, in 2 vols. crown 8vo. price 8s.

146

LORD MACAULAY'S MISCELLANEOUS WRITINGS : comprising his Contributions to *Knight's Quarterly Magazine*, Articles contributed to the Edinburgh Review not included in his *Critical and Historical Essays*, Biographies written for the *Encyclopædia Britannica*, Miscellaneous Poems and Inscriptions. 2 vols. 8vo. with Portrait, 21s.

THE REV. SYDNEY SMITH'S MISCELLANEOUS WORKS: Including his Contributions to The Edinburgh Review. Four Editions, viz.

1. A LIBRARY EDITION (the *Fourth*), in 3 vols. 8vo. with Portrait, 36s.
2. Complete in ONE VOLUME, with Portrait and Vignette. Square crown 8vo. 21s.
3. Another NEW EDITION, in 3 vols. fcp. 8vo. 21s.
4. The PEOPLE'S EDITION, in 2 vols. crown 8vo. 8s.

By the same Author.

ELEMENTARY SKETCHES OF MORAL PHILOSOPHY, delivered at the Royal Institution. Fcp. 8vo. 7s.

THE WIT AND WISDOM OF THE REV. SYDNEY SMITH: A Selection of the most memorable Passages in his Writings and Conversation. 16mo. 7s. 6d.

ESSAYS SELECTED FROM CONTRIBUTIONS TO THE *Edinburgh Review.* By HENRY ROGERS. Second Edition. 3 vols. fcp. 8vo. 21s.

By the same Author.

THE ECLIPSE OF FAITH; or, A Visit to a Religious Sceptic. *Tenth Edition.* Fcp. 8vo. 5s.

DEFENCE OF THE ECLIPSE OF FAITH, by its Author: Being a Rejoinder to Professor Newman's *Reply.* Fcp. 8vo. 3s. 6d.

SELECTIONS FROM THE CORRESPONDENCE OF R. E. H. GREYSON, Esq. Edited by the Author of *The Eclipse of Faith.* Crown 8vo. 7s. 6d.

ESSAYS AND REVIEWS. By the Rev. W. TEMPLE, D.D., Rev. R. WILLIAMS, B.D., Rev. B. POWELL, M.A., the Rev. H. B. WILSON, B.D., C. W. GOODWIN, M.A., Rev. M. PATTISON, B.D., and Rev. B. JOWETT, M.A. Fcp. 8vo. 5s.

ESSAYS AND REVIEWS, *Ninth Edition,* in 8vo. price 10s. 6d.

REVELATION AND SCIENCE, in respect to Bunsen's *Biblical Researches,* the Evidences of Christianity, and the Mosaic Cosmogony. With an Examination of certain Statements put forth by the remaining Authors of *Essays and Reviews.* By the Rev. B. W. SAVILE, M.A. 8vo. 10s. 6d.

THE HISTORY OF THE SUPERNATURAL IN ALL AGES AND NATIONS, IN ALL CHURCHES, CHRISTIAN AND PAGAN: Demonstrating a Universal Faith. By WILLIAM HOWITT, Author of *Colonisation and Christianity,* &c. 2 vols. post 8vo. [*Nearly ready.*

THE MISSION AND EXTENSION OF THE CHURCH AT HOME, considered in Eight Lectures, preached before the University of Oxford in the year 1861, at the Lecture founded by the late Rev. J. Bampton, M.A. By J. SANDFORD, B.D., Archdeacon of Coventry. 8vo. price 12s.

PHYSICO-PROPHETICAL ESSAYS ON THE LOCALITY OF THE ETERNAL INHERITANCE: Its Nature and Character; the Resurrection Body; the Mutual Recognition of Glorified Saints. By the Rev. W. LISTER, F.G.S. Crown 8vo. 10s. 6d.

134
BISHOP JEREMY TAYLOR'S ENTIRE WORKS: With
Life by Bishop Heber. Revised and corrected by the Rev. C. P. Eden,
Fellow of Oriel College, Oxford. 10 vols. 8vo. £5. 5s.

135
MOSHEIM'S ECCLESIASTICAL HISTORY. The Rev.
Dr. Murdock's Literal Translation from the Latin, as edited, with
Additional Notes, by Henry Soames, M.A. *Third Revised Edition*,
carefully re-edited and brought down to the Present Time by the Rev.
William Stubbs, M.A. Vicar of Navestock, and Librarian to the
Archbishop of Canterbury. 3 vols. 8vo.   [*In the press.*

136
A COURSE OF ENGLISH READING, adapted to every
taste and capacity; or, How and What to Read: With Literary
Anecdotes. By the Rev. J. Pycroft, B.A. Trin. Coll. Oxon. Fcp.
8vo. 5s.

137
PASSING THOUGHTS ON RELIGION. By the Author of
Amy Herbert. New Edition. Fcp. 8vo. 5s.

By the same Author.
SELF-EXAMINATION BEFORE CONFIRMATION: With
Devotions and Directions for Confirmation-Day. 32mo. 1s. 6d.

**READINGS FOR A MONTH PREPARATORY TO CON-
FIRMATION**: Compiled from the Works of Writers of the Early and
of the English Church. Fcp. 8vo. 4s.

READINGS FOR EVERY DAY IN LENT; Compiled from
the Writings of Bishop Jeremy Taylor. Fcp. 8vo. 5s.

138
LEGENDS OF THE SAINTS AND MARTYRS, as represented in Christian Art. By Mrs. Jameson. Third Edition, revised;
with 17 Etchings and 180 Woodcuts. 2 vols. square crown 8vo. 31s. 6d.

By the same Author.
LEGENDS OF THE MONASTIC ORDERS, as represented
in Christian Art. New and improved Edition, being the Third; with
many Etchings and Woodcuts. Square crown 8vo.   [*Nearly ready.*

LEGENDS OF THE MADONNA, as represented in Christian
Art. Second Edition, enlarged; with 27 Etchings and 165 Woodcuts.
Square crown 8vo. 28s.

**THE HISTORY OF OUR LORD AND OF HIS PRECURSOR
JOHN THE BAPTIST**; with the Personages and Typical Subjects of
the Old Testament, as represented in Christian Art. Square crown 8vo.
with many Etchings and Woodcuts.   [*In the press.*

CATS' AND FARLIE'S BOOK OF EMBLEMS: Moral Emblems, with Aphorisms, Adages, and Proverbs of all Nations: Comprising 60 circular Vignettes, 60 Tail-pieces, and a Frontispiece composed from their works by J. LEIGHTON, F.S.A., and engraved on Wood. The Text translated and edited, with Additions, by R. PIGOT. Imperial 8vo. 31s. 6d.

BUNYAN'S PILGRIM'S PROGRESS: With 126 Illustrations on Steel and Wood, from Original Designs by C. Bennett; and a Preface by the Rev. C. KINGSLEY. Fcp. 4to. 21s.

THEOLOGIA GERMANICA: Translated by SUSANNA WINKWORTH. With a Preface by the Rev. C. KINGSLEY; and a Letter by Baron BUNSEN. Fcp. 8vo. 5s.

LYRA GERMANICA. Translated from the German by CATHERINE WINKWORTH. FIRST SERIES, Hymns for the Sundays and Chief Festivals of the Christian Year. SECOND SERIES, the Christian Life. Fcp. 8vo. price 5s. each series.

HYMNS FROM LYRA GERMANICA. 18mo. 1s.

LYRA GERMANICA. FIRST SERIES, as above, translated by C. WINKWORTH. With Illustrations from Original Designs by John Leighton, F.S.A., engraved on Wood under his superintendence. Fcp. 4to. 21s.

THE CHORALE-BOOK FOR ENGLAND; A Complete Hymn-Book for Public and Private Worship, in accordance with the Services and Festivals of the Church of England: The *Hymns* from the *Lyra Germanica* and other Sources, translated from the German by C. WINKWORTH; the *Tunes*, from the Sacred Music of the Lutheran, Latin, and other Churches, for Four Voices, with Historical Notes, &c., compiled and edited by W. S. BENNETT, Professor of Music in the University of Cambridge, and by O. GOLDSCHMIDT. Fcp. 4to. price 10s. 6d. cloth, or 18s. half-bound in morocco,

HYMNOLOGIA CHRISTIANA: Psalms and Hymns for the Christian Seasons. Selected and Contributed by Philhymnic Friends; and Edited by BENJAMIN HALL KENNEDY, D.D., Prebendary of Lichfield. Crown 8vo. [*Just ready.*

166

LYRA SACRA; Being a Collection of Hymns, Ancient and Modern, Odes, and Fragments of Sacred Poetry; compiled and edited, with a Preface, by the Rev. B. W. SAVILE, M.A. Fcp. 8vo. 5s.

167

LYRA DOMESTICA: Christian Songs for Domestic Edification. Translated from the *Psaltery and Harp* of C. J. P. SPITTA. By RICHARD MASSIE. Fcp. 8vo. 4s. 6d.

168

THE WIFE'S MANUAL; or, Prayers, Thoughts, and Songs on Several Occasions of a Matron's Life. By the Rev. W. CALVERT, M.A. Ornamented in the style of *Queen Elisabeth's Prayer-Book*. Crown 8vo. 10s. 6d.

169

HORNE'S INTRODUCTION TO THE CRITICAL STUDY AND KNOWLEDGE OF THE HOLY SCRIPTURES. *Eleventh Edition*, revised, corrected, and brought down to the Present Time. With 4 Maps and 22 Woodcuts and Facsimiles. 4 vols. 8vo. £3. 13s. 6d.

> VOL. I.—A Summary of the Evidence for the Genuineness, Authenticity, Uncorrupted Preservation, and Inspiration of the Holy Scriptures. By the Rev. T. H. HORNE, B.D. 8vo. 15s.

> VOL. II. by AYRE.—An Introduction to the Criticism of the *Old Testament* and to *Biblical Interpretation*. Revised and Edited by the Rev. JOHN AYRE, M.A. 8vo. 25s.

> Or—VOL. II. by DAVIDSON.—The Text of the *Old Testament* considered: With a Treatise on Sacred Interpretation; and a brief Introduction to the *Old Testament Books* and the *Apocrypha*. By S. DAVIDSON, D.D. (Halle) and LL.D. 8vo. 25s.

> VOL. III.—A Summary of Biblical Geography and Antiquities. By the Rev. T. H. HORNE, B.D. 8vo. 18s.

> VOL. IV.—An Introduction to the Textual Criticism of the *New Testament*. By the Rev. T. H. HORNE, B.D. The Critical Part re-written and the remainder revised and edited by S. P. TREGELLES, LL.D. *Second Edition*. 8vo. 18s.

170

HORNE'S COMPENDIOUS INTRODUCTION TO THE STUDY OF THE BIBLE. *Tenth Edition*, carefully re-edited by the Rev. JOHN AYRE, M.A., of Gonville and Caius College, Cambridge. With 3 Maps and 6 Illustrations. Post 8vo. 9s.

171
INSTRUCTIONS IN THE DOCTRINE AND PRACTICE
OF CHRISTIANITY. Intended chiefly as an Introduction to Confirmation. By the Right Rev. G. E. L. COTTON, D.D., BISHOP of CALCUTTA. 18mo. 2s. 6d.

172
THE TREASURY OF BIBLE KNOWLEDGE : Comprising
a Summary of the Evidences of Christianity; the Principles of Biblical Criticism; the History, Chronology, and Geography of the Scriptures; an Account of the Formation of the Canon; separate Introductions to the several Books of the Bible, &c. By the Rev. JOHN AYRE, M.A. Fcp. 8vo. with Maps, Engravings on Steel, and numerous Woodcuts; uniform with *Maunder's Treasuries.*   [*Nearly ready.*

173
BOWDLER'S FAMILY SHAKSPEARE ; in which nothing
is *added* to the Original Text, but those words and expressions are *omitted* which cannot with propriety be read aloud. Cheaper Genuine Edition, complete in 1 vol. large type, with 36 Woodcut Illustrations, price 14s. Or, with the same ILLUSTRATIONS, in 6 volumes for the pocket, price 5s. each.

174
GOLDSMITH'S POETICAL WORKS. Edited by BOLTON
CORNEY, Esq. Illustrated with numerous Wood Engravings, from Designs by Members of the Etching Club. Square crown 8vo. 21s.

175
MOORE'S LALLA ROOKH. With 13 Plates, engraved on
Steel, from Original Designs by Corbould, Meadows, and Stephanoff. Square crown 8vo. 15s.

176
TENNIEL'S EDITION OF MOORE'S LALLA ROOKH.
With 68 Woodcut Illustrations, from Original Drawings, and 5 Initial Pages of Persian Designs by T. Sulman, Jun. Fcp. 4to. 21s.

177
MOORE'S IRISH MELODIES. With 13 highly-finished
Steel Plates, from Original Designs by Eminent Artists. Square crown 8vo. 21s.

178
MOORE'S POETICAL WORKS. People's Edition, complete
in One Volume, large type, with Portrait after Phillips. Square crown 8vo. 12s. 6d.

POETICAL WORKS OF LETITIA ELIZABETH LANDON

(L.E.L.) Comprising the *Improvisatrice*, the *Venetian Bracelet*, the *Golden Violet*, the *Troubadour*, and Poetical Remains. New Edition; with 2 Vignettes. 2 vols. 16mo. 10s.

LAYS OF ANCIENT ROME; with *Ivry* and the *Armada*.

By the Right Hon. Lord MACAULAY. 16mo. 4s. 6d.

LORD MACAULAY'S LAYS OF ANCIENT ROME. With

Illustrations, Original and from the Antique, drawn on Wood by G. Scharf. Fcp. 4to. 21s.

POEMS. By MATTHEW ARNOLD. FIRST SERIES, Third

Edition. Fcp. 8vo. 5s. 6d. SECOND SERIES, 5s.

By the same Author.

MEROPE: A Tragedy. With a Preface and an Historical

Introduction. Fcp. 8vo. 5s.

SOUTHEY'S POETICAL WORKS; with all the Author's

last Introductions and Notes. *Library Edition*, with Portrait and Vignette. Medium 8vo. 21s.; in 10 vols. fcp. 8vo. with Portrait and 19 Vignettes, 35s.

By the same Author.

THE DOCTOR, &c. Complete in One Volume. Edited by

the Rev. J. W. WARTER, B.D. With Portrait, Vignette, Bust, and coloured Plate. Square crown 8vo. 12s. 6d.

CALDERON'S THREE DRAMAS: *Love the Greatest*

Enchantment, The Sorceries of Sin, and *The Devotion of the Cross*, attempted in English Asonante and other Imitative Verse, by D. F. MACCARTHY, M.R.I.A., with Notes, and the Spanish Text. Fcp. 4to. 15s.

A SURVEY OF HUMAN PROGRESS TOWARDS

HIGHER CIVILISATION: a Progress as little perceived by the multitude in any age, as is the growing of a tree by the children who sport under its shade. By NEIL ARNOTT, M.D., F.R.S., &c. 8vo. price 6s. 6d.

COLONIZATION AND COLONIES: Being a Series of Lectures delivered before the University of Oxford in 1839, '40, and '41. By HERMAN MERIVALE, M.A., Professor of Political Economy. Second Edition, with Notes and Additions. 8vo. 18s.

C. M. WILLICH'S POPULAR TABLES for Ascertaining the Value of Lifehold, Leasehold, and Church Property, Renewal Fines, &c.; the Public Funds; Annual Average Price and Interest on Consols from 1731 to 1861; Chemical, Geographical, Astronomical, Trigonometrical Tables, &c. &c. *Fifth Edition*, enlarged. Post 8vo. 10s.

THOMSON'S TABLES OF INTEREST, at Three, Four, Four and a-Half, and Five per Cent., from One Pound to Ten Thousand and from 1 to 365 Days. 12mo. 3s. 6d.

A DICTIONARY, PRACTICAL, THEORETICAL, AND HISTORICAL, of Commerce and Commercial Navigation. By J. R. M'CULLOCH, Esq. Illustrated with Maps and Plans. New Edition, containing much additional Information. 8vo. 50s.

By the same Author.

A DICTIONARY, GEOGRAPHICAL, STATISTICAL, AND HISTORICAL, of the various Countries, Places, and principal Natural Objects in the World. New Edition, revised; with 6 Maps. 2 vols. 8vo. 63s.

A MANUAL OF GEOGRAPHY, Physical, Industrial, and Political. By WILLIAM HUGHES, F.R.G.S., &c., Professor of Geography in Queen's College, London. New and thoroughly revised Edition: with 6 coloured Maps. Fcp. 8vo. 7s. 6d.

Or, in Two Parts: PART I. Europe, 3s. 6d.; PART II. Asia, Africa, America, Australasia, and Polynesia, 4s.

By the same Author.

THE GEOGRAPHY OF BRITISH HISTORY: Comprehending a Geographical Description of the British Islands and the Colonial Empire of Britain, treated historically, in successive periods, from the earliest times to the present day. Fcp. 8vo. [*Nearly ready.*

A NEW BRITISH GAZETTEER; or, Topographical Dictionary of the British Islands and Narrow Seas: Comprising concise Descriptions of about 60,000 Places, Seats, Natural Features, and Objects of Note, founded on the best Authorities. By J. A. SHARP. 2 vols. 8vo. £2. 16s.

A NEW DICTIONARY OF GEOGRAPHY, Descriptive, Physical, Statistical, and Historical: Forming a complete General Gazetteer of the World. By A. K. JOHNSTON, F.R.S.E., &c. *Second Edition*, revised. In One Volume of 1,360 pages, comprising about 50,000 Names of Places. 8vo. 30s.

AN ENCYCLOPÆDIA OF CIVIL ENGINEERING, Historical, Theoretical, and Practical. Illustrated by upwards of 3,000 Woodcuts. By E. CRESY, C.E. *Second Edition*, revised and extended. 8vo. 42s.

THE ENGINEER'S HANDBOOK; explaining the Principles which should guide the young Engineer in the Construction of Machinery, with the necessary Rules, Proportions, and Tables. By C. S. LOWNDES, Engineer. Post 8vo. 5s.

USEFUL INFORMATION FOR ENGINEERS: Being a FIRST SERIES of Lectures delivered before the Working Engineers of Yorkshire and Lancashire. By W. FAIRBAIRN, LL.D., F.R.S., F.G.S. With Plates and Woodcuts. Crown 8vo. 10s. 6d.

SECOND SERIES: Containing Experimental Researches on the Collapse of Boiler Flues and the Strength of Materials, and Lectures on subjects connected with Mechanical Engineering, &c. With Plates and Woodcuts. Crown 8vo. 10s. 6d.

By the same Author.

A TREATISE ON MILLS AND MILLWORK. VOL. I. on the principles of Mechanism and on Prime Movers. With Plates and Woodcuts. 8vo. 16s.

AN ENCYCLOPÆDIA OF ARCHITECTURE, Historical, Theoretical, and Practical. By JOSEPH GWILT. With more than 1,000 Wood Engravings, from Designs by J. S. Gwilt. 8vo. 42s.

LOUDON'S ENCYCLOPÆDIA of Cottage, Farm, and Villa Architecture and Furniture. New Edition, edited by Mrs. LOUDON; with more than 2,000 Woodcuts. 8vo. 63s.

THE ELEMENTS OF MECHANISM, designed for Students of Applied Mechanics. By T. M. GOODEVE, M.A., Professor of Natural Philosophy in King's College, London. With 206 Figures on Wood. Post 8vo. 6s. 6d.

URE'S DICTIONARY OF ARTS, MANUFACTURES, AND MINES. Fifth Edition, re-written and enlarged; with nearly 2,000 Wood Engravings. Edited by ROBERT HUNT, F.R.S., F.S.S., Keeper of Mining Records, &c., assisted by numerous gentlemen eminent in Science and connected with the Arts and Manufactures. 3 vols. 8vo. £4.

AN ENCYCLOPÆDIA OF DOMESTIC ECONOMY: Comprising such subjects as are most immediately connected with Housekeeping. By THOS. WEBSTER; assisted by Mrs. PARKES. With nearly 1,000 Woodcuts. 8vo. 31s. 6d.

MODERN COOKERY FOR PRIVATE FAMILIES, reduced to a System of Easy Practice in a Series of carefully-tested Receipts, in which the Principles of Baron Liebig and other eminent Writers have been as much as possible applied and explained. By ELIZA ACTON. Newly revised and enlarged Edition; with 8 Plates, comprising 27 Figures, and 150 Woodcuts. Fcp. 8vo. 7s. 6d.

A PRACTICAL TREATISE ON BREWING, based on Chemical and Economical Principles: With Formulæ for Public Brewers, and Instructions for Private Families. By W. BLACK. 8vo. price 10s. 6d.

ON FOOD AND ITS DIGESTION: Being an Introduction to Dietetics. By W. BRINTON, M.D., Physician to St. Thomas's Hospital, &c. With 48 Woodcuts. Post 8vo. 12s.

HINTS TO MOTHERS ON THE MANAGEMENT OF THEIR HEALTH DURING THE PERIOD OF PREGNANCY AND IN THE LYING-IN ROOM. By T. BULL, M.D. Fcp. 8vo. 5s.

By the same Author.

THE MATERNAL MANAGEMENT OF CHILDREN IN HEALTH AND DISEASE. Fcp. 8vo. 5s.

LECTURES ON THE DISEASES OF INFANCY AND CHILDHOOD. By CHARLES WEST, M.D., &c. *Fourth Edition*, carefully revised throughout; with numerous additional Cases, and a copious INDEX. 8vo. 14s.

THE PATENTEE'S MANUAL: A Treatise on the Law and Practice of Letters Patent, especially intended for the use of Patentees and Inventors. By J. JOHNSON and J. H. JOHNSON, Esqrs. Post 8vo. 7s. 6d.

THE PRACTICAL DRAUGHTSMAN'S BOOK OF INDUSTRIAL DESIGN. *Second Edition, Enlarged.* By W. JOHNSON, Assoc. Inst. C.E. 4to. 28s. 6d.

THE PRACTICAL MECHANIC'S JOURNAL: An Illustrated Record of Mechanical and Engineering Science, and Epitome of Patent Inventions. 4to. price 1s. monthly.

THE PRACTICAL MECHANIC'S JOURNAL RECORD OF THE INTERNATIONAL EXHIBITION, 1862. A full and elaborate Illustrated Account of the Exhibition, contributed by Writers of eminence in the Departments of Science and Art. In 12 parts, 4to. price 2s. each.

COLLIERIES AND COLLIERS; A Handbook of the Law and leading Cases relating thereto. By J. C. FOWLER, Barrister-at-Law; Stipendiary Magistrate for the District of Merthyr Tydfil and Aberdare. Fcp. 8vo. 6s.

THE THEORY OF WAR ILLUSTRATED by numerous Examples from History. By Lieut.-Col. MacDOUGALL, late Superintendent of the Staff College. *Third Edition*, with 10 Plans. Post 8vo. price 10s. 6d.

PROJECTILE WEAPONS OF WAR AND EXPLOSIVE COMPOUNDS. By J. SCOFFERN, M.B. Lond. late Professor of Chemistry in the Aldersgate School of Medicine. *Fourth Edition.* Post 8vo. with Woodcuts, 9s. 6d.

SUPPLEMENT, containing New Resources of Warfare, price 2s.

A MANUAL FOR NAVAL CADETS. By John M'Neil
Boyd, late Captain R.N. Published with the Sanction and Approval
of the Lords Commissioners of the Admiralty. Second Edition; with
240 Woodcuts, 2 coloured Plates of Signals, &c., and 11 coloured Plates
of Flags. Post 8vo. 12s. 6d.

PROJECTION AND CALCULATION OF THE SPHERE.
For Young Sea Officers; being a complete Initiation into Nautical
Astronomy. By S. M. Saxby, R.N., Principal Instructor of Naval
Engineers, H.M. Steam Reserve. With 77 Diagrams. Post 8vo. 5s.

By the same Author.
THE STUDY OF STEAM AND THE MARINE ENGINE.
For Young Sea Officers in H.M. Navy, the Merchant Navy, &c.;
being a complete Initiation into a knowledge of Principles and their
Application to Practice. Post 8vo. with 87 Diagrams, 5s. 6d.

A TREATISE ON THE STEAM ENGINE, in its various
Applications to Mines, Mills, Steam Navigation, Railways, and Agriculture. With Theoretical Investigations respecting the Motive Power
of Heat and the Proportions of Steam-Engines; Tables of the Right
Dimensions of every Part; and Practical Instructions for the Manufacture and Management of every Species of Engine in actual use. By
John Bourne, C.E. Fifth Edition; with 37 Plates and 546 Woodcuts
(200 new in this Edition). 4to. 42s.

By the same Author.
A CATECHISM OF THE STEAM ENGINE, in its various
Applications to Mines, Mills, Steam Navigation, Railways, and Agricul-
ture; with Practical Instructions for the Manufacture and Manage-
ment of Engines of every class. *New Edition,* with 80 Woodcuts.
Fcp. 8vo. 6s.

HANDBOOK OF FARM LABOUR: Comprising Labour
Statistics; Steam, Water, Wind; Horse Power; Hand Power; Cost
of Farm Operations; Monthly Calendar; Appendix on Boarding
Agricultural Labourers, &c.; and Index. By John Chalmers Morton,
Editor of the *Agricultural Gazette,* &c. 16mo. 1s. 6d.

By the same Author.
HANDBOOK OF DAIRY HUSBANDRY: Comprising
Dairy Statistics; Food of the Cow; Choice and Treatment of the
Cow; Milk; Butter; Cheese; General Management of a Dairy Farm;
Monthly Calendar of Daily Operations; Appendix of Statistics; and
Index. 16mo. 1s. 6d.

216

CONVERSATIONS ON NATURAL PHILOSOPHY. By
JANE MARCET. *13th Edition.* With 84 Plates. Fcp. 8vo. 10s. 6d.

By the same Author.

CONVERSATIONS ON CHEMISTRY. 2 Vols. fcp. 8vo. 14s.

CONVERSATIONS ON LAND AND WATER. Fcp. 8vo.
5s. 6d.

CONVERSATIONS ON POLITICAL ECONOMY. Fcp. 8vo.
7s. 6d.

217

BAYLDON'S ART OF VALUING RENTS AND TILLAGES,
and Claims of Tenants upon Quitting Farms, at both Michaelmas and
Lady-Day. *Seventh Edition,* enlarged. 8vo. 10s. 6d.

218

AN ENCYCLOPÆDIA OF AGRICULTURE : Comprising
the Theory and Practice of the Valuation, Transfer, Laying-out, Improvement, and Management of Landed Property, and of the Cultivation and
Economy of the Animal and Vegetable Productions of Agriculture. By
J. C. LOUDON. With 1,100 Woodcuts. 8vo. 31s. 6d.

By the same Author.

AN ENCYCLOPÆDIA OF GARDENING : Comprising the
Theory and Practice of Horticulture, Floriculture, Arboriculture, and
Landscape Gardening. Corrected and improved by Mrs. LOUDON.
With 1,000 Woodcuts. 8vo. 31s. 6d.

AN ENCYCLOPÆDIA OF TREES AND SHRUBS : Con-
taining the Hardy Trees and Shrubs of Great Britain, Native and
Foreign, Scientifically and Popularly Described. With 2,000 Woodcuts.
8vo. 50s.

AN ENCYCLOPÆDIA OF PLANTS : Comprising the
Specific Character, Description, Culture, History, Application in the
Arts, and every other desirable Particular respecting all the Plants
found in Great Britain. Corrected by Mrs. LOUDON. With upwards of
12,000 Woodcuts. 8vo. £3. 13s. 6d.

219

THE CABINET LAWYER : A Popular Digest of the Laws
of England, Civil and Criminal : Comprising also a Dictionary of Law
Terms, Maxims, Statutes, and much other useful Legal Information. *19th
Edition,* extended by the Author ; with the Statutes and Legal Decisions to *Michaelmas Term,* 24 and 25 Victoria. Fcp. 8vo. 10s. 6d.

THE EXECUTOR'S GUIDE. By J. C. HUDSON. New and
enlarged Edition, revised by the Author. Fcp. 8vo. 6s.

By the same Author.

**PLAIN DIRECTIONS FOR MAKING WILLS IN CON-
FORMITY WITH THE LAW.** New Edition, corrected and revised
by the Author. Fcp. 8vo. 2s. 6d.

THE BRITISH FLORA: Comprising the Phœnogamous
or Flowering Plants, and the Ferns. 8th Edition, with Additions and
Corrections; and numerous Figures engraved on 12 Plates. By Sir
W. J. HOOKER, K.H., &c.; and G. A. WALKER-ARNOTT, LL.D., F.L.S.
12mo. 14s.; with the Plates coloured, 21s.

BRYOLOGIA BRITANNICA: Containing the Mosses of
Great Britain and Ireland, systematically arranged and described
according to the method of *Bruch* and *Schimper*; with 61 illustrative
Plates. By WILLIAM WILSON. 8vo. 42s.; or, with the Plates coloured,
price £4. 4s.

HISTORY OF THE BRITISH FRESH-WATER ALGÆ:
Including Descriptions of the Desmideæ and Diatomaceæ. By A. H.
HASSALL, M.D. With 100 Plates of Figures. 2 vols. 8vo. £1. 15s.

By the same Author.

ADULTERATIONS DETECTED; or, Plain Instructions for
the Discovery of Frauds in Food and Medicine. By ARTHUR HILL
HASSALL, M.D. Lond., Analyst of *The Lancet* Sanitary Commission.
With 225 Woodcuts. Crown 8vo. 17s. 6d.

CORDON-TRAINING OF FRUIT TREES, Diagonal, Vertical,
Spiral, Horizontal, adapted to the Orchard-House and Open-Air Culture.
By Rev. T. COLLINGS BRÉHAUT. Fcp. 8vo. with Woodcuts, 3s. 6d.

THE THEORY AND PRACTICE OF HORTICULTURE;
or, An Attempt to Explain the Principal Operations of Gardening upon
Physiological Grounds. By J. LINDLEY, M.D., F.R.S., F.L.S. With
98 Woodcuts. 8vo. 21s.

By the same Author.

AN INTRODUCTION TO BOTANY. New Edition, revised
and enlarged; with 6 Plates and many Woodcuts. 2 vols. 8vo. 24s.

THE ROSE AMATEUR'S GUIDE : Containing ample
Descriptions of all the fine leading varieties of Roses, regularly classed
in their respective Families; their History and Mode of Culture. By
THOMAS RIVERS. *Seventh Edition.* Fcp. 8vo. 4s.

THE GARDENERS' ANNUAL FOR 1863. Edited by the
Rev. S. REYNOLDS HOLE. With a coloured Frontispiece by JOHN LEECH.
Fcp. 8vo. 2s. 6d.

THE TREASURY OF NATURAL HISTORY ; or, Popular
Dictionary of Zoology : in which the Characteristics that distinguish the
different Classes, Genera, and Species are combined with a variety of
interesting information illustrative of the Habits, Instincts, and General
Economy of the Animal Kingdom. By SAMUEL MAUNDER. With above
900 accurate Woodcuts. Fcp. 8vo. 10s.

By the same Author.

THE SCIENTIFIC AND LITERARY TREASURY : A
Popular Encyclopædia of Science and the Belles-Lettres; including all
branches of Science, and every subject connected with Literature and
Art. Fcp. 8vo. 10s.

THE TREASURY OF GEOGRAPHY, Physical, Historical,
Descriptive, and Political; containing a succinct Account of every
Country in the World. Completed by WILLIAM HUGHES, F.R.G.S.
With 7 Maps and 16 Plates. Fcp. 8vo. 10s.

THE HISTORICAL TREASURY : Comprising a General
Introductory Outline of Universal History, Ancient and Modern, and a
Series of Separate Histories of every principal Nation. Fcp. 8vo. 10s.

THE BIOGRAPHICAL TREASURY : Consisting of Memoirs,
Sketches, and Brief Notices of above 12,000 Eminent Persons of All
Ages and Nations. *12th Edition.* Fcp. 8vo. 10s.

**THE TREASURY OF KNOWLEDGE AND LIBRARY OF
REFERENCE :** Comprising an English Dictionary and Grammar, a
Universal Gazetteer, a Classical Dictionary, a Chronology, a Law Dic-
tionary, a Synopsis of the Peerage, useful Tables, &c. Fcp. 8vo. 10s.

Uniform with the above.

THE TREASURY OF BOTANY. By Dr. J. LINDLEY.
[*In the press.*

THE TREASURY OF BIBLE KNOWLEDGE. By Rev.
J. AYRE, M.A.
[*In the press.*

INDEX.

New Works published by Longman and Co.